PERSONALITY
IN THEORY AND PRACTICE

OTHER WORKS BY A. A. ROBACK

THE INTERFERENCE OF WILL-IMPULSES. 166 pp. — $2.75

BEHAVIORISM AND PSYCHOLOGY. 285 pp. — Out of Print.

PSYCHOLOGY WITH CHAPTERS ON CHARACTER ANALYSIS AND MENTAL MEASUREMENT. Out of Print.

ROBACK MENTALITY TESTS FOR SUPERIOR ADULTS (8th edition). COMPREHENSION TESTS (3d ed.), SCIENTIFIC INGENUITY AND JURISTIC APTITUDE TESTS. $2.00 Sample Set. (Manuals: 75c; 50c; $2.25)

THE PSYCHOLOGY OF CHARACTER. (3d rev. and enlarged ed.), 724 pp. — $8.00

PISCOLOGIA DEL CARACTER. (Madrid), 654 pp. — $6.00

A BIBLIOGRAPHY OF CHARACTER AND PERSONALITY. 340 pp. — $4.00

POPULAR PSYCHOLOGY. Illustrated. (Out of Frint), 267 pp.

JEWISH INFLUENCE IN MODERN THOUGHT. 506 pp., illustrated — $4.50

PERSONALITY: THE CRUX OF SOCIAL INTERCOURSE (o.p.)

BUSINESS PSYCHOLOGY. (Correspondence Course), Eight Booklets for Commonwealth of Massachusetts

SELF-CONSCIOUSNESS, SELF-TREATED. 265 pp. (2d ed. in press)

VARFOR HAMMAR JAG MIG SJALV, (Swedish translation of above), 160 pages (Stockholm) — $2.50

CURIOSITIES OF YIDDISH LITERATURE. 227 pp. (Out of Print)

I. L. PERETZ: PSYCHOLOGIST OF LITERATURE. 458 pp. — $4.00

BEHAVIORISM AT 25. 256 pp. (Out of Print)

THE PSYCHOLOGY OF COMMON SENSE. 350 pp. — $3.80

SENSE OF HUMOR TEST. (2d ed.) 50 cents

THE STORY OF YIDDISH LITERATURE. (Illustrated) 510 pp. — $5.00

APOLOGIA PRO VITA YIDDICIA. 98 pp. — $1.50 (300 numbered copies)

WILLIAM JAMES. (500 numbered copies), 340 pp. — $3.50

A DICTIONARY OF INTERNATIONAL SLURS. 394 pp. — $6.25

PSYCHORAMA; A PSYCHOLOGICAL ANALYSIS. 365 pp. — $3.75

EDITED

PROBLEMS OF PERSONALITY. (Second ed.), 443 pp. — $7.00

Collected papers of the late Dr. Morton Prince, under the title of CLINICAL AND EXPERIMENTAL STUDIES IN PERSONALITY 672 pages (2d revised and enlarged edition)— (Out of Print)

THE ALBERT SCHWEITZER JUBILEE BOOK. 508 pp. — $7.50

HANNS SACHS'S MASKS OF LOVE AND LIFE. 306 pp. — $4.25

TRANSLATED AND EDITED
(With Introduction and 169 Notes)

BASTIAT-SCHULZE VON DELITZSCH (F. Lassalle), 434 pp. — (Out of Print)

POPULAR PAMPHLETS ON PERSONALITY AND FOLKLORE
(some illustrated with many cuts)

Improving Your Personality

Readings For Cultural Personality

"I Am Winning Friends"

On Reading Character

Psychological Aspects of Jewish Protective Phrases

Physicians in Jewish Folklore

The Yiddish Proverb

Getting More Out of Life

Success in Handling Types

Overcoming Inferiority Complexes

Personality in Handwriting

The Use and Meaning of Dreams

The Psychology of Confession

SCI-ART PUBLISHERS   Harvard Square, Cambridge 38, Mass.

PERSONALITY

IN THEORY AND PRACTICE.

by
Abraham Aaron
A, A, ROBACK

Professor of Psychology, Emerson College, Formerly
Professor at Northeastern University and
Instructor at Harvard University.

SCI-ART PUBLISHERS
HARVARD SQUARE
CAMBRIDGE, MASS.

TO

SAMUEL D. ROBBINS

PREFACE

BOTH *Personality; the Crux of Social Intercourse*
and the much larger work *The Psychology of
Character* have been out of print for a number of
years, and even used copies were unavailable within
the past three or four years. Revising a text is
generally an irksome task but to the present author
it is an ordeal. Writing a text anew would have
been the more expedient thing to do. On the
other hand, however, there is often so much good
material in a first edition that the author is hard
put to it to cover the same ground in different
language. Occasionally the job comes out better.
More often, the spontaneity of the earlier statements is missing, and an author longingly harks
back to the first attempt.

In the writing of the present text, a compromise
was achieved in that a large part of *Personality
the Crux of Social Intercourse* was incorporated,
but it constitutes hardly more than a fifth of this
volume; and even that portion has been thoroughly
revised. The original essay which forms the
groundwork of both the small book and the

[7]

expanded text appeared in *The Century,* a quarterly of literary distinction (which probably led to its extinction) and had a cultural setting. To this cultural slant was added later the applied aspect required for university extension students. Both of these points of view were retained in the preparation of the present text. Perhaps a paragraph or two from the Foreword to its predecessor would be in order here.

"There is always a danger that writing which is addressed to the popular mind, and particularly that type of writing which has a practical aim, will descend to a conventionally inspirational level. For this reason, academic people seem to avoid such discussions, and, as a rule, confine themselves to theory, where they lay themselves less open to objection on the part of their colleagues. The result is that the layman, even when fairly educated, in his quest for wholesome counsel, turns to questionable sources for his information.

"The situation is gradually improving in that more people are becoming discriminating and that scientists and educators no longer consider it beneath them to touch upon everyday topics in a practical vein. Furthermore, it is possible to dwell on such subjects seriously without necessarily beclouding the issue through the use of a formidable terminology and a cumbersome or diffuse phraseology. Lucidity, accuracy and precision are the *sine qua non* of science, whether humanized or not. The interest value is secondary but should not be lacking in matters of such vital importance as personality. It sometimes happens, however, that irrelevant material or not altogether accurate data are introduced in order to fascinate the reader. For this reason, popularizations are most reliable when made after the author had engaged first in solid research (Faraday, Helmholtz, Ball), otherwise the temptation is too great to write cleverly and to make a bid for popularity."

The present text is not a condensation of the *Psychology of Character,* published by Kegan Paul and Routledge (International Library) London, which incidentally is forthcoming in an enlarged third edition, and dealing for the most part, with similar topics, historically conceived, and treated in a more extensive manner, with special emphasis on character rather than on personality, in general.

The Bibliography, with few exceptions, includes only the more recent titles, those not to be found in my *Bibliography of Character and Personality,* which appeared in 1927, nor in *Personality; the Crux of Social Intercourse,* 1930; and thus may be regarded as a supplement to the close to 3400 titles contained therein.

[9]

Part of what is in the introductory chapter might have been reserved for the preface, but it is a well-known fact that few instructors and practically no students read the foreword to a textbook, and some of the discussion on the nature of textbooks on personality and the criterion of includability is germane to the course as a whole.

A. A. ROBACK.

Cambridge, Mass.
October 20, 1949

ACKNOWLEDGEMENTS

Mr. William James has kindly placed at my disposal a portrait of his father, which had never appeared in print, and Prof. Robert Ulich has heeded my request for a photograph of the late Elsa Brändström Ulich. To Prof. Clark L. Hull, of Yale University, I am indebted for an extended statement in regard to a handwriting experiment which he directed many years ago at the University of Wisconsin. Prof. Blumer, of the University of Chicago, has been good enough to permit publishing the questionnaire and my replies, which appear in Appendix B, relative to a case study.

To the various publishers, whose publications have been cited, Macmillan, Harper, Thomas, Harvard University, Rutledge (London), College Press, Holt, Paul Elder, and the Readers Digest, thanks are due for permission to reprint brief passages in quotation.

CONTENTS

[13]

CONTENTS

CONTENTS

CONTENTS

PART ONE

CHAPTER I

INTRODUCTORY

THERE was a time, within the memory of the older psychologists, when textbooks were scarce. Even as late as 1910, perhaps a dozen textbooks is all that an instructor could select from for a course in general psychology, and only the foremost in the field would dare to cover the ground of a subject that required such delicate handling. William James had set a high standard, and Titchener, Dewey, Münsterberg, Royce, Baldwin, and Thorndike (*The Human Nature Club*) had each almost a system of their own.

The Value of a Text

Within a generation, textbooks in general psychology alone multiplied so that they could be counted in the many scores, if not in the hundreds, and practically every college or university of some standing or size can boast of, at least, one home-made textbook in psychology. Some day, if the process goes on at the same pace, the

Biblical comment "And to the writing of books there is no end" will have to be amended so as to read "And to the writing of *textbooks*, there is no end." Textbooks are necessary evils. When classes are small, collateral readings might be recommended, but it is out of the question with classes of several hundred to a thousand or more students. Many textbooks answer their purpose very well, others consist of only a series of extracts or paraphrases from others with interpolations by the author. Textbook writing can be as lucrative as putting out "whodunit" novels, and if the writer is on the staff of a very large university, and his students, subsequently specializing, become attached to the book so that they use it in the classes they teach, at any rate until they write a text themselves, many thousands of copies might be disposed of, in the course of a decade.

If more textbooks are not written, it is because relatively few psychologists are satisfied to pour old wine from numerous bottles into a single new flask. Many are research men; other are pure professionals. Then a number are adapted to producing treatises. Of the textbooks which do get written, a large proportion is on a high level in that they are suitable as sources of information for students, but in surprisingly few is there to be found the independent orientation which was characteristic of the early texts written by authorities who had a grip on the subject as a whole. The pioneers of the science in America were "self-made men"; even though they nearly all had sat at the feet of Wundt. The next generation saw the bumptious climb of behaviorism; and most textbooks became colored with the stimulus-response thinking—no! "implicit speech"; for thinking, according to real behaviorists, is a misnomer — as many of the writers came from the ranks of the behaviorists or their students. The stimulus-response circuit, so widely appealed to, has really been a short circuit which is calculated to blow out the psychological fuse.

A behavioristically tinged text may possess some excellent qualities. It may be methodical, well supplied with experimental references and diagrams, notes and bibliography, but it is apt to ignore other points of view or minimize them. To a certain extent, this will be true of any text; yet the fact remains that the mechanists, environmentalists, and their affiliates, while not hailed with enthusiasm, are nevertheless extensively discussed and given great consideration by their opponents, among whom the present author has the honor of counting himself. To receive attention and eventually to be dismissed is certainly better than not to have gained the slightest hearing. The more influential schools (psychoanalysis, gestaltism, operationalism) are often incorporated, or at least befriended, although the combination is scarcely a felicitous one, and the actual *modus vivendi* of these incongruous systems is never cleared up. Power politics in the international situation thus becomes a "power psychology" in our own sphere, with the clinical psychologists divided in their loyalties.

Playing "Hamlet" Without Hamlet

Under the circumstances, no wonder that while we have "personalized" cigarettes, "personalized" handkerchiefs, "personalized" matches, perfume; and one brand of razor blades is even called by a name that figures much in the early chapters of personality texts — the books on personality are not only far from being "personalized," but seem to be depersonalized. Perhaps it will be said "that is what science purports doing, in the first place," to which we should all assent, if the reference is to the method. Unfortunately, however, in a good many textbooks on personality, it would seem that everything is treated of but personality. We may find the inevitable sketch of Pavlov's heroic dog, we are indoctrinated with all the commonplaces of conditioned reflexes and habits, and receive a good deal of information about memory, intelligence, perception, and other topics of general psychology, which, no doubt, touch upon personality, but the core of the subject is missed or cavalierly moved out of the danger zone.

Textbooks of the better sort are heavy with quotations. Sometimes these extracts instead of clarifying the issues serve to bemuddle them, and the pabulum becomes indigestible, for if the authorities don't agree, and *no settling attempt is made,* the material will not agree with the student. The personality textbook, in the majority of cases, is a sort of omnibus where you can obtain a bit of biology, a little sociology, a dose of psychoanalysis, a capsule of anthropology and of course, a modicum of general psychology, but we should prefer to learn a little about personality too.

General Flaws in Textbooks on Personality

It was with such misgivings as these that I set out to produce a small text for elementary students in personality that might fill some of the gaps, even though I realize full well that it exhibits some lacunae of its own, and does not measure up to two or three large textbooks, which, however, are too advanced for first courses and contain altogether too much that is suitable for a treatise rather than a compendium. There is no need, for instance, to exhaust a topic in several chapters. Only the most relevant issues should be dealt with, and after ranging them on both sides, the author should make known both his own stand and the reason for taking it. The various disciplines which abut on personality should be introduced only insofar as they are required to throw some light on the central question. A digest of each of these allied sciences is out of place. The various topics handled in separate chapters should present a unitary picture, and problems should not be introduced simply because they happen to be much discussed *at the present time,* which means that perspective is essential in the writing of a textbook. The question is not what type of article is frequently seen in this or that journal, but what is *permanently going to be a significant item* in the study of personality.

The Technical is Not Necessarily Scientific

That the present volume fulfills its purpose I should be the last one to assert. I can anticipate a good deal of criticism on the part of those who are accustomed to the conventional textbook. In the first place, I have made little use of the terminology and phraseology which stud the psychological articles and texts, and one might gain the impression that the treatment of personality is on a popular level. If the layman can understand the development of the subject, then I have reason to feel satisfied. I do not think it necessary to resort to "Newspeak" in order to write scientifically. The psychological and sociological "lingo," as Morton Prince used to call it, which clutters up most of the literature in our field, is a liability rather than an asset. It is impressive rather than expressive, and can often be exchanged for an ordinary phrase which means something to the intelligent man in the street. To be sure, the terms and phrases are often steeped in a definite theory, but that is just the difficulty. We begin with the phrase and, before we know it, we are entangled in the theory.

The naïve suppose that to employ a quasi-physiological word is to make psychology scientific. Others, who have had special training in the physical sciences, like the *Gestalt* pioneers, have introduced terms from those sciences: *topology,* from mathematics; *valence* from chemistry; *"dynamic" field* from physics. We ought to know what these terms mean while discussing the various theories they represent, but to bandy them about throughout as if they were not only the last word but the alpha and omega for all time to come, and through them we might understand the working of the personality dynamism, is to deceive ourselves and others. There are some textbooks which adapt the behavioristic, the gestaltist, and the psychoanalytic terminology, rolling them all into one compact system; and the result is a farrago which bids fair to vie with the phraseology of Rabelais. Whatever these words stand for in their respective sciences, in psychology they are only metaphors.

Pseudo-Objectivity

That objectivity does not consist in the use of such terms is attested by a recognized authority in neurology who is too experienced to be taken in by supposedly scientific words; and the whole so-called objectivistic position is exposed trenchantly in the following passage:

> All this strikes me as hemianopic physiologizing. Jacobson applauds accurate description and precise use of terms, discarding "figurative terms" such as "conflicts" and "escape." He does not see that he is using just as figurative language in

his "neuromuscular hypertension complicated by pathological habit formation." Take the word "tension." Precisely used, this means the state of being stretched. Jacobson uses it figuratively, and poetically to signify a state of nerve and muscle that has nothing to do with stretching, but with an increase in number and strength of nerve impulses and a contraction of muscle fibres. His phrase "pathological habit formation" is worse; I do not see just how he could define it in "precise and descriptive terms" without using psychological metaphors. The whole concept of "habit" is psychological, excepting perhaps the conditioned reflex of Pavlov (another physiologizer, who made a great contribution to psychology, but never would admit that there was such a science as psychology.

His conditioned reflexes, however, were almost entirely observed in dogs; some workers have applied them to other animals, and a few observations on man show that similar mechanisms can be elicited in the human nervous system. But the whole idea that habit formation and the learning process are now understood because of Pavlov's work is largely reasoning by unverified analogy. In the honest observation of human behavior, clinical or physiological, one finds just as good evidence for "conflict" and "escape" as for "habit." One cannot arbitrarily simplify the problem to fit "physiological conceptions" when the facts are many and complex. [1]

Changed Roles

It is remarkable that physiologists like Sherrington and Cannon, neurologists like Lashley and Coghill, neuropathologists like Cobb and other noted authorities, including Freud, who have been trained in the anatomical and physiological fields, do not think of their own territory as a place of refuge where psychological mysteries could be unraveled, while psychologists are constantly looking to other sciences for their salvation, with the result that the problems are only shorn of their significance, and the solution is often like the temporary disappearance of a stain in clothing after it has come from the cleanser's.

That the answer to the riddle of personality must eventually be found in physiology almost goes without saying. Nay more, perhaps it is even to be sought in the physics and chemistry of the organism, but, for the present, let us concentrate on what is accessible. In other words, physiology is not the same as physiologizing, but is based on

[1] Stanley Cobb: *"Borderlands of Psychiatry,"* (Harvard) 1943, p. 124.

actual laboratory research, and when the results are obtained, the conclusions are not transferable to another science, like psychology or sociology, except as suggestive cues of heuristic value. Pavlov, great physiologist that he was, was no better psychologist than hundreds of others.

Latterly, psychology has been enriched by a vocabulary from sociology and anthropology; and whether or not this will add to the gayety of nations (or, perhaps better, *notions*), we know, at least, that such a practice tends to dilute psychology to such an extent that it would consist of a conglomeration of disciplines, so that while it is shedding more and more its philosophical feathers, it has been decking itself out in other plumes which are even less its own. To refer to concepts in cognate sciences is one thing; to take the theories for granted that revolve around those concepts and adapt them to explain something that is puzzling in personality is something different again. Acculturation, to take one instance, has its honored place in sociology and anthropology, but when it is brought in to solve a problem of distinct individuality, it becomes an intruder.

Priority of Topics

One of the strictures, I imagine, which will be

directed at this book is that there is a philosophical thread running through it. Yes, I have substituted common sense, if that is philosophy, based on everyday living for the speculative physiologizing which is rampant in our thousands of articles and scores of textbooks. Besides, in the physiologizing and physicizing there is implicit a philosophy, too, viz., that we are all the products of circumstances, and that values are fictions beyond the ken of psychology, and only that which has been measured is to be considered scientific, regardless of what it portends, and its bearing on the real issue.

The criterion of personality is the nubbin of the subject, but what textbooks consider it? The adequacy valence, again, is of cardinal importance, because on it hinges our recognition of worth, not merely the existence of minor traits. The matter of rigidity, which has been excluded for the present, in spite of the controversies it has called forth in the journals, is only an interesting adjunct, but all one can do at present is to tell what it's all about and produce the arguments on both sides, thus adding to the already highly controversial pile; and after this is done, we still are apt to wonder whether the personality status is affected by the extent of the rigidity found in a given individual.

Why Not Measure Greatness?

While discussing one of the truly great personalities of our age with a highly esteemed colleague, himself a pillar of our scientific structure, my interlocutor exclaimed "If only we could establish what greatness consists of?" I think it would be possible to do that if a part of the huge funds assigned to the measurement of this or that attitude were diverted to the study of values in personality, as manifested in self-denial and social constructiveness, or, negatively, in aggressiveness, exploitation, and rapaciousness. Our task would be well begun, at least. F. L. Wells, in one of the most thoughtful papers on the subject of personality, addressing the American Orthopsychiatric Association, pointed out that the "the name of this society implies a valuation." He further stated that

> The multiplicity of approaches to the social functions of the individual is patent enough to a group like this one; the topic of immediate concern is the tendency to instrumentalize or exploit the social milieu. That it must be to some extent instrumentalized, in its very study, is so obvious as to be easily overlooked; to the ethical issues here involved, the enthusiastic student

is apparently quite insensitive. The problems would, however, shape themselves something like this: what might we expect of experimental methods in disclosing the pattern of exploitation, such as predatism and parasitism, likely to be utilized; and what are the meanings of varying degrees of measurable intelligence for planfulness and patience? [2]

If only a few advanced students will be steered into somewhat different channels from the usual ones, the book will have served its purpose, but it may also call attention, in general, to the proposition that a course in personality should not neglect the guidance angle in ordinary social relations. If that can be called preaching, then any type of counsel may be designated by the same name.

Coming Back to Fundamentals

Perhaps we are beginning to come to closer grips with the problems I have in mind. E. R. Hilgard, [3] in his recent Presidential Address before the American Psychological Association,

[2] F. L. Wells: "Evaluation of Personality and Character Tests. *Amer. Journal of Orthopsychiatry*, 1932, vol. 2, p. 332.

[3] E. R. Hilgard: "Human Motives and the Concept of Self" *Amer. Psychologist*, 1949, vol. 4, pp. 379-380.

has outlined a program of psychodynamics, in which a number of vital issues come to the fore, and some of his proposals would support the position taken here. He sees, for instance, that we must recognize the *continuity of motivational patterns,* and that this is one of the presuppositions for the sorely needed concept of a self, an "inferred self," which is to go beyond the obvious and draw upon the genotypical ingredients in us. It is also gratifying that he draws the distinction between the integrated and the integrative self, which is in line with the underlying tenet in this book, particularly the criterion of personality, which is essentially social. "An Integrated personality soon leads to its own isolation or destruction, if it is not also integrative." Let us hope that the first psychodynamic laboratory to be established, in Berkeley, with D. W. MacKinnon as its Director, will, especially as the latter has had such excellent training, devote itself to the study of this inferred self and some of the socio-ethical problems it implies. That would mean the ushering in of a new era for our field.

Why Psychodynamics Has Been Eliminated

There is one limitation in the book which may disappoint a number of instructors, and that is the absence of a long chapter on psychodynamics, which seems to be the *pièce de résistance* of textbooks, nowadays, in personality; for it allows the play of imagination and affords the opportunity of introducing all sorts of theories and diagrams to explain motivation. But that is just the reason why this phase of personality has been omitted in an elementary book. Only those who have already been initiated into the subject may be expected to cope with the intricate material. For, let us see what it would involve.

Certainly the whole territory of psychoanalysis must be covered, including the seceded areas of Jung, Adler, and Rank, long out of bounds to orthodox Freudians. Other dynamic psychologies must surely find a place here too. There is the elaborate system of Lewin, with other *Gestalt* accessories, to be dealt with. Nor can we dispense with Tolman's purposive and molar Behaviorism, the theories of Mowrer, Young, MacKinnon; but why name them all? There are dozens who have something to offer in this psychological stratosphere where there is little resistance, and the subject can no longer be crowded into a single chapter or even two.

In a first course, the student is bound to become confused and suffer from mental indigestion. For

INTRODUCTORY

him, the theories are but theories; and even the
ingenious diagrams which purport to explain the
processes, either the passing of impulses along a
nerve circuit, or the relationships of objects and
the self in a given situation, have nothing factual
about them. There is not a shred of evidence that
this or that diagram is a correct representation of
what actually occurs. The many circles or squares
with arrows and coils, which resemble the blueprint
of some complicated apparatus, are just one man's
guess, which may be as good as the next man's,
represented by another set of geometrical figures
and letters. These conjectures and hypotheses may
all be interesting. The beginner in personality
study, however, should not be compelled to venture
in the deep waters of psychological speculation,
but, according to the proverb, keep nearer the
shore of descriptive fact and more or less accepted
explanations. If, on the other hand, the author
happens to be a partisan, a votary of a single
theory, then the student is cheated of a range of
information that rightfully belongs to him, when
every other attempt at explanation is suppressed.

Would it not be better to reserve such speculations for a course in dynamic psychology or
motivation, where the abnormal aspects of
personality, at least the psychoneuroses, might

receive due attention? The elementary course should be confined to the description of facts, the explanation of topics, the discussion of general issues, the outlining of methods and the mention of applications. The chapter on motivation, in this book, is merely a brief introduction to the large field of psychodynamics, which, however, must be treated separately.

Nativism Not Extreme

There is one more contestable feature about the book which I must allude to — its seemingly strong nativistic leaning. Many naïve people ask, "Why, if we are born that way, then what's the use of schools and home guidance, church precepts, etc?" As a matter of fact, I don't know of anyone who believes that we are born with ready-made traits. Nor have I ever met a psychologist who denies that the environment shapes the individual to a large extent, but fortunately there are still a few who hold that the individual can shape his environment too. The question is not whether it is easy or difficult, and how many people have affected their environment — in a sense, most have — but whether it can be done; and if feasible, then a strictly deterministic point of view must be modified in face of the facts.

We who adhere to the primacy of heredity simply say that the physical structure and neural pattern are such in every one that only specific traits will develop, varying of course, with conditions. I should be willing to concede more, that many traits are derived from combinations of two or more primary ones. Thus refinement may be the result of one pronounced and one practically absent trait. Strong aggressiveness and strong sympathy will produce a trait quite different from that distilled from a combination of strong aggressiveness plus weak sympathy. Thus, it would scarcely be just to charge hereditarians with an all-out nativism. Our propensity for constructiveness is better satisfied by a genetic, empirical, or environmental theory than by a nativist view, which, in my student days, I felt was too lazy, e.g. in explaining space or time perception. To build up a perception from non-perceptive elements is like meeting a challenge, and I often wondered, as a youth, why Wundt's genetic explanations were not universally accepted; for they appeared so plausible and even convincing, but "not all is gold that glitters"; and at a more mature age we can adjudicate a situation not on the strength of its thought-provokingness alone. We must have a sound basis for acceptance. Of course the issue of nativism and geneticism as applying to certain phases of perception is only indirectly related to the problems dealt with here, and we may be geneticists in the one case and not in the other. Our dispute is not with a moderate geneticism, but with an immoderate environmentalism.

A Curious Divergence

Incidentally, as often happens, when a term is shared by two sciences, the sense of genetics in biology is so unlike that of "genetic," as applied to space and time perception, as to almost suggest a contradiction. The geneticist, who specializes in problems of heredity, is of the opinion that most of our traits and capacities are contained, in one form or another, in the genes; and the environment merely acts as an extraeous agent in modifying them.

The genetic theory in perception, on the other hand, in opposition to the nativist theory, holds that our interpretation of the third dimension, movement, time intervals is built up on the basis of experience in the course of life, that three or more elements might give us the product we call perception. The nativistic theory thinks of the capacity to perceive as something *fundamental,* which does not require a gradual building up from more elementary cues.

[40]

The student should learn to distinguish the biological sense from the psychological. The semantic common denominator is the Greek word, *gennaô*, *to produce*, the sense of which bifurcates, as shown above, in (a) the *birth* of a new being, with incipient capacities and traits, and (b) the *growth* of a special adaptive function to interpret sense data as perceptions of one type or another.

Chapter II

EVOLUTION OF CONCEPT

IT IS RATHER strange that psychology, which deals with experiences closest to man, was among the latest sciences to develop, while the study of personality, which is the very nucleus of psychology, is scarcely more than thirty, at most, forty years old. The acres of diamonds have been in our scientific back yard all along, yet we did not recognize them as such. That is not to say that personality, as a term, has only recently been coined, or that some of the elements of personality have not been discussed, in one connection or another, *e.g.,* in treatises on ethics, or philosophical disquisitions, but the study *as a unit* came into being only of late, and the fragments found in the older philosophical and theological disciplines appear to us today like fossils of a by-gone age.

Neglect of Term in English Literature

In English, for the first time, the term "personality" was used, by Wyclif, in 1380, to designate the quality peculiar to a human being or person, and yet it was not until five centuries later that the word began to enjoy any popularity. Neither Shakespeare, wielding as he did an extraordinarily comprehensive vocabulary, nor Milton, with his stupendous command of the English language, even to its most recondite recesses, ever employed the word that has had such a long history and more recently came to acquire an interesting past in assuming the abbreviated and piquant form "it."

Theological Conception

The vicissitudes that the word, or rather the concept (idea) of personality has undergone are not without significance. There was a theological stage when personality nearly always referred to the Deity. It was in the course of the Middle Ages, when human beings were regarded only as reflections of a Supreme Being, that individuality was envisaged solely as a finite aspect of God. To speak of personality in terms of man was little short of blasphemy. To this day, the conception of God as forming the personal substratum of the mass of human waves is preserved, in one form or another, in idealistic systems of contemporary times.

Under the Aegis of Philosophy

The chief locus, however, of this word was to be found in philosophy, and we may look upon Hegel as the initiator of the philosophy of personality. For nearly a century, the concept of personality was steeped in a philosophical setting.

We need only turn to the term in one of the latest editions of the *Encyclopedia Britannica* to convince ourselves that the philosophical note is still dominant enough to drown all other claims; and for all the readers might gather, personality is not a matter for discussion in a psychological universe of discourse.

It was not until the cases of double and multiple personality began to crop up that a beginning was made to divert the word from the purely philosophical to the psychological, but as yet weirdly psychological.

Changing Interest and Problems

Books on personality which appeared in the first quarter of our century show little bearing on the problems of personality as we see them today. F. B. Jevons's *Personality* (published in 1913) *e.g.*, deals with the *self*, the *I*, and the *me*, the question whether there is a percipient, or whether the self consists only of successive states.

of consciousness. In 1918, there appeared G. T. Ladd's *The Secret of Personality.* A psychologist who is unfamiliar with the historical development of the subject might wonder why the book was so titled, when its author had introduced, for the most part, matter relating to God and faith.

To compare a recent textbook on personality with a treatise on the subject written some thirty years ago is like viewing two different universes of discourse. One may readily understand that a term like personality can cover a vast territory because of the different slants and approaches it suggests. Philosophy has had a lien on it for centuries, but theology has also had a close contact. The personality of God has been a favorite topic with theologians for centuries. Indeed, it would not be far from the truth to assert that the denial of the person-equality of the three members of the Trinity, as was done by Arius and his followers, at the beginning of the fourth century, could result in martyrdom, or might even lead to massacres. In C. C. J. Webb's Gifford Lectures, *God and Personality,* a full chapter is devoted to the elaborate discussion of "Divine Personality."

During the Middle Ages, when theology ruled science and occupied the mind of most educated

men, the human individual was regarded in many
quarters as a sort of reflection of the divine
personality; a mode, or monad, or occasion, but
scarcely as an independent entity, although the
definition Thomas Aquinas puts forth in his
Summa Theologia, namely as "a distinct being
subsisting in an intellectual nature, [1] might seem
to argue against such a view. Nevertheless the
trend during the Middle Ages and Renaissance
has been to envisage man not as a full-blown and
really independent personality — a doctrine which
has even influenced philosophy to the extent that
Leibniz's "Supreme Monad" encompasses all the
other monads, and Hegel's "Absolute Idea"
occupies a similar position.

Personalism as a World Outlook

Out of this idealistic conception, there emerged
the ramified, or perhaps three-cornered, system
of personalism in three different countries: Charles
Renouvier's in France, which, as is well-known,
was not without its impress on William James
in America: B. P. Bowne's in the United States,
and William Stern's in Germany; and although
each system is something apart and has its own
postulates and objectives, they are all related by

[1] This is almost a verbatim borrowing from Boethius.

virtue of the tenets that the starting point or central idea in philosophy and psychology must be the person. Even a sociology could be developed in terms of personal forces. Some of the sociologists are now inclined to turn the tables, making out of personality proper a central station of social forces.

Personality has crawled into the sphere of groups, like corporations, as a fiction *via* jurisprudence. Only a person is supposed to have rights and assume responsibility, and if a corporation or any other body is to exercise such rights, it must be considered a person. Hegel, in his *Philosophy of Law* spent some time on this point.

Personality In Literature

To a man like Hegel, who, when confronted with the account of the discovery of a new planet, despite his doctrinal finality about the number in existence, is reported to have replied, "So much the worse for the facts," the artificiality of the application of a purely personal concept to a fortuitous group, like a corporation, was not too obvious, but to the ordinary mortal of common sense, it is apparent why the contact between law and personality has been, at best, a nominal one.

The relationship of personality to literature, on

the other hand, is both real and vital, even if literature, as an art, and psychology, as a science, are supposed to be poles apart. Recent years have seen a closer *rapprochement* between the two; and it may be said that it was the psychoanalyst who served as the *liaison* officer in this instance. But even without him, the distance would have dwindled in the course of time.

The literary phase of the term was ushered in through the great German writers of the early nineteenth century, and their biographers. It was with a special intonation indicative of awe and dignity that the German would pronounce *"Persönlichkeit,"* with drawn accent on the second syllable, when coupled with the names of Goethe and Schiller. The late Kuno Francke's *Personality in German Literature before Luther* is an excellent example of the literary exploitation of the term.

The British literary and art critic, Herbert Read, basing his discussion on Roback's conception of character, has developed a theory of poetic personality which is to give us a clue to many puzzles regarding artistic creativeness.[2] It is only lately that the relationship of personality to talent[3] or

[2] H. Read: "The Personality of the Poet," in *Collected Essays in Literary Criticism*.

[3] A. Lewisohn: *Painters and Personality,* (*rev. ed.*) 1948.

[48]

genius has been gone into extensively; and it has been clearly demonstrated that there is no gap between the two, even where contradictions are apparent, as, let us say, in Georges Sand and Flaubert, whose mode of life and thematic treatment seem to be disparate, and whose writings would, consequently, be a poor index to their personality.

The contacts between personality and literature may be gathered from the fact that certain types and characters in fiction have become handles, so to speak, for everyday illustrations. Aside from such figures as Hamlet, Tartuffe, Don Juan, Shylock, who have become household references, there are whole outlooks, philosophies of life, general attitudes which are labelled according to this or that hero or heroine in fiction. Bovaryism, which has been so realistically described by Gustave Flaubert or Oblomovism, which is only another name for the irresponsibility, goallessness, and almost infantile existence of the average Russian official about a century ago whom Gontcharov knew so well — what are these designations but types of personality, seen through the spectacles of the artist and brought out in relief, even in the local color, whether gay and picturesque, or drab and hazy, that sets them off?

Personality and Performance Inseparable

It is true, too, that the author or artist is often unable to refrain from injecting his own experiences, incidents out of his own life, into his play, novel, short story, or painting. There is much more that is autobiographical in fiction than is ordinarily supposed. Strindberg has made a practice of wearing his heart on his sleeve, and has done so with a vengeance (perhaps even revenge), but others, while making no pretense to such self-exposition, have given us here and there a glimpse into their *Vita*. In between, stand such widely studied authors as Marcel Proust, Franz Kafka, and James Joyce, whose complex personalities have precipitated the experimental writing they have initiated, which to them, however, was no experiment, but virtually a demoniac urge.

The study of personality is indebted to the lights of literature in an extraordinary degree. Their visions, caught on a film, are sometimes taken into the dark room of the laboratory to develop, but the print, in most instances, lacks the essentials of the original insight. Instead of presenting a clear picture, it is often a shadow of the meaningful illumination, after being treated quantitatively, statistically, or broken up into factors and drives and reflexes. And yet such is the business of psychology. If it is to be a science, it must seek to explain. It takes the slice of life provided by the artist, whether literary, pictorial, or plastic, and cuts it up so as to allow of collation and correlation. When the experimentalist has no understanding of life or literature, he is likely to make a botch of it, use the wrong instruments for the most delicate operations; for experimentalists who are broad and intuitive as well are rare.

Psychological Exploitation

It is only within the last two decades that the concept has been encased in an applied setting; and it is somewhat curious that such an abstract word should have caught the fancy of the masses and made its way into the vocabulary of the street. In fact, such a degree of popularity has this term attained that writers of psychological and semi-psychological or pseudo-psychological books need only label their production "The Psychology of Personality" and the book has already found a market. Forty years ago, when psychology was just beginning to step out of its swaddling-clothes, the word "personality" was scarcely mentioned even by the masters of the science. To-day it is a household term, frequently heard among typists, stenographers, and even frequenters of the arenas and boxing gardens.

Vulgarization of Concept

The concept, thanks to the cinema, and writers like Elinor Glyn, has been vulgarized to mean nothing but sex appeal; and we shall see later that this view is not so far away from the position of the behavioristic wing in psychology. When a mere school-girl boasts of having "it," she means simply that she is the possessor of a personality which would attract men.

What is evident is the fact that this quality is the most important asset to her, and this, therefore, represents the all-in-all of the human race. Does she understand the real meaning of "personality"? Would she be able to frame a satisfactory definition of the word, without resorting to such vague phrases as "something about one (you know)," or to such one-sided qualities as charm, appeal, fascination, etc.? Our answer must be "Emphatically, no."

None but a mature mind can grasp the full import of *personality;* and although the dictionary definition, as "the quality or state of being a person," can be understood by a street urchin, he no more catches the meaning of the term than I can picture to myself the fourth dimension.

Child's Definition of Personality

Let us ask a child what constitutes a person, and the reply would be the enumeration of the most important features and limbs: head, nose, mouth, ears, hands, legs, etc. As we grow older we begin to appreciate that personality is more than external appearance, although a great many people have not been able to outgrow this childish notion.

We discover personality just as we become aware of the presence of electricity by its effects. In the rough and tumble of life we notice that one gets ahead with little ability, while another, incapable though he be in many respects, "has a way" with him. Those lacking insight attribute such inconsistencies in life to luck or fate, especially when they themselves are the unfortunates; but luck can play a part in at most two or three instances. Occasionally one is favored by Dame Opportunity or, in the language of the street, "gets a good break." Likewise, a misfortune may befall one quite unavoidably. If, however, misfortune pursues one constantly with dogged footsteps, we may be quite certain that the pursued is a *schlemihl* and is the bearer of some personality-defect.

Slow Grasping of Concept

I must confess here that I had managed to

graduate from college with the highest possible honors, to amass knowledge the very contemplation of which was awesome to most students, that I had gained my majority in years, had written and published extensively, without realizing what a part personality plays in social contacts, indeed without knowing that there is such an article except as the outward appearance of a person. Intelligence and character, it seemed to me, could take care of any residue, and therefore these, together with the physical expression of an individual, would constitute his or her personality.

But it was not long before I observed that intelligent men, possessed of a high degree of character in the ordinary sense, and not even lacking in the physical qualities, did not impress me or others; and I could not but conclude that there is something very important apart from intelligence, character, and physical appearance, which "makes the man." What this something is — *that* seems the very crux of human relationship, the *nervus vivendi* which keeps eluding us at every turn. We all act as if we knew what personality meant, but when asked to explain, much less to define the term, we are usually content with translating it into another perhaps much-meaning but equally unexplained word. To say that "personality is "it" betrays the uncritical attitude of the speaker in matters logical. One might as well use the symbol "X," "Y" or "Z" to designate that avowedly unknown quantity.

Those of the masses who have not yet adopted this nondescript jazz definition of personality, will probably resort to the childish refrain: "It's something, you know, that makes you winning," or "that makes you take with people," or "when people take to you."

Subjective Interpretation

The truth is that, with the general run of people, just as "beauty is in the eye of the observer," so personality is in the mind (perhaps better, affective system) of the judge. We estimate others not only according to our own lights, but in the light of our constitutional make-up, our wishes, desires, purposes and aspirations. The dapper ne'er-do-well with ruddy cheeks, expressive gestures, voluble speech and smart clothes, who dances his way into the heart of the *ingénue,* of course, possesses for her a wonderful personality; his employer or business acquaintances may think otherwise. The probability is that both are looking at this individual from extreme angles. He may have an interesting personality, defective at some points, particularly in the character segment. On the other hand, his choreographic, sartorial, and physical virtues do not comprise, by any means, all of his personality traits.

Great Men as Seen by the Masses

Beethoven, the man who personified music and whose name might easily serve as a synonym for "musical personality," could not have impressed the jeering boys who would gather mornings before his open window and view him standing before them in his night clothes. When one of Beethoven's brother's hired men was told that the eccentric man gesticulating to himself was *Herr* van Beethoven's brother, his remark in peasant dialect, which would be equivalent to "Some brother the boss has," was quite in keeping with the opinions of the waiters, servants, housekeepers, transcribers, and others who had come in contact with Beethoven in a menial way, and indeed even those of the uncultured who had no relations with him. To men, however, like Schubert, von Breuning, Schindler, Moscheles and Czerny, Beethoven's personality bore a halo of divinity which caused them to overlook all his faults and treat him with such fulsome reverence as if he were in a world apart from them.

One can list illustration after illustration of

such "diphasic" personalities. Although Carlyle's influence is beginning to wane rapidly, none of his readers will countenance any disparagement of his towering personality; but Frank Harris, in his *Portraits,* paints a picture of the famous writer that is slightly off color, and even the vastly more charitable and far less egotistic Emerson does not mince his disappointment when relating his first meeting with Carlyle at the latter's cloistered retreat.

Nor does Samuel Johnson's personality, rugged and picturesque as it is, stand out against a less sombre background. Had it not been for Boswell, there is no doubt that Johnson's arrogance, clumsiness and dogmatism would have appeared to posterity in greater relief, for the portrait would have lacked the colorful figuration which Boswell could so well handle.

From an examination of our concrete instances, we may have to conclude that personality does not permit of objective appraisal because of the lability and subjectivity of our standards. Were it to come to such a pass, the study of personality would indeed be a hopeless undertaking, but there is no need of despairing so soon. Despite the complications, we may yet, in fact, we are under obligation to, come to grips with this problem and settle it at least tentatively.

CHAPTER III

THE CASTLE AND ITS APPROACHES

PERSONALITY, though the closest thing to us *in concreto,* as a study may be envisaged as a remote castle with many avenues of approach. Some of the roads are direct; others are winding; a few are hardly more than blind alleys; some bifurcate while others, starting independently, meet at a certain point half way; some are steep and rocky, while others are smooth, yet even the most devious road is not to be avoided, for each approach reveals something which could not be perceived elsewhere; and the nature of the castle, remarkably enough, is grasped adequately only in the light of its approaches. Yes, even the philosophical road, which has been abandoned by the travelers of late, has something to offer.

The Psychological Road Not Enough

One might, at first blush, suppose that the psychological avenue alone should direct our steps, but on reflection we should find the psychological broadway, ideal in prospect, criscrossed by the other roads, so that at times we have before us a labyrinth. The reason is that psychology is a complex of many patterns, and the various schools have each their own path and recourse, and almost each of the schools is associated with some other scientific field which guides its destiny.

Small wonder, then, that textbooks on personality will differ both as to content and interpretation, with the result that students who have been trained along certain lines will be astonished to learn from those who took their courses in another institution that another point of view was reasonably possible.

To enhance the picturesqueness of our metaphor and the force of the analogy, we might even imagine the castle surrounded by a moat, which is no easy obstacle to surmount. The castle is well protected against invasion by divers scientists. Only those who are suitably equipped can reach the gate.

Religious Experience

It is not necessary to recount all these explorations. One might start with the theological, or at at least the *religious,* which involves a sudden flash of experience (vision, revelation, illumination leading to conversion) that to the experiencing subject might mean all there is to be known, while to the skeptical outsider, the religious seizure might signify nothing more than an abnormal quirk or a clinical situation. The *theological* slant is a theoretical elaboration stemming, of course, from dogmas and postulates surrounding the concept of deity.

Explorations from All Sides

Since personality has so many points of contacts — biology, sociology, anthropology, psychiatry, and even organic medicine, it can readily be seen that from all these spheres, there will radiate influences sufficiently powerful to block out almost every view which does not tally with the principal tenets of each respectively. Thus biology will stress the heredity angle, while sociology and its affiliates (education, penology, social work, etc.) will apotheosize the environment and discount the effect of heredity. Anthropologists, with rare exceptions, are inclined to get on the sociological band-wagon, collecting data among primitive tribes calculated to confound the upholders of heredity in a large degree, the instinctivists, and the advocates of unitary traits. Other anthropologists join forces with the psychoanalysts and seek evidence to bolster their cause. There are, however, some who do devote themselves to their task of discovering, through physical measurements, the personality factors of individuals, constitutionally grounded.

The Medical Approach

Clinical psychology, at the present moment, has become a sort of king's highway; and there is some justification for the honor. In the first place, the study of personality, in a psychological sense, has received its first impetus through the interest in dissociation and alterations found in individuals — the so-called multiple personality cases. But abnormal psychology has further presented the claim of shedding a flood of light on normal psychology by displaying exaggerated states and conditions so as to facilitate comparison and investigation. Thus schizoid behavior, or more particularly schizophrenia, gives us a clue to the ordinary idiosyncrasies found in average people who share this particular type, which Kretschmer called *schizothymia*. Psychosomatic medicine, although its principle is almost hoary with age, has recently become the coping stone of clinical psychology. There was a time when mental disorders were

ascribed to malnutrition, infection, and other
physical defects and deficiencies. At present, the
pendulum has swung around the other way, and
the psychogenic factors (i.e., of a mental origin)
of organic disease are stressed via the emotions
(tensions and conflicts and frustrations) so that
Goethe's dictum

Die Natur hat weder Kern noch Schale;
Alles ist sie mit einem Male [1]

is now applicable to medicine, which no longer
has a physical and a mental department, but is
organismic, including the bodily and psychic
aspects as different facets of the same thing. The
latest offshoot of psychosomatic medicine is
psychosurgery, as when the removal of a frontal
lobe in the brain (lobectomy) or the cutting away
a slice of white matter in either frontal lobe in
the plane of the coronal, suture i.e. severing the
pre-frontal lobe from the thalamus (lobotomy)
produces a different kind of personality. [2]

The endocrinological lane had also its traffic,

[1] *Nature has no shell nor core;*
It's all at once — nor less nor more.

[2] W. Freeman and J. W. Watts: *Psychosurgery,* but especially
G. Rylander: *Personality Changes after Operations on the Frontal
Lobe.*

and it was scarcely pedestrian; for it always held a fascination for adventurous spirits, ever since the days of Brown-Séquard. Its main attraction was ushered in by the fanfare of a book by L. Berman, [3] but that road had lost its popularity and is almost abandoned by the personality folk.

Meeting of the Sciences

Psychoanalysis certainly cuts a wide swathe, and is a sort of boulevard, leading us through all sorts of alluring spots and making a bid for the only real entrée into the recesses of our castle. Sometimes the other roads converge into it at one point or another: the sociological, the anthropological, at times even the behavioristic, in its modified phase. Without psychoanalysis, though much of its speculation must be taken with a grain of salt, the study of personality would have offered even greater puzzles than we are confronted with today.

Intersecting Schools

Finally we come to the purely psychological approaches, which are not necessarily close to each other. The hormic and the reflexological or behavioristic are on opposite sides, and correspond to the heredity and environment angles, in a more

[3] L. Berman: *The Glands Regulating Personality.*

[63]

specialized or restricted area. Typology offers a new avenue which will be shunned by those treading on either of the other two. *Gestalt* psychology, again, presents another course to be traversed especially by those who manipulate with "vectors" and "valences" and "fields." While *Gestalt* psychology devotes itself to the dynamics of personality, just as do psychoanalysis and the hormic doctrine of McDougall, it is differently equipped. Factorial analysis, with its testing and statistical accessories, is another alley which has been broadened lately from different quarters.

There are even philosophical tracks to the castle, which cannot be ignored. Personalism has had more than one dignitary to sponsor it; and its slant will at least be helpful in understanding the goal of our pursuit.

Literature

But surely we cannot overlook perhaps the longest of all roads — literature. If all the avenues of approach were to be traversed without taking advantage of the great tunnel that fiction has been excavating, our knowledge of personality would have been scant if not superficial. From earliest times, but, more articulately and intimately, during the past two centuries, the *belles-lettres* have provided us with cues and clues which had not been dreamt of by science. Dostoyevsky's *Crime and Punishment* or his *Brothers Karamazov,* Poe's depictions of the psychoneurotic, R. L. Stevenson's study of double personality, Maupassant's and Balzac's psychological situations, Kipling's outlandish and exotic characters, Thomas Hardy's fateful ironies, strange and fantastic as they seem, approach the truth perhaps more closely than the experimental techniques which often deal with reality in an unrealistic way. What Israel Zangwill once said about the difference between history and fiction, *viz.,* that in history the names and dates are true, while the events described are false, whereas in fiction, the names and dates are false while the accounts are true, may apply to laboratory results too, where the statistics and tables are correct, but the actual conclusions are very much in doubt. Good literature always succeeds in grasping the real thing; the best laboratory often manages to catch the shadow. Let us combine the two methods and spheres for an accurate picture of what does happen.

The manner in which personality has been treated by famous writers is a topic which has not been done justice to as yet. Nevertheless a few sporadic studies like Le Breton's,[4] Martin-Chauffier's,[5] and Roback's[6] would indicate that at least a beginning has been made. On the other hand, it is not always that we can rely on the title of a book, e.g., R. A. Scott-James's *Personality in Literature* (1913) is merely taking the name in vain. The volume consists of a series of literary reviews or, at best, critical essays, which do not even bear a tangential relation to our subject.

Biography

Biography, however, and especially autobiography, cannot but become a source of personality study. It is the raw ore which must be sifted and refined. The yield may be scant in an adequate literary performance, but at least a few grains of relevant information may be picked up. The same may be said for diaries, memoirs, and intimate journals of one type or another. Anything which one writes about himself is bound to be a revela-

[4] M. Le Breton: "Problème du Moi et technique du roman chez Virginia Woolf." *Jour. d. Psychologie,* etc., 1947, vol. 44 pp. 20-34.

[5] L. Martin-Chauffier: "Proust and the Double 'I'." *Partisan Review,* 1949, vol. 16, pp. 1011-1026. (This article is translated from the French).

[6] A. A. Roback: "Peretz's Treatment of Personality" in *I. L. Peretz, Psychologist of Literature,* pp. 356-383.

tion. The case history is a sort of controlled biography for a definite purpose, and is, therefore, on a scientific rather than a literary level.

Here, however, an elementary student may become not only bewildered but exasperated and exclaim that such a labyrinth is more than he had bargained for, that if there is no short and single route he would rather stay home and leave the castle to the adventurous.

Vast Labor Well Repaid

Perhaps it is true that there are too many roads to traverse. It would be a desideratum, indeed, if all roads led to personality as they proverbially lead to Rome; and once there, you can look about for yourself. We are living, however, in a paradoxical world, and our very personality, our own self, is inaccessible to us except through laborious travel on the various roads designated. It would seem as if the only thoroughfare consists of many paths and alleys, but if we took one of them alone, we might arrive at one entrance and be unable to see the castle as a whole. Through the elaborate and circuitous pilgrimage, we might glimpse many hidden nooks and crannies which are unknown to the general public.

Or to apply another analogy, personality is the

mammoth elephant, and we psychologists are the proverbial blind groping about. If we are not to fall into the same blunders as the interpreters in the fable, it is incumbent upon us to cover the whole surface of our subject, which can be done only through a manifold approach.

Nor must we suppose that because of our different avenues, we should become confused. Many of the views do not conflict, but dovetail into or supplement each other; and what is more, when there is a clash, our experience would enable us to thresh out the issues and select the more reasonable and, therefore, soundest interpretation.

CHAPTER IV

THE SEMANTICS OF PERSONALITY

Etymology

FOR A VERY complex and highly human, not to lay oneself open to a tautology by adding the phrase "deeply personal," thing as personality, it is somewhat disappointing that the very significant term should be derived from the Latin word *persona*, a mask. True, there have been other etymologies suggested, like *personare* (to sound or speak through) and *per se una* (self-containing), but in spite of the authorities who choose the one or the other, it seems most likely that *persona*, the mask, which the actors wore on the ancient stage was the source of the term now in the forefront of the mental sciences. The word *persona*, itself, however seems to have been derived from the Greek, *prosôpon*, the countenance, the facial appearance. *Persona* and *prosôpon* do not sound closely related, but through Etruscan channels and assimilation to the Latin prefix *per*, we can very well see that such a change is plausible. The old

Latin word for face or head is *persum,* the shift from *prosô(pon)* to *per(son)* is not difficult to follow.[1]

Now what does the Greek word, *prosôpon,* mean originally? If we take it apart according to its roots, we shall see that all it implies is that which we *see in front* of us, viz., the face. The Hebrew *panim* is also "the front," or exactly what "face" is (Latin, *facies*). The ancestor of our term, personality, was nothing but *face, appearance,* and oddly enough, in the Latin, not even in the sense of genuine, but as a *mask,* as something "put on" for a certain purpose.

A Protean Word

It will not be necessary to trace and classify, as G. W. Allport has done, all the meanings of the word *person,* which, according to him, total exactly 50. That they should aggregate such a round number is, in itself, suspicious; but even after making allowance for a scholastic tendency to pull out as many stops as possible in playing on this theme, we can readily accept a number of these meanings as distinct and clear-cut, *e.g.,* "person"

[1] Prof. Werner Jaeger, privately, has suggested that the Etruscan language was, in this instance, the intermediary between the two words; and it stands to reason from the circumstances of the case.

[70]

may be a reference of esteem, and it may be a mark of contempt or hate, a cover epithet. During the Nazi war, Hitler would constantly be spoken of, by many in England, as "that person," which was too flattering at that.

The Greeks had No Word for it

What, however, does seem noteworthy is the fact that the concept of personality was not known in ancient Greece or Rome; and certainly not in other countries of antiquity. This time, we may say, for once, that the Greeks had *no* word for it. To be sure, there were words to designate certain qualities, not only the external or physical, but virtue or excellence (*aretê*). Nevertheless, personality, in our sense, was *terra incognita* until recent times. If a Greek wished to speak of Socrates' personality, he would be obliged to point out several components, lacking an over-all word.

It is because the Greeks had no word for it, that we have no term for the field of science which covers personality, unless we coin the word *prosoponology,* for the occasionally seen "personology" is a hybrid (Latin and Greek), which is discouraged in coinages. A term to embrace the portion of psychology devoted to the subject-matter of personality is a desideratum.

The Chaldaic and Syriac equivalent, *partsufa,* is suspiciously close in sound to *prosopon,* especially as p and f, in the Semitic languages, are the same letter, and *on* in the Greek word, is merely a suffix; while, in the Talmud, the Chaldaic-Aramaic *partsufa* has received priority over the Hebrew *Panim,* in designation of the physiognomy. To this day, *partsuf* is used by the Jews in the sense of "character," "nature," or "face," the latter, however, in a derogatory sense, as in the exclamation "I can't bear the sight of him."

From Appearance to Reality

Our next puzzle is: Why should the mask, the mere "false-face" have been adopted to render that which is so inward, "down-beneath?" Surely a personality is not a mask, but an honest-to-goodness being. Such deviations from the original concept take place in our own day, too; and Archbishop Trench has presented a large number of similar transformations of meaning in his widely read *Study of Words,* but as regards the semantics of the word "person," it may be assumed that the *persona,* or mask, became a convenient symbol to mark off each individual as a separate entity with a special characteristic, such as the mask represented. Later on the *persona* lost its pristine meaning, and simply *meant* the individual; and when the abstract noun was formed, in consequence of the need of the concept to characterize the state, it grew in dignity and significance. Religion had invested it with spirituality; and ethics with inwardness, so that it was no longer a mere pointing to an individual, or his outward mien and manner, but signified something submerged, which nevertheless was bound to reveal itself in due course.

Linguistic Ramifications

Any one who wishes to delve into the history of the word *persona* might turn to H. Rheinfelder's monograph on the subject [2] of 200 pages (provided with several hundred footnotes and copious illustrations), and survey the vicissitudes of the word, or rather the kaleidoscopic succession of senses which the term touched off among the European nations. There is scarcely a word which has shown such a wide range of applications; and what is more, the Romans have brought its significance home almost everywhere. Apparently the Germanic tribes had no word to express the concept, as *Mannsbild* ("form of a man") was

[2] H. Rheinfelder: "Das Wort 'Persona.' " *Beihefte zur Zeitsch. f. roman. Philologie,* 1928, No. 77.

too corporeal. Gaelic, too, apparently was not too well adapted in this respect. The very name McPherson signifies the son of a parson, i.e., the person of the parish; and the English *parson* is derived from the French, through Norman channels, *persone* or *personne,* who was the curate or vicar. In England, the word parson took on a somewhat pejorative or jocular coloring; for if we consult our *Oxford Dictionary,* we shall find that many animals or birds with black coat or markings would be called "parson." (e.g., parson bird; parson gull). Parson, to the country folk, might mean a guidepost, which is not too complimentary.

In Italian and Spanish, we meet the same evolution of the concept — from the mask, in the classical Latin, through the theological and ecclesiastic meanings, to the juridical and philosophical, including the psychological. Rheinfelder has even found an astrological sense in the old Spanish word *persona* which represents a force or influence attributed by astrologers to planets which stand in a certain relation to each other. In Yiddish, curiously enough, *parshoin* often denotes a very attractive individual (ironically too, a homely person), but also a man of questionable character.

In comparison with Rheinfelder's almost exhaus-

tive study, Bayet's brief article[3] on the history of
the word "person," published twenty years later,
is jejeune and practically redundant, and probably
would not have been written had the author
known of the German work, even though in the
French article, there is a slight psychological lead.
He points out, for instance, that the *person* was
the master, while those who worked for him
were collectively designated as his *personnel,* those
who, in the manner of personal effects, belonged
to him — a sort of feudal remnant. Individuality,
or to be an individual, is a social creation which
rests uncertain in the face of 'circumstances.' In
the opinion of Bayet, many people cannot be
thought of as individuals by the social group.

Personality in Relation to the Semantic Movement

The semantics of personality recalls that in the
Semantic movement, at least in the American
applied section, which was founded by the Polish
engineer, A. Korzybski, personality occupies a
niche of its own. What was his toy-like gadget,
the anthropometer, but an instrument for gaining
an understanding of important concepts in order
to arrive at an integrated personality? Among
the other semanticists, the most direct approach

[3] A. Bayet: "Note sur l'histoire du mot 'Personne.'" *Jour. de
Psychologie,* etc. 1948, vol. 41.

to the problem has been made by C. W. Morris[4]. He combines in his little book many currents, like the sociological, the psychoanalytic, and the philosophical. His thesis is that "we need new selves and new relationship between selves . . . . . We can subordinate impersonal forces to human ends only if we recover the standpoint of the personal. We must become person-centred in order to construct a person-centred society . . . . . We have made over the material environment, and now we cannot evade remaking ourselves." Of course all this is sheer rhetoric, as all "we must" talk invariably is, but he tries to implement his injunctions by a semantic instrument.

Further Developments of the Signification

It is by no means to be assumed that the word "person," with its derivatives, has passed through all its stages in sense and connotation. In antiquity, "personality" was not known at all in our denotation. But when it did become a term for a concept which may have been dimly sensed, no one could have foreseen that the same word, in the plural, might some day come to mean "personal references of an unfavorable sort," such

[4] C. W. Morris: *The Open Self*, 1948; also in his earlier *Signs, Language and Behavior*, 1946.

as are bandied about in political campaigns. Similarly the *personnel* today enjoys a higher standing than when it stood for the employees of a person. Even the chief of a great institution is now part of the personnel; and *personnel psychology* is perhaps another name for the branch which deals with the relations among employees and between them and the administrative staff. The phrase "in person" could scarcely have had a vogue before the cinema became popular. To see an actor or actress "in person," half a century ago, would have been regarded as an absurd statement, but it has become such a stock phrase that at one time, as one might recall, it could be said of dogs "in the public eye" like Rin-Tin-Tin, Laddie Boy, or Igloo, that they would appear "in person."

It would be idle to speculate on the semantic evolution (or involution) of the words "person" and "personality" centuries hence, but we can be reasonably certain that the concept will not remain static; and as the world progresses technically and new vistas are opened up, there are bound to be certain accretions, offshoots, derivatives which we cannot imagine today.

CHAPTER V

HOW IS PERSONALITY TO BE DEFINED?

FIRST of all, what do we understand by personality from a psychological point of view? That there are many different avenues to approach the subject, even under the psychological purview, has already become obvious; but at least when we know what we are about, what it is that we are seeking, the search is not so confusing, and we are not so apt to be misled as on the popular view, where personality is taken to mean anything in an individual that makes a special appeal to us.

It has long been noticed that the more fundamental the phenomenon, the more difficult it is to define it. Some phenomena, the most important of all, defy all attempts. "Life," e.g., has been defined variously by philosophers, biologists, and lay thinkers who have pondered on this drawn-out process; and no definition satisfies the majority. Consciousness baffles one especially, and only demonstration, or better, inner experience, in the form of awareness, can actually tell the story.

So Many Slants — So Many Definitions

Personality is also one of these fundamentals which will allow of a score or more definitions, depending on the particular slant of the definer. In fact, one could tell something about the personality of the definer by studying the definition; and an investigation might be instituted on the peculiarities of defintions of personality. There is, of course, the philosophical psychologist who stresses the *idea* of the *self;* perhaps even its *ideal,* as envisioned by each individual. There is the psychologist who tries to construct it out of the functional components, and there is the sociologist (even though professionally he might be a psychologist) who sees it only as a *relationship to society.*

We are here not dealing with theological, juristic, or philosophical conceptions of personality, but with the psychological reference; and yet within this framework, there are such vast differences that the impatient student might be tempted to throw up his hands in despair or disgust.

Definitions Galore

G. W. Allport endeavors to classify a number of such definitions, and presents categories such as sociological, juristic, biosocial, psychological; and as subdivisions in the latter, "integrative and configurational definitions," "hierarchical definitions," "omnibus definitions," "definitions in terms of adjustment," and "definitions in terms of distinctiveness." Of the two score or more definitions which confront us in the literature, at least half say the same thing in different words. That applies to the so-called omnibus definitions of which a representative example is Morton Prince's, *viz.*, "Personality is the sumtotal of all the biological innate dispositions of the individual and of all the acquired dispositions and tendencies — acquired by experience" [2]. This is a psychological definition, honoring both the heredity and environmentalist doctrines, but it lacks the dynamic or operational click, which is the life of the personality.

The Social Prism

The sociologists have appropriated personality for themselves and persist in highlighting the social milieu. Thus, Burgess defines personality as "the sum and coördination of those traits which determine the rôle and the status of the individual

[1] G. W. Allport: *Personality; a Psychological Interpretation*, chapter II.

[2] M. Prince: *Clinical and Experimental Studies in Personality* (edited by A. A. Roback) 2nd edition, p. 181.

in his social group"[3]. It would seem as if
personality amounted to reputation, according to
this definition. Psychologists with the social
bias are somewhat more circumspect in their
phraseology. Thus F. H. Allport, in his *Social
Psychology,* makes personality equal the "individual
characteristic reactions to social stimuli and the
quality of his adaptations to the social features of
his environment." In this definition, the behavioristic influence is also apparent in the stimulus-
response formulation.

The social stimulus aspect of personality is
stressed particularly by M. A. May, who tells
us that it is the responses made by others to
the individual as a stimulus that defines his personality[4]. Similarly, H. C. Link sees the high
personality quotient (P. Q.) in the number of
social activities which an individual can lay claim
to. "He has developed a collection of activities
and standards which he values above his personal
impulses, and a momentum of habits and skills
which enables him to do those things which are
desirable rather than those which are merely

[3] E. W. Burgess: "The Delinquent as a Person." *Am. Journal
of Sociology,* 1922-1923, vol. 28, p. 66.

[4] M. A. May: "The Foundations of Personality" in *Psychology
at Work,* 1932 (edited by P. S. Achilles) p. 82.

pleasant"[5]. The extreme position in defining personality will be found in the following by A. E. Sheffield, for whom, as a social worker, personality is "the centre of interpenetrating social forces"[6]. I suppose it would be possible to define a boat in terms of winds and water only, something like a "vehicle disturbing the waters under suitable wind conditions;" or a king as "an individual to whom courtiers pay homage," but would this tell us what a king is? Some of the definitions exhibit poetic fancy in that a certain detached or displaced imaging of a phenomenon supervenes over the everyday reality, e.g., the throngs rushing to the subway in the morning hours might be seen as a caravan entering a cavern.

An Elaborate Definition Analyzed

A carefully thought out definition is contained in G. W. Allport's *Personality*, which reads as follows: "Personality is the dynamic organization

[5] H. C. Link: *The Rediscovery of Man,* 1947, p. 200.

[6] A. E. Sheffield: *Case Study Possibilities,* p. 10. Since Mrs. Sheffield was ministering to unmarried mothers, the psychoanalyst might see something symptomatic in the definition, but actually John Dewey's influence is probably at the bottom. In his essay "Reality as Practical" (*Essays Philos. and Psychol. in Honor of William James,* p. 65), he defines the organism as "the active centre of a system of activities."

within the individual of those psychophysical systems that determine his unique adjustments to his environment," but as I have pointed out a dozen years ago, in a lengthy review, "The definition seems to be both abstract and redundant. Every psychophysical organization may be said to be dynamic. The organization is naturally within the individual. Where else could it be? And if we are speaking of systems within an individual, they would have to be psychophysical. Furthermore, all adjustments are unique; and every psychophysical system determines adjustments to an environment.

"We thus see that in spite of the explanations which follow every term in the definition, nothing remains of it after we take it apart."[7]

Personality Not Merely a Distinguishing Mark

Individual differentiation figures in such definitions as Schoen's, which reads: "personality is the organized system, the functioning whole or unity of habits, dispositions, and sentiments that mark off any one member of a group as being different from any other member of the same group"[8]. As we shall see presently, this is not enough. Schoen

[7] A. A. Roback: *Character and Personality*, 1938, vol. 6, p. 244.
[8] M. Schoen: *Human Nature*, p. 397.

might refer to birds and insects in the same way, and the definition is excellent if we bear in mind individuality, but personality is to individuality as electricity is to magnetism, or maybe as energy is to mass.

Some people are scarcely more than individuals. They remind us of prepositions and colorless adjectives, while others are like words fraught with meaning. Or a word, e.g., culture, may be understood to some extent by a philistine, but what does culture mean to a Goethe? In the same way, the two different comprehensions of the same word, even in the same sense, may represent the difference between individuality and personality.

Yet Another Trial

It may be surmised that the present author, too, has participated in the sporadic contest of definitions; and his own attempt figures as the first of several definitions for this term in H. C. Warren's *Dictionary of Psychology,* where the task of defining and revising the personality and psychoanalytic terms fell to him. This definition partakes of the (a) summational, (b) dynamic, (c) social, and (d) differential phase; but first of all, let us see what it is. "Personality is the integrated organization of all the cognitive, affective, conative, and physical characteristics of an individual as it manifests itself in focal distinctness to others." [9] It will be seen that I have not made reference to the environmental factors nor to adjustments. They are to be taken for granted, are corollaries or, what logic calls, *propria,* but are as unnecessary as the enumeration of all the possible elements. On the other hand, I should now amend the definition by adding the words "and carrying a special meaning" after "focal distinctness," since this latter phrase may not imply what it has intended to express, viz., *meaning.* In other words, every personality has his or her own significance, which permits of characterization, often in a single word or phrase.

The Social Implication Not to be Ignored

It will be observed perhaps that while Allport introduces "adjustments to the environment," the

[9] H. J. Eysenck, in his *Dimensions of Personality,* (1949) p. 23, supposes that the first definition of personality in the *Dictionary of Psychology* is Warren's own. For the sake of accuracy, it may be pointed out that Warren would have preferred another, making no use of the term "conative," but emphasizing, rather, adjustments to the environment. In point of fact, definitions 1 and 4 (the latter relating to the popular view) are my own, and it is gratifying that Eysenck has adopted it "throughout this book," all the more so because he had at his command a veritable library of reference books and treatises.

social manifestation is an integral part of my own definition, and although one might argue that you have personality whether other people see it or not (I believe G. W. Allport made this point, although perhaps not in writing) it may readily be countered that without a social validation in the course of history, if not during the lifetime of the individual, the personality remains problematic and lacks the polarization of meaning, which is, so to speak, the emblem or signature of personality. The matter of meaning will be treated in another chapter.

When we come to sift out the various components of personality, we shall note that there are some which rate more, and others less, e.g., memory is an important function of the individual, yet in the evaluation of personality, other things being equal, it would not make a particle of difference whether one had the memory of a Macaulay or that of his "proverbial schoolboy." Intelligence in the abstract sense, e.g., in solving problems is not nearly as significant as insight, which is the type of intelligence that can perceive relations between oneself and others in a proper perspective. In every one of the departments from which personality draws its ingredients, it is *that item which can affect others that counts.* On a deserted island, it may still be the animals, the birds which represent "others," or the affections toward and thoughts of distant people may serve the purpose of the definition. An attitude toward Negroes, Catholics, Fascists, or Communists is more revealing of personality than merely a depressed mood, although such a mood too has an active social bearing. At any rate personality cannot be a gem shining in a social vacuum, nor is it enough to speak of reactions or adjustments to the environment. The social phase enters prominently into the understanding and interpretation of personality.

Demarcating Other Areas in the Field

In the *Psychology of Character*, a whole chapter has been devoted to "Defining the Terms" and demarcating the lines between character, personality, and temperament; and since these words are often used interchangeably, and therefore incorrectly, it is just as well to paraphrase a passage in this chapter, with additional comments. The position taken here, as has been seen, is that personality means an *integrative combination of all our cognitive (knowledge), affective (feeling), conative (volitional) and even physical qualities,* focused in a social medium and bearing an intrinsic meaning, as the result of the individual's make-up and experiences. Every quality, in its *operative* phase, and in relation to other qualities, enters into this complex whole. And herein lies the difference between the psychological approach and the general notion that, while the latter usually singles out one item and elevates it to the ruling concept, the former treats all the qualities as a complex, integration, *Gestalt,* or configuration working, as a rule, more or less harmoniously, but occasionally in the direction of discord, which denotes that the person is maladjusted, neurotic, or even psychotic.

Temperament

By temperament, I understand the *sum-total or blend of one's* affective qualities *as they impress others.* Character — the chief stumbling-block in modern psychological theory — I conceive of as that part of personality which coincides with the *volitional and inhibitory phases* of behavior. In other words, it is the residue of personality after the cognitive, affective, and physical ingredients have been removed. Some of our behavior falls distinctly under the one rubric, and some under the other two rubrics. An uncontrollable tic, such as blinking or heaving the shoulders, is decidedly a personality flaw; but the moment a man has, through sheer will-power (with the assistance of auto-suggestion, self-discipline, and other measures), been able to overcome his muscular contraction, he has manifested a mark of character.

Character

Character has too often been identified with morality, on the one hand, and confused with personality, on the other. Nearly all the American investigators of character and personality do not differentiate between the two concepts they are operating with. To them character is a "characteristic mode of human behavior," i.e., any individual difference, whether a habit, an idiosyncrasy, or peculiarity, would indicate character. It is evident that character and characteristic, in the biological sense, become so merged into one another in this picture, that we are, in a sense, outside the psychological field.

Chief Difference between Man and Animals

It is my own conviction that character is not only a characteristic mode of behavior. It must be shown to be a *significantly* potential mode of behavior, and in order to be significant it can apply only to that sphere of behavior which

[89]

distinguishes man from animal; and until it has been proved that animals are able to inhibit their natural impulses, drives, or instincts, of their own accord, i.e., without the help of powerful and frequent incentives (reward and punishments), we feel safe in limiting the concept of character to human endowment and endeavor. As a corollary from the foregoing, we may further deduce that animals cannot be said to have any personality, notwithstanding the recent book-titles, *The Personality of Insects, Personality of Plants,* etc. Even plants may be invested with individuality, but personality is strictly an attribute of persons, endowed with a modicum of intelligence and character. The faithfulness of the dog, the "independence" of the cat, etc., is common to the species or breed. The individual dog or cat does not decide after deliberation one way or another.

In according the endowment of personality to man alone and not to animals, we might take cognizance of the fact, too, that to be a person implies to be aware of oneself. In German philosophy, the term *"Selbstbewusstsein"* (consciousness of oneself) is akin to McDougall's sentiment of self-regard; and it is very doubtful whether dogs, horses, or even apes, are conscious of themselves as individuals, any more than

[90]

infants are. We might experiment with apes
seeing their reflection in the mirror, but the
awareness of being an "I" alongside other "I's"
can scarcely be proven objectively. A further
sequel of this circumstance is the absence of self-
consciousness, in the sense of being observed
critically by others to the embarrassment or distress
of the individual involved, in animals, although
sometimes we do hear an anecdote referring to
such a case.

Futility of Behaviorist Theory

Behaviorists and mechanists, who are always
looking out for the interests of infra-human organisms, will, of course, refuse to consider any such
distinctions between *homo sapiens* and the lower
species. In their democracy, they apply the same
methods of research to both, and, as practically
all personality testers are behavioristically inclined,
we find that there is a great deal of activity going
on in measuring and comparing behavior with
respect to fatigability, speed of reaction, persistence,
rhythm, likes and dislikes, sensory discrimination,
and so forth. The rigidly behavioristic conception
of personality is that it is the sum-total of habit
patterns, woven by means of conditioned reflexes
on what is practically a *tabula rasa* — a blank

slate. Hence the boastful cry, "Give me the child," which reminds us of the circus illusionist, who promises to produce pancakes and rabbits out of a handkerchief or a top-hat. From the very nature of things, the psychological hawker cannot even create the illusion, but his theory, were it as correct as it is comforting and buoyant, would surely, when applied, work protean wonders.

It is on the basis of childhood fixations that the behaviorist explains our personality attitudes. Personalities are appreciated, claims J. B. Watson, in terms of likes, which gives evidence of the sexual conditioning, or else in terms of respect, which harks back to the awe the commanding presence of our father would call forth in us as children. In other words, our present estimation of personality is governed by ingrained memory patterns. The psychoanalytic outlook, while taking a much deeper view of personality, nevertheless has much in common with this doctrine of childish fixation. It would probably be nearer the truth to say that Watson, while disavowing any kinship with the Freudians, has borrowed from them the very foundation of his philosophy of personality.

CHAPTER VII

THE DETERMINANTS OF PERSONALITY

IN THIS SECTION we are concerned with the very important question of what is at the root of the millionfold varieties of personalities: for it has truly been said that there are no two alike, although similarities may be found quite abundantly. The moment we ask the question, we become entangled in all sorts of difficulties. In the first place, it stands to reason that we must leave the psychological sphere, and begin anew in other territory; for the determinants must somehow be possible tangibles, biological entities or else stimuli and conditions which are demonstrable.

Nature and Nurture

We shall also find ourselves involved in an interminable controversy between the biologically-minded who stake practically all upon heredity and the sociologically disposed who minimize the influence of innate qualities, seeking the causes of the differences in the environment; in other words, the age-old dispute between the geneticists and the environmentalists on the respective rôle of nature and nurture is on again with theory and counter-theory cited, objection met by counter-objection, and so our answer will depend on our own scientific bent or training.

It is scarcely necessary to incorporate, as many textbooks do, a chapter on the biology of repro-duction, introducing the process of fertilization and such terms as zygotes, gametes, allelomorphs, etc., which may be dispensed with for our purpose. It is sufficient to begin with the chromosomes, of which there are forty-eight in man, because it is in the nucleus of these chromosomes contributed by each of the parents that are to be found the genes or carriers of the individual's qualities. The cells (cytoplasm) in which these genes are imbedded are said by many to have some influence too. In USSR., the dominant, one might say, state-sponsored, view is that the cytoplasm or soma-toplasm, indeed, all the cells in the organism, can offset the effects of the genes under favorable conditions, but as against Mitchurin and his fol-lower, Lysenko, who has opened a campaign against the accepted theories, based on experimental results, of Mendel, Weismann, Morgan, and other pioneers in genetics, it is the latter who have the facts on their side.

Environmental Bias

The environmentalists tend to discount the claims of heredity, and, while not denying the importance of the genes, think, nevertheless, that the intra-uterine conditions and reactions during gestation, the impacts on the cytoplasm and later environmental influences, shape the personality of the individual to a much greater extent than the genes. In other words the "original stock," as we refer to it in conversation, is only subsidiary to what happens to it.

No geneticist will disregard the fact that the environment plays a part in moulding the individual, and that even prenatal, intra-uterine conditions enter in to modify the original characters, but nearly all environmentalists prefer to make the most of the changes and little of what the genes have contributed, in the first place.

Temperature and Personality

One scientist who stands high in scientific circles, Ellsworth Huntington, the anthropogeographer, has been zealously propagating a view that has some slight contact with astrology, viz., that the season of birth has a marked effect upon a person's entire life, his attitudes, intelligence, and personality in general. "Persons who achieve unusual success show an exceptional tendency to be born in winter" and his book "might be better," avows the author, if he "had been born in February instead of September." [1] Had he merely seen a relation between temperature and temperament, we might have gone along with him a short way, but it is difficult to countenance a theory which takes on such a bold form, when the evidence is overwhelmingly against it; for after a fervid plea fortified with copious illustrations, he explains all the negative instances by an appeal to heredity!

Psychoanalysis Takes a Hand

To make matters worse, the psychoanalysts, who emphasize the solitary experience, (say) the primal scene, i.e., when the infant observed for the first time the sexual union of his parents—or others—only add to the confusion. One dissident psychoanalyst, Otto Rank, even goes so far as to attribute many of the ills we develop in later life to the

[1] E. Huntington: *Season of Birth* (Wiley) 1938, p. 2.

[96]

55306

trauma of birth; [2] and there are of course the theorizing physiologists who concentrate on the visceral nerves and muscles and interaction in the sympathetic nervous system, in general, as the source of personality manifestations of one kind or another. This is certainly a case of too many cooks spoiling the broth. We have on the one hand, perhaps thousands of genes, with which the fetus is endowed or afflicted, as well as the reactions from the cytoplasm, which is generally not believed to possess any hereditary function. Then there are the numberless intra-uterine processes which must affect the embryo — to what extent, however, we can never know — and finally the forces of the environment, in the broadest sense of the word, must be reckoned with.

And thus there is a tug of war, the biologists pulling in the direction of heredity; the sociologists pulling on the side of environment; and as psychologists, we belong either in the one camp

[2] The birth trauma doctrine of Otto Rank, according to which each child at the time of birth experiences a peculiar anxiety, which is often responsible for the neurotic states in adult life, has nothing to do with the *physical injury* some children receive during parturition, and which may or may not be a contributing cause of maladjustment in later life. Where there is no definite injury, the testimony of the mother as to the difficulty of the labor, is scarcely acceptable as evidence for or against the natal influence on the temperament of the child.

or in the other. Of course, a compromise is usually made, but on close scrutiny it will be seen that a man "convinced against his will is of the same opinion still." Our scientific position depends on our original inclinations and training.

Difficulty of Positive Proof

The human individual lives his life only once; and experimentation to decide what he might have been under different conditions is out of the question. Experiments on sub-human species, like rats, are, first, particularized and reduced to low-level activities; secondly, even there the results are not decisive; thirdly, the applicability of the conclusions — should they be regarded as valid — to the human sphere is contestable.

Common sense in interpreting scientific data is still, even in the age of atomic fission, our most essential instrument, and it is disconcerting to follow the tortuous expositions of the environmentalists who find all sorts of difficulties in the genetic position, but glibly spin out fantastic theories which can never be proven, even if the scaffolding were much less elaborate than what they set up.

A Crucial Instance

Let us take a very simple case. When two

children in the same family turn out to resemble one another not only physically, but mentally and temperamentally or in character traits, the biologist would attribute such resemblance to the same stock of genes. Thus, two girls, years apart, might both have inherited the make-up of the father. A boy born in the interim has a different physique and mentality because he has taken after the mother *i.e.,* has inherited her genes for the most part. Let us admit that intra-uterine play and environmental influences have had their share, and even what I should call idio-empirical occurrences, *e.g.,* a severe injury, a shock, or a grave disappointment, but would it not be more reasonable to suppose that if these were the deciding factors, the boy should have had more in common with that sister approximating him in age than should the two sisters whose environmental influences, including intra-uterine conditions, because separated by a greater interval, would likely have been quite different? [3] Or let us take the instance of individuals who, though coming from diagonally opposite parts of the world and of different ethnic stocks, show a kinship in many ways, which the environment, as

[3] Idio-empirical" is the word coined to designate the type of experience which is peculiar to a given individual, and scarcely in the same category as the usual environmental happenings in the course of social development.

known from records, cannot account for, but the combination of genes (a simpler matter than the millions of possible conditions which arise in the course of development, beginning with the prenatal period, and are supposed to effect more and more significant changes in a compound manner) can, by virtue of the uniformity of nature, turn out to be somewhat alike, since certain characteristics go with others, and the constellations are such as to range people into types. It is thus quite possible that a person from Denmark and one from Holland might exhibit markedly similar characteristics, in fact far more similar than in the case of individuals in the same family who have inherited each from a different parent.

The Pot Calling the Kettle Black

Environmentalists will often refer to the genes and their functions as mystical. They vociferously deride any form of instinct theory, particularly McDougall's, as if such a view presupposed the transmission of mental qualities in a vacuum, and not through a physical substrate in the form of genes. But when they get under way to expound their own hypothesis, they take *carte blanche* and ride roughshod over the most elementary canons of logic, and crash the gate of youthful gullibility, which feeds on far-fetched explanations of ordinary behavior, highlighted by a psychoanalytic terminology and bias.

How Scientific Are the Following Statements?

An exemplification of this business of straining at a gnat and swallowing a camel, quite typical of many of our textbooks, will be found in the following passages which are reeled off, as if the evidence were abundantly supplied. The author is a dyed-in-the-wool environmentalist who misses no opportunity to poke fun at "heredityists," as he calls them. Yet descanting on the mechanisms of frustration and identification in the development of personality, he leads us into all sorts of vagaries.

> Since a boy is more loved and less frustrated by the mother, the boy's early identification is easily made with the father. If the father is an actively masculine person, the boy will develop a masculinoid type of personality.
> If, on the contrary, the mother is the dominating member of the household, that is to say, a person of masculinoid make-up, the boy's original identification with her tends to continue. The result depends on the stage of identification. If the latter occurs in the pre-genital stage, on an anal

basis, the boy will develop into a passive type of personality. If, however, the identification is on a genital level, that is at the time when the inhibited energy is shifted from the other appetites to the genital region, the identification, being on a phallic basis, leads to a narcisstic or self-admiring complex which is of course in keeping with the phallus as a pleasure-giving entity.

*　　*　　*　　*　　*　　*

When a boy happens to be exposed to parents that are equally severe, the fear of a severe father, combined with the hatred of the father, leads to a personality that is feminine and passive but ever striving to be masculine. This is where Adler's 'inferiority complex' and 'masculine protest' have probably had their origin.

In the girl the development proceeds along somewhat different lines. If the female child has an indulgent or accom-modating father, she easily overcomes her envy of masculine structures, by identifying with the mother and taking on a feminine role. The girl who is faced repeatedly with a strict or indifferent father, is forced to identify with him, under protest. Her envy of masculine structures is greatly increased, and her behavior becomes clearly masculin-oid in character.

One great difference in the personality development of boys and girls is that the boy's co-conditioned love-object is the mother, and continues to be that throughout the infantile period, while the girl whose co-conditioned object is also the mother must break away at an early stage. The boy's development, if normal, does not change this fixation, but requires a father identification to strengthen it. The girl however must break away from the infantile attachment, make her identification on a homosexual basis, but shift (recondition) her fixation (love-object) to a person of the other sex, namely—effect an adjustment on a heterosexual basis. Moreover, the girl must not only give up her primary love-object (the mother) but must establish an attitude of rivalry and hatred for her. [4]

Deleterious Effects on Students

All this of course is unsubstantiated, and can never be proven, because in order to isolate all the variables for observational and statistical treatment, let alone experimental procedure, an army of researchers would be required over a long period of time, yet students lap it up, because the whole account dramatizes their young life. It makes out

[4] M. H. Krout: *Major Aspects of Personality*, pp. 233, 234, 235.

of all of them heroes and heroines. They "know" now why they can't get along with the "old man." They can "see" now why they are so dissatisfied, why they do so poorly. Who would not, in their place, *i.e.,* when frustrated by a dominating mother or after fixation, and identification with this or that parent, have turned out the same way? The youth makes his parents the guilty ones for his own defects or delinquencies, and has no difficulty in condoning every culpable act of his.

This, we must bear in mind, is textbook material, and furthermore, the text is not that of a psychoanalyst, but presumably general in character. The series of unproven statements may be justifiable in an article or treatise on psychoanalysis, but a book which is so intolerant of comparatively simple and sensible views should at least make an effort to sift interpretations which are of a purely subjective nature, even if presumably based on clinical observations. (How many; and what controls were used in checking on negative instances will never be ascertained.)

Conjecture vs. Fact

Environment certainly must be taken into account in the understanding of personality development, but first of all, the facts must be known, not merely surmised. In the case of intra-uterine influence, other than physiological deficiencies or injuries, they cannot even be surmised, so that one is bound to grope in the dark. Evidently many writers in the non-physical sciences delight in drawing out the ingenious, no matter how devious the explanations, as, e.g., when a prominent psychologist explained Charles Darwin's achievement not as a result of an inherited endowment and interest[5] in natural science but by reason of a fixation upon his mother who had leanings in that direction. But why would she possess such interests? Shall we say, by the same token, that it was due to

[5] The interest usually comes with the endowment. In other words, one who is musically gifted will become interested in music, but aside from that it is not too much to assume that our constitutional build, a particular brain structure or a certain combination of genes, or both will incline the growing child in a given direction. Why, e.g., should one child have his gaze directed upward, while another child looks down toward the ground as he walks? Why should the outdoors have a special appeal for one, and indoors for another?

The fact that adolescent genius is never discouraged by carping teachers (e.g. Paderewski, who was ridiculed by his piano teacher and told to study the violin instead, while the violin teacher equally disdainful recommended composition) nor coerced by domineering parents should at once suggest to us that environmental influences are secondary once interests are inherent. Many of the great literary men have been forced into the study of law or medicine by their practical fathers only to abandon their profession after graduation.

fixation, on her father, and so on *ad libitum?*

It surely is more in keeping with common sense to assume that a certain combination of genes would yield a particular type of constitution or, perhaps better, a nervous system and brain structure, which would incline the individual toward certain situations, as he became mature, and would render him more adaptable to the comprehension and interpretation of certain phenomena. And if this applies to the cognitive or intellectual sphere, how much more to the social, attitudinal, and character phases? We do not inherit the perceptions or the views but the susceptibilities in a given direction just as diatheses, and not diseases are inherited in the sphere of pathology.

The Broken Home Argument

The genes are the ground; the environment the figuration. Both combined present the particular pattern of personality. Poverty and humble circumstances may hamper an individual in his progress, yet frequently they spurred genius and near genius to accomplishment. Broken homes have often been said to cause juvenile delinquency. If statistics show a high correlation between the two, it yet does not follow, by any means, that the one is the cause of the other, at least not until we have satisfied ourselves as to the rôle *heredity plays in causing the broken home,* in the first place. [6]

There is also a difference between direct and indirect environmental influence. Usually the environmentalist plays up the unfavorable condition as directly affecting the psyche of the individual, causing tension, frustration, etc., which in its turn leads to the delinquency. But it is also possible that the broken home, or a domestic set-up with a drunken and irresponsible father, may simply send the unsupervised child, with an unstable character, to join delinquent companions, and thus the outcome is not the effect of a direct mental impact but a sequel of negative circumstances. A broken home *could* be a blessing sometimes in comparison with an inferno of an unbroken home but much divided house.

It would seem necessary for those environmentalists who discount the force of biological inheritance to account for the numerous instances of fine character despite the poor environment, broken homes, an oversevere or derelict parent, etc. Sometimes one obtains the impression that environmentalists eschew the reading of biography, lest

[6] N. D. M. Hirsch: *Dynamic Causes of Juvenile Delinquency.* A full discussion of this question will be found in this book.

the facts gleaned might militate against their pet theory. The researches which are so copiously cited to bolster it are frequently undertaken with the same purpose in view but may easily be matched by others which apparently happened to strike the blind spot of the selector. The most fruitful information might be gathered from investigations of identical twins raised in altogether different environments as compared with siblings brought up by the same parents under relatively similar circumstances.

The problem of heredity and environment in the light of published investigations on twins and foster children has been critically surveyed by R. S. Woodworth in a report prepared for the Committee on Social Adjustment (Social Science Research Council). In this comprehensive review which comprises about 75 separate studies, (among the studies missing in this summary is N. D. M. Hirsch's extensive monograph on twins [1]) we are confronted with diverging views through which the clear-headed and experienced author guides us with cautious steps. His methodological suggestions constitute the most valuable sections in the report

[1] N. D. Hirsch: *Twins; Heredity and Environment.* "Neither the extreme hereditist nor the extreme environmentalist is correct, but the contribution of heredity is several times as imporant as that of environment."

more than half of which is taken up with correlations of intelligence and I. Q., as if that were the crux in the controversy.

The summing up reminds one of the judicial charge to a jury. Woodworth is loath to favor either side. Nevertheless some of the expressions coming from veteran psychologists are definitely giving more weight to heredity, and his own conclusion, in spite of his capacity as a moderator, a role to which he seems to have been born, reveals what we have been anticipating all along. It reads:

> To assure a gifted young couple that they could do as much for the next generation by adopting any "normal infant" as by having a child of their own would be a scandalous exaggeration of the known facts. [8]

Of course, environmentalists always have a trump card up their sleeve, because the original reaction of an infant to some occurrence is, to them, part of the environment. Thus if the Dionne quintuplets, whose environment is as equal for all insofar as a painstaking control, on the part of

[8] R. S. Woodworth: *Heredity and Environment,* p. 86. (Social Science Research Council 1941, Bulletin 47).

trained supervisors could make it, will nevertheless show marked individual differences, the "solution" will be that the voice of the nurse, the
chirping of the bird, the color of the gift, the
pat of a parent or nurse, had a different effect
(conditioning) in each case. But why and to
what extent? In other words, here heredity is
reduced to environmental conditions, to begin with.

Indeed, the resourcefulness of environmentalists
in meeting arguments matches that of little Sammy
Kaplan, who was always bringing home a poor
report card while promising that the following
month he would have nothing but A's. When
his ambitious father, after months of patient
waiting, took him severely to task for not making
good his promise, the lad confided to him that
it was all due to his teacher who was a "terrible
anti-Semite" and would not give a decent grade
to a Jewish pupil.

"All right" decided his businesslike parent "By
next September, you'll be baptized, and that will
settle your teacher." But September and October
went by, and the boy, now called Seymour, still
received C's and D's. His father was furious.
"What now?" he thundered, "You're a full-fledged
Christian, aren't you? No prejudice, no bias.
What excuse is there now?"

"But dad" calmly interposed (Sammy)-Seymour, "How can you expect me to beat those smart Jewish kids?"

The study by Barbara S. Burks of monozygotic twins (i.e. fertilized in the same ovum) and reared almost from birth by different foster parents under different environmental conditions, confirms the claims of geneticists, as may be seen from the following statement:

> In certain aspects of temperament and social behavior, the twins showed some striking parallels in behavior sufficiently unusual to suggest congenital predispositions, especially since the environments of the twins were quite dissimilar in many variables clinically related to personality development. They had similar histories with respect to nail biting, enuresis, and early puberty; they were similar in observed expressive movements — gait, handshaking, writing tempo, and, to some degree, graphic form, and in a group of traits (ratings) that appeared to rest on an underlying physical vitality and non-adaptive irritability. [9]

[9] Barbara S. Burks: "A Study of Identical Twins Reared Apart" in *Studies in Personality* (in honor of Lewis M. Terman) p. 67.

What is more, and of special significance for the evaluation of graphology, the writing specimens at different ages of the twins, who were reared far apart, show such marked similarity that this, in itself, would furnish ample proof of a gene-determined nervous system, especially as the writing for both twins changes *in the same direction,* as the girls get older.

A Puzzle Seldom Posed

One question which crops up here is; why are there so many scientists seeking the secret of personality in the environment rather than in the genes? Next to USSR and its satellites, of course, this country is most affected by the view that external circumstances make the man or woman. An extended article or monograph might be written on this subject, but among the reasons, the following may be mentioned as likely:

(1) The fact that heredity is associated with a species of fatalism. If we are born with a particular constitution, then nothing can be done about it, whereas if heredity is a negligible factor and environment dominates the scene, all that has to be done is to change the environment, and presto the personality improves. This is in line with the mechanistic, behavioristic, conditioned-

reflexological outlook, and in the United States, that attitude, philosophy, or whatever one chooses to call it, is rampant.

The fatalism of heredity has, of course, been much exaggerated. It is true that "you cannot make a silk purse out of a sow's ear," but education in a broad sense can benefit both the best and those not-so-good. A better environment is, to be sure, desirable, but let us not mawkishly suppose that the many parolees who end up their career in murder before they are committed again would have been model personalities if their early environment or intra-uterine conditions had been entirely different, while inheriting the genes they have.

Insurmountable Handicaps of Environmentalism

One advantage which the heredity conception has over its rival is that we have something tangible to go by through the comparison of parent and offspring, barring mutations and atavistic occurrences. Aside from physical resemblances, there are records which we might consult and check. There is no way, however, of keeping tabs on environmental conditions so that they might be correlated with the behavior of the individual, except in the most obvious cases of general organismic reaction. A child who has tasted poverty will, as an adult, appreciate comfort; but will all underprivileged individuals develop the same traits, habits, or whatever you wish to dub them, as a result of these handicaps?

August Strindberg has definitely made an attempt, in his autobiography, *The Son of a Servant,* to show how much his environment was to blame for his disposition, attitudes, temperament, and outlook. But the environment was the same for all his brothers and sisters, yet his two elder brothers were well adjusted, while he kept entangling himself in difficult situations. A loving atmosphere and less austere father might have made him perhaps a little happier, but was he not interpreting conditions to suit his fancy, and was he not often making it hard for his parents to understand him, so that he might play the martyr? And if we read between the lines, we shall find that Strindberg's father was just and paternal in his attitude, certainly devoted.

And yet this same Strindberg, in his ghastly and soul-searing autobiographic narrative of his late forties, so serenely labelled *Legends,* goes to the other extreme and proclaims that he would never ask for justice, never seek to have a wrong redressed because he was predestined to suffer, so that his bitter life was accepted as a penance for some original sin.

> The disturbances last till morning. Why don't I complain to the manager? Because never once in my life have I succeeded in obtaining justice. Being born and pre-destined to suffer injustice, I have ceased to complain. [10]

On the other hand, because of Strindberg's emphatic position on this matter, we have no way of evaluating the heredity situation in that family. Heredity, in this instance, might not give us the clue, any more than it would explain his genius, unless we assumed that the accumulation of certain traits and the elimination of others could produce the particular end-result which spelled that gifted paradox, August Strindberg.

(2) The influence of sociology, which has infiltrated everywhere, not only in academic life, but in the most diverse agencies: social, govern-mental, educational, labor etc., is another promi-nent factor. Sociology, if it does not deal with it exclusively, certainly stresses the environment in every connection.

(3) Psychoanalysis, while not studying the

[10] August Strindberg: *Legends,* p. 20.

environment in the same sense as the others enumerated, derives all significance from the early experiences of the child. Inasmuch as the original nature of an individual is considered as secondary to what happens to him or her at a tender age, these experiences might well be subsumed under the general head of environment.

Useful in Acquiring Mass Data

(4) *Expediency* is another motive in the worship of the environmentalist doctrine. The culture or civilization of a people yields valuable information for strategic purposes. Knowing the historical and social conditions of the Russians will give us a clue as to what to expect in general, and how to handle them. This is especially true of more remote civilizations such as the Japanese or Hindu, but what has this mass information to offer us in the way of studying an *individual personality?* And personality does deal with the individual. The personality of Rabindranath Tagore is not merely the product of his surroundings. Nor is Lenin just another Russian.

Some time ago, a great ado was made of the fact that a young American, who had been adopted by a Chinese family as a two-year-old child, after his missionary parents were killed by bandits, on arriving in the United States, to all intents and purposes, acted like a Chinaman and found the country of his birth so foreign to him, that he returned to China.

Assimilation and Acculturation

There is, however, nothing startling about this incident. The cultural accoutrements, the distinct Chinese manners, style of food, language, gestures, gait, and all the other more or less surface attachments certainly could not but change his appearance and outlook *as regards China and the United States.* The question is whether his individual traits, temperament, more intimate attitudes, were patterned after his foster parents or resembled those of his real parents. An extreme geneticist does not deny the process of assimilation or acculturation. We do not have to go to China to find evidence for it, but if the more particularized traits of personality: timidity, or bravery, faith or distrust, generosity or miserliness, tactfulness, hypocrisy or sincerity, moroseness, envy or unbegrudgingness, benevolence or malice etc., are to be shown as independent of the personality of the parents, something more substantial than the spectacle on the boat arriving from China would have to be undertaken. C. Kluckhohn, who reports the case, expressly states that the "biological heritage was American, but the cultural training had been Chinese." [11]

(5) The Nazi exploitation of genetic principles for their nefarious purposes has been, to some extent, responsible for the abhorrence, in many circles, of references to "stock." Let us not forget, however, that Hitler and his co-villains believed in environmental influences, too, as the arrangement of the youth camps would indicate.

Historical Determinism

(6) The halo of Marxism and its deterministic philosophy lends support to the environmentalist doctrine. In communist circles, to stress heredity smacks of a reactionary tendency. Idealism and mysticism are tagged on the generally received accounts of gene transmission. The curious thing about it is that the new policy in USSR "politbiol" circles, viz., to advocate the erstwhile universally rejected theory of the transmission of acquired characteristics, through the somatoplasm, is of a piece with the esoteric and hazy notions of Samuel Butler and Semon on the genesis of instinct, and C. G. Jung on the inheritance of the collective unconscious in the form of arche-

[11] C. Kluckhohn: *Mirror for Man,* 1949, p. 19.

types, which harbor symbolically the experiences of the group.

Queer bedfellows, Lysenko and Jung! Weismannism subservient to Neo-Lamarckianism, and heredity subsidiary to environment!

Strange portents of our time

Personality vs. Social Forces

Another paradox of the environmental ideology is that while the individual is supposed to be a mere function of mass action, and is, therefore, looked upon as only one among many in the vast human collective, shaped by the impacts of social and historical forces, there is actually no country which is as guilty of leader worship as USSR. Indeed, Marx, Lenin, and Stalin are simply a Communist counterpart of God, the Father, the Son, and the Holy Ghost. This is only another instance in which theory and practice are at odds with one another, and one more indication that something is wrong either with the theory or the practice, or possibly with both, considering the misplaced emphasis on power and its fountainhead.

Dialectical materialism in USSR, taking its lead from some of Engels's writings, at least makes an attempt to allow for an article like consciousness or personal initiative in the evaluation of historical phenomena. The more mecanistically inclined American environmentalists do not go even that far; and are intent upon finding the causes, for the most part, determined by what had happened to the individual in the course of his or her experience, beginning with the intra-uterine pressures and tensions.

CHAPTER VI

THE UNIT OF PERSONALITY

THE HUMAN being is a unit which should be treated as such, but which must be analyzed into components, if we are to learn anything about it. The anatomist and the physiologist divide the body into muscles, nerves, bones, cells, various organs, etc., the chemist finds, in the body, phosphorus, salts, carbon, etc.

The psychologist discovers other things not in the body, but in the psychophysical organism and principally the mind. We have perceptions, images, ideas, emotions and mental associations. All these are the constituents of the mind. Personality, however, has its own constituents.

Mind and Personality Not Equivalent

If asked to make an inventory of personality, one who has not had much training in psychology would be apt to include, as is frequently done in books under the title of personality, many items which are not essential. In one sense all mental processes are part of our personality. Everything we do and even the clothes and furnishings we select reflect our personality. Indeed, the things we fail to do or refrain from doing may also be counted in, but rather than take such an all-embracing view, we might just as well eliminate those functions of the mind which do not have a private angle, more closely *related to the self as affecting other selves* than, let us say, memory, sensation, imagination, perception, mechanical intelligence, not that these do not shed light on one's personality, but they are *not the characteristics of personality.* Nor is every mode of behavior to be considered as basic. Even emotions and the various aliases of instinct cannot fill the bill. We are looking for a generic term that will express the unit of personality more than anything else — and that is the *trait.* The *trait* (originally a French word derived from the Latin *tracto*) is the line (something drawn) many of which constitute the individual's sketch.

Patterns Differ and Why

Thus a man sits opposite you and boasts of his conquests, of his achievements, of his aspirations. He has had a good schooling; in fact he has several degrees, but he cannot eradicate this inborn tendency to brag about himself.

Another man, while speaking to you, wonders how much he can get out of you. His whole life seems to be a question mark symbolising, "What is there in it for me?" He reads the same newspaper as the altruistic person, the man who has devoted himself to serve his fellow-men, he listens to the same sermons, belongs to the same organizations, yet his acquisitive trait, paralleled by the intelligence counterpart of shrewdness, is dominant at every step.

We all have an assemblage of traits going to make up our personality. One pattern is different from every other. In other words, as the fashion advertisers say, "only one of a kind is made." Our traits are the same, but they appear not only in different proportions but in different groupings and settings. In the one case we have wisdom, perspicacity, intuition; in another the principal direction of intelligence lies in craftiness, cunning and scheming. One set of traits will affiliate with another which is kindred to it; and thus we may truly say that we are like loaded dice, not only loaded, but magnetized so as to attract or repel.

Outwardly the differences may not show so much, because those who are aware of their shortcomings will try to polish the dice so as to conceal their respective weights. They will be plausible, they will say, "What can I do for you" when they mean just the opposite; but the psychologist, the psychoanalyst, the psychiatrist and the graphologist can see deeper, because the individual under test conditions cannot help revealing his true self.

Each of us has thousands of traits, some relating to the physique or appearance (tall, short, stout, slim; fair, dark) others belonging to the intelligence department (bright, dull; acute, obtuse; cultured, philistine) while many traits deal with the emotional, social, and characterial phases of man. Every deliberate act points to a trait, and even habits can be subsumed under the same category. When it is said of someone that "he makes a habit of not paying his debts," it is not the habit which is significant, but the trait of irresponsibility. The incorporation of the word "habit" is only for the sake of emphasis, to show that the trait has had several occasions for manifestation. A trait will, in general, show its true colors through the repeated behavior, but it may not have had the opportunity, or else it might have been checked or disguised, so that it is not detectable to the "naked" or inexperienced eye.

Some traits don't amount to as much as others so far as personality is concerned. Often it depends on the particular judge or perhaps victim. To A, aggressiveness may be just "terrible;" to B, it is mildly censurable, while C may even admire it. To say that we differ in our evaluation of these units or elements is not to deny that they exist, but as we shall soon see, there are quite a few psychologists grouped around the powerful Columbia school who question them in all seriousness.

Definition of Trait

What, however, is a trait? Again I consult the *Dictionary of Psychology* and find my own definition as No. 2, viz., "A distinctive mode of behavior, of a more or less permanent nature, arising from the individual's native endowments as modified by his experience." What does this imply neurologically or genetically? Simply that we have inherited a certain physical structure and probably also a neural pattern which will determine our reactions to the various experiences. In other words, there is a mould which will shape our reactions, and Tom and Dick are different not because they have been trained differently or were subjected to disparate conditions, but because their neural structure is different in various respects. Cleanliness is a trait, just as is honesty, cheerfulness or miserliness. That seems elementary, obvious to the man in the street, but the Columbia psychologists, taking their cue from the late E. L. Thorndike, would have no truck with traits, and their spokesman, P. M. Symonds[1] thinks that all our acts are specific, depending on a particular situation and condition. An individual may be tidy in one respect and untidy in another, officious to colleagues and subordinates and cringing to superiors; deceitful in one sphere and honest in another. What consistency, he asks, can there be under the circumstances? In an extensive and laborious investigation, covering several years of experimentation, H. Hartshorne and M. A. May have attempted to prove that the specificity theory was correct, that children will cheat and yet not lie; or steal and not cheat, hence they have no scruples in throwing overboard the general trait of dishonesty.

The Specificity School and Its Weak Position

If this were really so, i.e., if we could not predict from previous acts the behavior of most individuals, the world would be a sorrier spectacle

[1] P. M. Symonds: *Diagnosing Personality and Conduct.*

than it really is. We should not have to be wondering about the date of Doomsday via the atom bomb. Fortunately for us, Symonds, May, *et alii* have proven only that if you are set on proving something, you will do so to your satisfaction by inadvertently disregarding some important factors. Elsewhere[2], I have shown that the Hartshorne-May research, conceived though it was on a grand scale, was marred from the beginning, because the *motives underlying a certain trait* were not examined, so that the trait-name, whether honesty or dishonesty, was in point of fact only a *conventional* term, as popularly employed, while, in reality, we were dealing not with one but with a *few* different traits. That there are certain individuals who are inconsistent goes without saying. August Strindberg, as his several autobiographical books abundantly show, is one of those paradoxes, but are we to frame a rule on the basis of the exceptions, which, for that very reason, offer good material for further scrutiny?

Common Sense Helps to Orient Us as to Traits

Luckily, too, everyday observation, in addition

[2] A. A. Roback: "Personality Tests — Whither?" *Character and Personality*, 1933, vol. 1, pp. 214-224.

to experimental evidence [3] tends to contradict the view that our behavior is nothing but a specific stimulus-response affair, that on Monday afternoon we might be brutal, and on Tuesday morning, our gentleness will surprise no one, least of all the specificist. The fact that Goering could be tender to a canary while engineering the extermination of millions of humans need not detain us for a moment. Even the devil purrs and coos on occasion. The whims and ruses of gangsters and psychopathic personalities should not be invoked to overrule the status of normal beings. These whims have their place under a separate bailiwick, and may be studied under the fluoroscope of psychoanalysis or some other dynamic system. Goering's motives, attitudes, etc., in the light of compensation or displacement, might then clear up much of the perplexity.

Genotype and Phenotype

Above all, we must learn to recognize a trait, and to trace it to the original motivational sources. Is a smile always a sign of cheerfulness or friend-

[3] The earlier experiments are cited in A. A. Roback's *Psychology of Character,* chapter 21, and in the same author's *Bibliography of Character and Personality.* Investigations by graduate students at the Harvard Psychological Clinic are described in H. A. Murray's *Explorations of Personality.*

liness? Shakespeare has recognized long ago that "he smiles and smiles and is a villain." There is the roguish smile and the smile of embarrassment, the vacant smile of the imbecile and the wistful smile of disillusionment, and a score of other varieties. In our conventional language, the behavior is designated by the same word, but some of the smiles are a world apart from one another.

From the sphere of biology[4], we have acquired a pair of correlates which are of considerable value in the treatment of traits. They are the *phenotype* and the *genotype*. The former exhibits the individual or the trait as is perceived right then and there — the man as he appears at any given moment of observation. He may be jolly or grim, but in either case we cannot take him at his face value unless we know more about him and judge him in the light of other traits. The genotype is what a careful scrutiny of underlying motives will reveal. It is what was originally there in the way of inherited tendencies as

[4] G. W. Allport, in his *Personality* textbook, seems to imply that Kurt Lewin was the originator of these concepts, but they are to be found in the biopsychological literature of Germany before 1927. In fact, H. Hoffmann, as early as 1923, in his monograph *Ueber Temperamentsvererbung* (Grenzfragen des Nerv.- und Seelenlebens, 1923, No. 122) speaks of phenotypical traits, as if it were a term in vogue at the time. G. Murphy in his recent bulky volume, *Personality* (1947), apparently has taken his cue, as to the origination of the concepts, from G. W. Allport.

ingrained in the neural and structural patterns, without the paddings and camouflages, although the modifications through training and other experience will, naturally, by a certain age, have become a part of the genotype.

A Sign-Post Which is Universally Ignored

There is one phenomenon which has always impressed me, and which does not appear to have had any consideration from anyone else, although surely it must have been noticed by a great many. We may have two friends who come from different parts of the world or from unrelated ethnic groups, who nevertheless resemble one another in inflection, tempo, and quality of voice (say a clicking or rasping but voluble and confident style of speech); moreover the play of mimique around the eyes and mouth is reminiscent of one another too, and there is something alike in the gait. Now, the most surprising thing is that certain attitudes, rationalizations, defense acts, excuses, and major traits like negativism, unreliability in keeping appointments on some irrelevant pretext, scatter-brainedness, snobbishness, or other traits are shared by the same individuals who have had a totally different environment. Yes, they might even have the same type of ail-ments, spinal or hip trouble. Often, a few gestures, the gait, or the voice will become an index as to what to expect of a new acquaintance.

If my observation is borne out by others, and if it is not a series of coincidences, then it suggests the operation of some law or principle implicit in the uniformity of nature, on an extensive scale, such that traits will be grouped in clusters, with the physical characteristics paralleling, or corresponding to, certain personality traits. Far from the atomized acts or habits that the specificists insist on, we should perhaps, have a hierarchical grouping [5], but, in any case, the concept of traits cannot be relinquished without doing violence to our whole system of social intercourse. It is my belief that just as David Hume did not presume, in his everyday living, to doubt the existence of the self or the operation of the principle of causation, which he questioned in his philosophizing, so our specificists take the traits for granted in their transactions with people. If they had to suspect every person who has "made good" in this or that connection lest

[5] H. J. Eysenek (*Dimensions of Personality*, p. 16) thinks of personality as hierarchically structured but along factorial lines involving (a) intelligence, (b) introversion-extraversion, and (c) neuroticism. His and his collaborators' results might fit into the typological scheme just as well.

he or she would, on future occasions, reverse their reputation, life would, indeed, be almost intolerable.

Are there Any Pseudo-Traits?

The most valiant defender of the trait view has been G. W. Allport, whose analysis of the subject is both penetrating and sound. His critique of the specificity school is, to say the least, damaging, and his classification of traits into cardinal, central, and secondary is, for the sake of convenience, acceptable. Strictly speaking, such categories might be multiplied or graded more finely. On the other hand, the division of pseudo-traits as contrasted with genuine traits, which F. Baumgarten introduces, is less appealing. Her distinction might have a certain value in ordinary conversation, but since every genuine trait might have its "phony" counterpart, our canvas would be so terribly crowded that we would be doing nothing but shoving traits around. Is not every pseudo-trait a manifestation of the *genuine* trait — insincerity, which will take on countless forms according to the situation and the particular individual's motives? On the other hand, if the "pseudo-trait" is not deliberately insincere, then some of the unconscious mechanisms must be brought into the story. As a temporary label, the pseudo-trait, might, for the sake of expediency, be retained, but unlike the ordinary trait, it is not a psychophysical entity, but merely a name for the fact that something bears watching or investigating.

ATTITUDES

For the past decade or more, there has been a growing interest in the psychology of attitudes. An attitude is very much like a trait, often indistinguishable from it, to the extent that it would not be wrong to call the element by either name. Pessimism is a trait, but it may also, as an outlook on life, become an attitude.

Differentiation of Trait and Attitude

An attitude is *directive* toward something or someone. It is more fraught with a readiness for action. *It is action in a congealed state, which any favorable occasion is apt to bring to a liquidation point.* That is why attitudes are, other things equal, more dangerous than traits. The attitude suggests a certain muscular tension, a posture, and an emotional relation to an individual or idea. A communistic leaning is an attitude, as is republicanism or prohibitionism, or anti-vivisectionism on the part of an individual.

An attitude, unlike a trait, is often rationalized. The anti-Negro in the South will give his reasons for putting the colored people "in their place." Traits are not always admitted. Very few people would own up to being lazy, stingy, or cruel. Attitudes, on the contrary, are largely proclaimed, except by the diplomat. Furthermore, attitudes are mainly specific, while traits, as has already been set forth, are general. We can take attitudes toward almost anything or anyone, boogie woogie music, the comic strip, spinach, or the king of Egypt, but a trait like generosity implies that charity does not begin at home, at any rate, that it does not stay there. A benevolent person who does not extend sympathy or aid to the lowliest, but only to those of his class, clan, or clique cannot be said to possess the trait. Specificity does, however, apply to attitudes. Let us note, nevertheless, that attitudes, too, may run in clusters. Reactionaries will generally prove to be anti-Semitic, anti-Negro, and xenophobic (opposing all immigration) as well as opponents of labor reforms. On the other hand, a liberal will be defending the rights of the underdog everywhere. It is very seldom that a radical will betray race prejudice. Thus, even attitudes can fit into a scheme of grouping which might be utilized in establishing where a given individual stands on social questions.

Momentous Issues in Collective Life

It is for this reason that attitudes have been common territory for social scientist and psychologist. The sociologist may be interested in traits only tangentially, but attitudes are decisive in matters of public opinion, propaganda, reducing international friction, or local strife. When riots break out at concerts because the performer happens to be both a Negro and a declared communist, we can well see how attitudes can cumulate into a crest and precipitate a feud, or even civil war. Just at present, there are many large organizations, including the UNESCO, financing collective investigations of attitudes with the purpose in view of ameliorating interracial, international, and interfaith relations. What these attitudes have been in the folk mind may be gathered from the present writer's compilation of thousands of slurs [6].

DISPOSITIONS

The term "disposition," as used in everyday life, should be accorded its place in the psychology

[6] A. A. Roback: *A Dictionary of International Slurs,* 1944.

of personality, but somehow it is swallowed up by other words and phrases, while various technical senses of "disposition" greet us in textbooks. In the *Dictionary of Psychology,* we find five meanings. None answers our purpose, although "an organized emotional attitude or tendency" approaches the common usage. The question is: What does one intend to say by the statement "John has a good disposition?" Is this *disposition* a trait or an attitude? Certainly it is more like an attitude because it is directed toward people, but it is so general, lacking the cognitive attribute which is inherent in the usual attitude, that we must needs discern the distinction between the two. The disposition in common parlance may be cheerful, bilious, or even "rotten," and is more spontaneous than the attitude, i.e., it is generally pleasant or unpleasant in a more or less uniform manner, although circumstances might aggravate or mitigate it. It is perhaps a phase of one's temperament which manifests itself at the first meeting of a new acquaintance, and since it is at such times that impressions are made, the kind of disposition one shows is of practical importance.

Mood

The attitude is a *conational aspect* of the personality built around, or fortified by, a *cognitive element;* that is to say, it presupposes some notion, right or wrong, which causes us to direct our energy toward or away from someone or something. Tension of some sort in the musculature and an incipient motor reaction are implicit in any attitude. The mood, on the other hand, is an *affective* cast of the personality which lingers for some time as the residue of an emotion that may have been, for the time being, forgotten. A cheerful mood may last for a day or a week or even a month, depending on the intensity of the emotion which induced it and the type of individual experiencing it. A moody person is one whose moods change frequently in a relatively brief period.

Humor

Humor and mood are often employed as synonyms in everyday conversation. Thus a state of depression may come under the head of either mood or humor, but humor usually denotes a passing fancy, which, unlike the mood, has had no external event to call it forth, but is rather due to periodic physiological processes (glandular, vascular, etc.). Thus the present usage is in keeping with the old doctrine of the humors in its more scientific evolution. The humor may be said to have its source in physiological caprice.

CHAPTER VIII

THE ISSUE OF INSTINCT AND MOTIVATION

THE PROBLEM of instincts is inseparably bound up with that of heredity. As a rule, environmentalists tend to make short shrift of the whole instinct theory or to reduce its applicability to a minimum, while geneticists, or biologists in general, set great store by it. Psychologists are divided, as we have seen in the chapter on "Determinants of Personality," and the "nays" are the more numerous, and especially the more strident.

It would take us too far afield to attempt threshing out issues in an elementary text on personality, especially as the subject has been worn threadbare in numerous books for the past fifty years, reaching its polemical peak in the early '20's. My purpose here is only to draw attention to a change of trend, and to clarify a few points for the sake of the general presentation of the conception of personality.

Earmarks of Instinct

Although every intelligent person knows what the word instinct means and has doubtless used it in conversation, it is just as well to establish its meaning in the more technical denotation, since it occasionally occurs in a wrong sense, as when someone says, "I instinctively raised my hand to tip my hat" where the word intended is, of course, "automatically." An instinct is, first of all, an unlearned mode of response, to a given situation, which stems from a definite physiological mechanism or structure. There are other qualifications which, however, are derivative, or else more hypothetical than the definition need sponsor. All we need adopt at present is the view that both man and beast, according to the species, do react in specific ways, to a situation without having been taught beforehand, and that these reactions are determined by the genes transmitted to us by our parents via the germ plasm.

William McDougall, unexceptionally the foremost English-speaking psychologist, has given us the most finished exposition of the theory, which, before him, had been accepted uncritically and without much analysis of the data. He has separated out the instincts, divided them into classes, linked them with the emotions, and showed their relation to the cognitive sphere like perception, at the same time stressing the part instinct plays in motivation. In other words, we are to understand that these instincts are the mainsprings of action, something we can readily grant.

The War on the Doctrine of Instincts

McDougall's *Introduction to Social Psychology* was one of the most widely used textbooks in the British Empire, as well as in the United States, and all went well until the Russian reflexologists (Bekhterev, Pavlov) began to exercise a considerable influence over American philosophers, via neo-realism, and psychologists via behaviorism. The phenomenal rise of sociology, at about the same time, and the defections of biologists like Jacques Loeb, Bethe, von Uexküll from the traditional course all contributed to create a large-scale rebellion against the doctrine of inherited tendencies.

Soon McDougall was tackled on all sides. "How do we know that such and such are instincts?" "Why, even an infant doesn't know enough to feed at it's mother's breast unaided." "On what authority do we have to accept a given number of instincts?" "How can we predict the means an instinct takes to realize itself, when

training, cultural traditions, and many other factors intervene?" The word "instinct" was shown
to have many meanings, and finally the view
began to take on the coloring of a taboo. It
loomed as a mystic entity which McDougall and
others were anxious to palm off on the psychological clientèle. "Give a dog a bad name and
hang him" was never so true. Indeed McDougall
was so affected by the onslaught against his pet
that he decided to save it by changing its name;
and in his *Energies of Men,* we find that instincts
have become *propensities.* King Solomon would
probably have given him this advice to save his
brain-child. I did not, however, deem it worth
while to follow the generally sound counsel of a
highly esteemed colleague to substitute another
word for "instinct" in the heading of this chapter,
so as to avoid the impression that the material
is outmoded.

Countering the "Objectivists'" Objections

It is not clear that a single charge could be
sustained, in the last analysis. We can find many
senses for the term "habit," "reflex," or any other
word in constant use over a long period of time.
Do we know how many reflexes or habits there
are? If instinct is something which persists in

the individual, it is also true that it is modifiable. No instinct but what could be subdued. If most instincts manifest themselves later in life, instead of at birth or in very early infancy, is it not because the situation must be to some extent *perceived before there can be a directive toward the goal,* except in the case of the purely bodily functions? Surely, at the age when the world is one "big buzzing blooming confusion," the infant could not be expected to make use of its instinctive apparatus. What motives has the neonate? Is it surprising if a one-week-old does not fear a ferocious animal, when the animal does not mean anything to it? The spontaneity and directness of an instinct must still have cognitive finger posts. Similarly, if a convinced fatalist or religious maniac with a Messiah delusion has sufficient faith in his dogma, there will be no situation to evoke his fear or to cause the reaction of his glandular, vascular, and motor systems, culminating either in semi-paralysis or flight. The foolhardy don't perceive consequences sufficiently so as to touch off the instinctive basis of fear. That is no argument against instinct.

The conflicts among the instincts, with one overwhelming the others, appears to have no place in the purview of the critics. When we are confronted with such evidence as the doing away with twins on the part of the mother among a certain primitive tribe because it is believed that twins are the offspring of the devil, implanted in a particular woman, it seems strange that the reason should not be apparent. If the child is the devil's, then it is not the woman's who bore it, and the maternal instinct is not operative. But why go so far afield for negative evidence? Are there not infanticides among us in this very country? And have we not had an instance in this very community of gross maltreatment of a boy, for many years, because his mother was terrified at the thought that the world might learn of her infraction of the conventions, if the child were allowed to be seen by the neighbors? No doubt the maternal instinct was there, as the other children were brought up with devotion and care, but instincts can be choked, crushed, perverted, or only inhibited. What apostle of the instinct theory would deny that? One might as well conclude that there was no universal food craving or need because a starved person will not eat something that had been soaked, to his knowledge, with cyanide of potassium.

Foregoing the Simple to Espouse the More
Hypothetical Complex

On the other hand, with all the possibilities of and devices for learning, we find it nigh impossible to explain many acts except by resorting to the doctrine of instincts, unless some of the more speculative hypotheses of psychoanalysis be invoked. Let us take one sample. A leading scientist enters someone's library. He glances at a number of book titles, but does not fail to look between the rows of books on top of the bookcase, where dust and dirt often collect, as if he were looking for something in particular. In the ante-room there is a screen; as he is about to walk out, he cannot resist craning his neck to catch a glimpse behind the scenes, but he catches himself in time. The man is well-bred, extremely tactful, and enjoys an excellent personal reputation. How can we account for this curious curiosity on his part? Was he conditioned as a child to look into nooks and crannies? Did he notice his mother going through such movements, or are his reactions symptomatic of some repression? How much simpler to see in this unsought seeking the expression of a specific instinct, which has not been sufficiently modified, despite his academic standing and unusual insight and maturity?

Hundreds of mechanisms might be thought of in this connection — from some vagrant element in the *id,* to frustration of some sort, or a dynamism of a topological-vector derivation, but why waste time on crossword puzzles, when common sense has a more direct solution?

One of the chief arguments against instinct seemed to be its purposive character. Perhaps it is the remote suggestion of teleology; possibly it is the long-range view which is repugnant to many psychologists of the younger set, but the whole biological structure of man and animals evinces a purposive plan, without necessarily making a deity responsible for it.

Meeting Half Way

Among the chief compromisers between the two groups — the "instinctivists" and the "learned-habit" advocates — is G. W. Allport, who has set up his doctrine of functional autonomy, which was suggested partly by William James's belief in the transitoriness of instincts (i.e. if an instinctive mechanism is not made use of when its maturation time comes, it is bound to become impaired and stop functioning) and partly by the tri-modal scheme of attention, viz., active, passive, and spontaneous, which means that what, at one time, had to be attended to with effort, (studying a case in school), later comes to us non-voluntarily — or spontaneously as when the now-graduated physician examines a patient or the full-fledged attorney pleads in court, although as students, the work went against the grain. I have pointed out the genealogy or affiliations of this view about a dozen years ago in a lengthy review of Allport's book.

The theory that motives succeed one another in the development of the individual, and that they may not have a common root, is in keeping with the elementary data of the goal idea and spontaneous attention. The motives may even seem to be at odds with one another. This reaction-formation in psychoanalysis, as when a character-trait assumes the opposite phase at a certain age, in the individual's life, points to the latitude even of Freud in the matter of heterogeneity of motives, but the question is whether the particular succession is not determined by the type of the individual, as well as the circumstances. There is ample experimental evidence that the chain of motives which is forged by the schizoid type, under identical conditions, is not the same as that of the cycloid type, in which case the constitutional factor is somewhat of a governor in this functional autonomy. Functional autonomy takes place within the autonomy of the particular individual. '

Allport takes a position midway between the *"acquisitionist"* (a word that might serve as a designation for those scientists who cling steadfastly to the view that all behavior is learned), and the *"innatist,"* between the mechanist and the purposivist. With the former, he rejects the original nature of motives as based on inborn instincts, but with the latter, he believes in the inner drive toward a goal as against stimulation from outside.

Critique of "Functional Autonomy" Arguments

To win his point, he confronts us with a formidable array of illustrations, and does an excellent job in laying the bricks, but the bricks themselves are not altogether solid. Almost every instance could be interpreted along hormic lines. "A good workman feels compelled to do clean-cut jobs even though his security or the praise of others no longer depends upon high standards." In what sense is the individual at issue a good workman? Does "good" mean "skilled?" Then

[1] A. A. Roback: *Character and Personality*, 1938, vol. 6, pp. 245-246.

we might question the universality of the proposition. Many skilled workers are not conscientious. But if it means a man who is more or less of what is called a "perfectionist," then I fail to see in what way such a tendency is acquired. Furthermore, to say that high standards are not required for security or praise, *at all times,* is a begging of the question. At least the "good workman" knows it. Allport's point might be proven if it could be shown that the poor workman will feel *compelled* to do a clean-cut job.

Similarly the other instances may be turned against Allport's principle. What *about* the businessman who keeps on driving himself until he ruins his health and loses his fortune? Is this proof that "What was once an instrumental technique becomes a master motive?" Or is the acquisitive drive or will-to-power perhaps so insistent and propelling that the rational consideration of leaving well enough alone does not get a chance of obtaining a hearing? Or may there not be a new regrouping of instinctive tendencies: rivalry, philanthropic impulses, excess devotion to family — which goad a man to continue at the grindstone long after he should have retired? An instinctive tendency does not, as a rule, operate in isolation from other drives.

Likewise, to take another of Allport's arguments, even though some women bear their children unwillingly, to whom later they become so much attached, does it mean that there is, therefore, no maternal instinct to begin with? No amount of learning would produce that mother love, if it were not inherent, in the first place. The instinct, however, might express itself, in modified ways, in various individuals. Other instincts may interfere with it; and in many cases, the instinct does not manifest itself until there has been some stimulation through sight, sound, or touch. It should not be supposed that the instinctive mechanism works like a trigger.

As far as other illustrations are concerned, there is even less conviction. If the erstwhile sailor who is now a banker still displays a craving for the sea, does it indicate that the means has become an end, or is it not more reasonable to see therein a *persistent motive?* Just think of it, of all the possible vocations, the young man has selected navigation. Was it sheer accident? But even so, would not the preoccupation of the now prosperous financier with the sea express the nostalgia, the desire to recapture his youth? And why, pray, should the musician "first having been stung by a rebuke or by a slur on his inferior performances into mastering his instrument" feel now that "there is no need to continue," so that we should be amazed when he still "loves his instrument more than anything else in the world?"

This bit of reasoning is not quite clear. Is Allport puzzled because a finished musician loves music and actually does play? Would we not be astonished if it were not so? As to the acquisition of the skill because of adverse criticism, there is again a fallacy lurking in the background. To a talented person, even at an early age, criticism is only incidental. There may be resentment, even of a lingering kind, toward the individual indulging in the slur or taunt, but the art itself will never suffer. Even Keats, who was practically killed by vicious criticism, did not turn against poetry. Nor do we know that the gifted made the grade just because they were ridiculed. The anecdotes about Demosthenes or Disraeli, should they be adduced here, are scarcely authentic. Suppose, however, they were spurred on by hostility, would we expect to have them rest on their laurels once they achieved initial success?

That motives change is almost self-evident, but only *in form* — hardly in content. The little boy who wants to be a policeman, because he sees authority vested in the uniform, may change his ambition later on, and enter politics or journalism. It is still the same *élan* which determines his course. He is seeking power. Hence, before we decide on a succession of motives, where the instrument takes the place of the former goal, let us break down the purpose into its protean phases, and we may find, as in the case of the vivid colors, they are all only components of white light.

Purposive Behaviorism

E. C. Tolman is another influential psychologist who has adopted a compromise position in the matter of motivation and instinct. In fact he has so many tourist tags on his traveling bags that he could gain admittance into almost every psychological circle. He is first of all a behaviorist, not of the crude variety of J. B. Watson, but on a more polished level; for since he has been working on mice for a good many years, he steers clear of mentalistic concepts, which would, of course, have involved introspection. But then he does make a great deal of goal-directed activities. In this regard, he approaches more G. W. Allport than the pure hormist, Wm. McDougall, although he does not commit himself on any theory like that of functional autonomy, except in the sense that "mechanism may become drive" as Woodworth has taught, and which, according to Tolman, approaches the principle of fixation, where "some of the intrinsic and final positive value of a more fundamental goal spreads and remains fixed upon what was initially a mere means activity or means technique." [2]

In his *purposive behaviorism,* as he calls his system, Tolman makes room for *Gestalt* psychology, particularly of the Lewinian brand, and for psychoanalysis, and even for a factor psychology, like Spearman's, but his chief object is to construct a model for what is happening in any task, not along the nerve-gland channels but on a molar basis, featuring the "sign — *gestalt* — expectation" triad. Thus the rat *perceives or recognizes* in an *object* before it the means for *getting to* some goal or *away from* its present situation. But in order to get to or away from, the animal must have a "sign-*gestalt*-readiness" which includes our old rejected instinct, for it covers "all such varieties or phases of response as are primarily due to innate endowment plus a biologically provided relatively 'normal' or 'standard' environment." [3] He further sees "these

[2] E. C. Tolman: *Drives Toward War,* p. 62.

[3] E. C. Tolman: *Purposive Behavior in Animals and Men,* p. 447.

main types of activity which qualify as instincts as thus defined."

In his more recent little book, he appears to have become reconciled to the doctrine of instincts which, in his younger days, he wished to abandon completely. Here we find his concession "we must suppose that the biological drives, and all the four types of social technique are all rooted, to some degree, in 'instinct.' " [4]

Return of the Prodigal

Tolman, however, is not the only one to have relented on the subject of instincts. There is a general swing of the psychological pendulum in its direction. Some will be amazed to read what the No. 2 behaviorist of a quarter-century ago, W. S. Hunter, has to say in a recent article in this regard.

It will come as a surprise to many psychologists that all five of the distinguished contributors to this Symposium have emphasized the rôle of heredity in the determination of behavior. Not one has insisted that environmental factors are of primary significance in shaping the psychological characteristics of the individual. I am

[4] E. C. Tolman: *Drives Toward War,* p. 56.

sure that all of them acknowledge the importance for behavior of the environmental factor whether it is called learning, practice, or the modification of the internal milieu. Historically, the interesting thing is that all of the speakers place their stress on heredity. * * *

Twenty-five years ago, the situation was quite different. Such writers as J. B. Watson and Z. Y. Kuo were conducting a great offensive against the accepted belief that inherited patterns of behavior existed in man and animals. * * *

The anti-instinct movement came not only from some of the behaviorists but also from numerous writers on social psychology like Bernard, Dunlap, Faris, and Kantor. I believe that a prime basis for the origin of this anti-heredity movement was the violent reaction against the presentation of the topic of instinct in William McDougall's (1908) *Introduction to Social Psychology.*[5]

McDougall Defended by Behaviorist!

The curious part is that Hunter should wish to take up the cudgels on behalf of the much abused William McDougall and to recognize with him that "evolutionary development has largely freed

[5] W. S. Hunter: Summary Comments on the Heredity-Environment Symposium *Psychological Review,* 1947, vol. 54, p. 348.

man from a dependence upon directly inherited behavior patterns except for those controlling reflex responses, emotions, drives and certain general capacities." In other words man has evolved a tremendous modifiability and adaptability which often occludes the original pattern and thus gives rise to the illusion that there are no inborn tendencies of any sort, as one might gather from a book like Holt's last volume,⁶ where the arch-neo-realist and Freudian behaviorist makes mincemeat or rather a habit-complex out of instincts. Yet he does not mind speaking of instincts, provided we assume that they are nothing but reflexes. As he puts it:

> They are all reflexes. And with this elementary equipment, the animal begins to evince what must be called 'conduct.' It is the various acquired habits of this rather elementary sort, which have commonly been called 'instincts.' ⁷

⁶ E. B. Holt: *Animal Drive and the Learning Process.* It is an irony that my invitation to the author to participate in the Prince commemorative volume, (*Problems of Personality,* which I edited in 1925) resulted in this book. Holt accepted with alacrity, and a year later, he had not an article but a few chapters of a book ready. Nevertheless it took him years to complete the volume.

⁷ E. B. Holt: *Animal Drive and the Learning Process,* p. 121.

THE ISSUE OF INSTINCT AND MOTIVATION

Lashley's Conclusions

Nor is Hunter the only veteran psychologist who has sung the palinode to instincts, and a genuine behaviorist who has to his credit numerous experimental researches on the nervous system, like K. S. Lashley, has no qualms about using the term *instinct* without quotation marks around it. In his article on "Structural Variation" there are many passages which will bear citing, but only two or three will be reproduced here to show that all is not over with the much belabored theory of instincts.

> Species — constant characters include not only reflexes and such complex instincts as are exhibited by arthropods and birds, but also differences in the level of activity, in motivation, in sexual and maternal patterns of behavior, in emotional and temperamental traits, and in general and special abilities, There is scarcely a variable in the range of human personality which cannot be matched as a fixed interspecies difference in other animals.
>
> Interspecies differences are obviously a result of hereditary constitution, and, if the same kinds of structural differences are found to occur among individuals of a

single species, they justify the inference of genetic determination of corresponding individual differences. [8]

Some of the more conspicuous structural differences have been shown to be hereditary.

*   *   *   *   *   *

There can be little question that some of the lesser variants in cerebral structure are likewise hereditary.

Even if this is not the case, if the variants are largely the result of development accidents, they still present a serious difficulty for the environmentalist. Discussions of heredity and environment have tended to regard the nervous system, if it is considered at all, as a vaguely remote organ, essentially similar in all individuals and largely moulded by experience. Even the limited evidence at hand, however, shows that individuals start life with brains differing enormously in structure; unlike in number, size, and arrangement of neurons as well as in grosser features. The variations in cells and tracts must have functional significance. [9]

[8] K. S. Lashley: "Structural Variation in the Nervous System in Relation to Behavior," *Psychol. Review*, 1947 vol. 54, p. 325.

[9] K. S. Lashley: *Ibid*, p. 333.

Leaving Lashley's article, our eyes fall on the title of the very next article, viz., "the Hoarding Instinct" by C. T. Morgan, who certainly is no old-fogey or mere theoretician but an experimentalist along physiological lines. In his attack on the problem of hoarding in rats, he states the facts as follows:

> This we can say, that it takes no teaching or conditioning to get a rat to hoard. In dozens of experiments by different people, all that is necessary to observe hoarding is to put a rat in a hoarding apparatus and give it sufficient opportunity. Adult rats, fully watered and fed, will hoard five to twenty pellets per day, if placed in hoarding apparatus and left there. Since the rat only eats one or two pellets a day, this is plainly hoarding. And since it comes out spontaneously without training, it is plainly instinctive. Of course, rats may have learned to hoard early in infancy because of competition for food in their home cages, but hoarding is so universal in laboratory rats, always fully fed and watered, that such learning is extremely unlikely. [10]

[10] C. T. Morgan: "The Hoarding Instinct," *Psychol. Review,* 1947 vol. 54, p. 335.

One could go on quoting and quoting from various recent articles and books to prove that the doctrine of instinct which has been buried by Russian physiologists, and by their disciples in this country, E. B. Holt, J. B. Watson, Z. Y. Kuo and others, more than twenty-five years ago, and has been thought to be as dead as a doornail by this time, is one of those die-hards in science, and every so often will pull a face at its pall-bearers, just as they are ready to consign the corpse to the grave.

Perhaps that is one reason why so many psychologists who are lured by the various schools of learning and the environmentalist trend are not willing to lay the ghost of instinct and are contriving means to satisfy the wolf while keeping the goat intact; and a whole vocabulary has sprung up to circumvent the opprobrium which attaches to the word *instinct*. There is a far cry from the taxes (Bethe) and tropisms (Loeb), conditioned reflexes (Pavlov), even to the personal reflexes of Bekhterev and the habit-products of E. B. Holt, or Sherrington's prepotent reflexes; but when we range the whole gamut of *wants* (Thorndike), *drives* (Woodworth, Prince), *alpha* or *beta* behavior (Hunter), *needs* (H. A. Murray), *autonomic sentiments* (G. W. Allport), *ergs* (R. B. Cattell), *propensities* (McDougall), etc., we wonder whether this is only a camouflage by way of an alias, or an essential differentiation. One cannot help recalling, at this point, the story of Cohen and Levy who were in business together. Cohen, for some reason, took the notion of changing his name to O'Kelly, whereupon Levy, with no imaginative bent, adopted the same name. Shortly afterwards, a call came in for Mr. O'Kelly. The girl at the switchboard answered it. "Yes, sir," she said "but which Mr. O'Kelly do you wish to speak to? Mr. Cohen O'Kelly or Mr. Levy O'Kelly?

CHAPTER IX

THE EXPERIMENTAL STATUS

LIKE EVERYTHING else in psychology, personality should be probed by experimental methods, and the proof of any hypothesis must be sought in the results obtained through a rigidly controlled procedure.

For the past thirty years, more than a thousand investigations have been conducted purportedly establishing some personality relation, whether positive or negative. In fact, of late, personality studies have been vying in number with those on learning or the sensory processes. Occasionally we come across a survey or summary of such investigations, but very rarely do we encounter a balance sheet, a critical estimate of the work as a whole. In the present chapter, no attempt will be made to discuss the many hundreds of experimental approaches — the phrase being used in two senses here; for in the majority of instances these laboratory activities were more approaches to an experiment than experimental approaches to personality. The ground has been gone over in the *Psychology of Character* (pp. 354-384) [1] nearly twenty-five years ago, and although the territory has more than doubled since, the situation has scarcely been improved, so far as significant results go.

Recent Stress on Tests and Measurement

The behavioristic bias in American psychology has lent considerable impetus to personality testing and so-called character measurement. Even the religious-minded investigators, whose researches are subsidized by church organizations, have adopted the semi-experimental method of testing character reactions and treating the results quantitatively, going beyond the comparatively modest dream of Spinoza to deal geometrically with human affects.

Motive and Trait

The campaign now bids fair to rival the intelligence-testing movement. Emphasis is placed on what an individual does, and not on what he is, or what traits he may be said to have. It is not

[1] In the forthcoming edition, the chapter will be much enlarged with references to the more recent literature, of course.

recognized that *acts are meaningless unless they are referred to a motive,* this motive pointing to a trait, which, in its turn, is the unit of personality, For this reason, the testing of discrete bits of behavior, despite the bustle in the American camp, has yielded thus far, to use a Latin phrase, *multa sed non multum.* The prospectors meanwhile are busy rejecting the sand. They are critical of the concept "trait." They suspect that a set of traits is a sort of fiction or illusion, like the bent stick in the water, and question much that has been accepted as common observation, but their own constructive findings betray glaring inconsistencies, and suggest that the assumptions underlying their methodological procedure are even farther away from the factual situation than the observations of the keen and observant layman. Perhaps these miners of human ore will yet strike gold. So far, however, their efforts have not impressed the other half of the characterological world, those who think experimental methods are not applicable to such a complicated organization of qualities as constitute personality, at least not before we have constructed a sort of topographical chart of the human mind.

In the first place, the so-called objective methods of measuring personality are, with few exceptions, not, strictly speaking, experimental. They consist, for the most part of ratings, tests, questionnaires, matchings, opinionaires, and other verbal attacks, implemented by factorial analysis and statistical treatment, necessitating a great deal of mathematical computation; and very frequently one finds that this mountain of work has given birth to a puny mouse.

At times, it might seem as if psychologists are casting about for something to construct or devise, and they think up a game — a questionnaire or opinionaire, which might be given to school children, for instance — but not always is the investigator certain even of the sphere of application. Do the results purport to enlighten us on the personality of the school children? Or is this an "experiment" in social psychology? Or is educational psychology to be the beneficiary in this connection?

Question of Indivisibility

One of our first problems is the consideration of whether personality is an indivisible entity, and as such cannot be plumbed piecemeal. Naturally, should such be the case, our position would be hopeless; and all we could do is to rely on intuitive methods alone, which in the last analysis, mean intuitive *talents or skills,* enhanced by seasoned experience. But this would place the study of personality in the realm of art rather than science; and other circumstances like the appeal to authority would be our only resort, which, again, would bring about a wide difference of opinion as to who might be set up as an authority, so that his judgment could be accepted as reliable.

The great advantage of the objective approach is that after the method and technique are described, any one might repeat the experiment and, under the same conditions, expect the same results. If such are not obtained, then we have a right to question the reliability of the methods or the interpretation or the investigator, or, in rare instances, even his scientific integrity. Certainly we must all welcome the empirical approach, but thus far the solid experiment in the sphere of personality has been not an accomplished fact but a desideratum.

Personality Zones Must Be Considered

Sometimes we may liken the subject of personality to a mountainous mass at which there is incessant nibbling or only tugging on the part of the small army of testers and measurers, while the mass is left practically intact. Thus one busies himself by submitting words in order to elicit associations; another measures a single attitude, like conservatism or radicalism; a third probes the amount of bias or prejudice in a given individual; a fourth measures interests; a fifth makes the presence or absence of perseveration his experimental objective. In a sense, all these items are components of personality, but to what degree, and in what connections? Some are merely tangential, unless we consider the fields of psychology and personality co-terminous. Is musical talent a phase of personality in the same sense as sociability, or refinement, or coarseness? It would seem that we ought to keep the different zones or levels of personality distinct, or we should be confusing intelligence, character, and the core of personality hopelessly.

If we map out an area which we designate as personality, then intelligence, talent, skill, and genius would occupy the more or less peripheral zone; the emotional, social and character traits would occupy the centre; and even then it would behoove us to arrange the clusters or departments of traits in some order, closer or less close to the focus. Persistence is a more decided personality trait than perseveration. We know what persistence will accomplish; whereas perseveration is something still to be toyed with; we are still trying to establish connections with it at the personality switchboard. If we do succeed in proving that perseveration correlates highly with persistence, or with negativism, or with radicalism, we should have arrived at a midway station, although it would still be difficult to demonstrate that we were operating with a single variable. Tapping such relations, however, in itself, requires some intuition and judgment. There is too much groping among the testers, although they at times devise ingenious techniques and have developed a formidable array of statistical formulas, but of what good is all that, if the problem posed rests on a shifting foundation, or on no foundation whatever?

Choosing Our Experimental Problem

While it is true that in physics or chemistry an unforeseen chance happening may lead to a great discovery, only a smattering of the history of science will convince us that every experimenter of any account has had a definite hypothesis to start out with; furthermore that this hypothesis was no wild-cat scheme, but a logically defensible thesis, on the evidence gathered to date. In psychology — and this is to some extent the advantage it has over the physical sciences — practically every problem, the silliest, the most far-fetched, or the most obviously settled (which would therefore ordinarily be no problem whatever) will come under the head of "all is grist that comes to the mill." If we obtain no positive results, the negative correlations might be said to have a certain value, or else the investigator's conclusions confirm what we always knew to be the case, e.g., that the children coming from prosperous homes are better dressed than those coming from the slums. It occurs to me, however, that in a world where *ars longa, vita brevis est,* the more problematic and yet consequential issues should have priority. It is not easy to state offhand which is pertinent and which is not, yet there is where the scientist's intuition and imagination should serve as a guide.

Let us take one sample: one might be impelled to examine the relation of hypnosis to perseveration. Offhand, I can see no close connection; but since such an investigation has been undertaken, then it could have been projected only on the basis that there is a possible common factor at the bottom of suggestibility and perseveration. That common factor would have to be recognized and tentatively formulated in the mind; otherwise it might be just as relevant to institute an investigation on the color preferred and left-handedness or habitual tardiness.

Personality Has A Central Core

On the strength of our original definition, it is possible to view every possible trait, whether cognitive, affective, physical, or volitional, as a personality quality, but in the economy of the whole domain, some components have a place in the forefront, while others are in the background. Genius is certainly among the greatest assets, if not the greatest, and yet it can be contrasted with personality. Even character may be compared with personality, thus suggesting that the *core of personality* does not ordinarily include these two most important departments. The area is deliberately circumscribed, not only as a concession to popular usage, but also in order to avoid including so much that nothing is left for the sister-disciplines. The fact that intelligence tests and personality tests are kept in separate compartments would indicate that psychologists appreciate the necessity of keeping the divisions apart.

An experiment may be significant in its own sphere, and yet have little bearing on the subject of personality. One of the most widely cited experiments is that of Zeigarnik who has shown that an unfinished task is remembered better than a completed piece of work, so that on its interruption, we are prone to be under some tension until the job is resumed and finished. This is apparently a general law, although individual differences may disclose various amounts of tension or degrees of memory recurrence; but it is hardly a personality experiment. Perhaps that is the reason why it could be so neatly handled. There are many other problems of a like nature which are treated as subject-matter for personality, but they are only cousins-german, if that close, to our field. Perhaps all roads eventually lead to Rome; nevertheless the more direct highways are, considering the complexity and expenditure of time and labor, the most expedient.

Such direct experimentation is still *Zukunft-musik,* but beginnings have been made in a modest way; and with the coöperation of related sciences, there is every expectation that human personality will, through the collective exploration of this or that segment, gradually yield more of its secrets, but that will entail a balanced and concerted effort where the intuitivists will not be ignored; for it may be said that an experiment is as strong as its weakest premise. When investigators arbitrarily decide that there are no congenital tendencies, or accept conventional terms without analyzing them into psychological derivatives, as when dishonesty is adopted as a *bona fide* generic term, after which it is easy to prove later that children are not generally honest or dishonest, but are so only in specific instances; and from that conclusion the testers set out to establish the even more disputable fact that most people are neither honest nor dishonest, but vary from occasion to occasion, or at least from sphere of operation (cheating at cards) to sphere of operation (marital unfaithfulness).

Indictment from Abroad

A British critic who has had ample opportunity to deal with tests and measurements has come to the same conclusions as the present writer, who had already threshed out the issue in the *Psychology of Character* a full decade before. Adverting to the application of word associations to correlate with such traits as fair play, honesty, loyalty to fellows, poise, mastery, regard for property rights, and school drive in children, he aptly remarks: "Although there is certainly need for objective and scientific methods in the study of personality, it is difficult to believe that this blind empiricism which takes no account whatever of the psychological significance of the test situation and the test responses can yield fruitful results."[1]

If different testers had at least obtained the same results and had arrived at the same conclusions, the agreement, even if unanimity is out of the question, would of itself serve as a reassuring sign. Regrettably, however, while occasional confirmation is secured by another investigator, it is not the rule, and the question comes up as to why "objective" investigations, carried out under the same conditions, should yield different results. Even if there were agreement, we could only be satisfied as to their reliability. Whether the results of the ratings, tests, and questionnaires are valid, that is, whether they have predictive value so that we could actually depend on the outcome to expect certain behavior in an actual life situation is something else still; and it is, naturally, the latter which is the test of the tests.

The Harvard Grant Study

As regards personality, we are still in the groping stage. The complexity of the subject does

[1] P. E. Vernon: *The Assessment of Psychological Qualities by Verbal Methods* — A Survey of Attitude Tests, Rating Scales and Personality Questionnaires, London, 1938.

not lend itself to simple or simplified approaches. It seems that, in order to lift the mass for the right kind of scrutiny, several different levers would need to be applied, and the operations would require to be extended over a period of years, in order to check up on results. The Grant Study at Harvard University, which has been going on for years, is an auspicious beginning. "Our plan is to follow the careers of participants for fifteen or twenty years or more,"[2] and the participants are students at Harvard, who are tested, observed, interviewed, and measured from various angles by psychologists, psychiatrists, physiologists, anthropologists and sociologists (for the socio-economic data); but in addition, Rorschach and graphological methods have been resorted to, for the collaborators in this study have thought it better to risk including too much than excluding some possibly useful aids; and graphology has proven of some value as a control, after its testimony has been checked and validated by the collaborators on the strength of what they knew about the students.

That is how it should be. We cannot afford to dismiss claims on the basis of reputation. If a

[2] A. V. Bock: Preface to C. W. Heath's *What People Are* (Harvard) 1945.

palmist or astrologer should be able to make significant predictions by the use of their methods, it is my opinion that they should be pressed into service despite our attitude toward their premises. The scientific skeptic is one who doubts but will not be so dogmatic as to deny any claimant a chance to prove his claim. Surely that risk costs little time and energy, and does not involve the vast expenditures of money which it takes to subsidize most experimental projects.

Experimental Tapping of the Hidden Mainsprings

It strikes me, too, that aside from tests and measurements of traits (whether physical or mental) experimental techniques, in the real sense of the word, will have to be devised, so that personality could be probed from the cognitive, affective and conative sides. Thus, if words, all jumbled up, representing crucial motivations (money, sex, power, learning, art, religion) were to be presented to subjects under uniform conditions (position, number of letters, size etc.) the unconscious mainsprings might be tapped without the individuals experimented on being aware, as they generally are, even in the most disguised tests, of the actual purpose of the problem. In some of my classes, such exercises have been assigned, but there was not the opportunity as yet of following up the technique on a long-range period. The time it takes to perceive the words from different motivational spheres correctly for each individual would suggest an index to his motivation. Or words could be arranged so as to be read upside down or at odd angles on a rotating sphere, and the order of the words recorded by the subject and the time taken would be another clue in the same direction. These experiments are not, as in ordinary perception or apperception, dealing with cognition, but rather with motivation as elicited by a cognitive approach.

Affective methods should be in line with a life situation. To find out what a man would do when startled, amazed, frightened, or terrorized, not a series of questions or words is to be presented to him. It would be more revealing if he could be confronted with an incident which would take him unawares. The "Invasion from Mars" affair was a real test. If only that had been exploited at the right time, but there are other possibilities; and once the experimental mind will be diverted a bit from the stereotyped test material, we shall have gained a vantage ground in regard to the plumbing of personality.

Vicarious Situations Unsatisfactory

On the conative side, persistence, endurance, self-discipline, and other character traits might be tested through direct means, provided we do not offer substitute devices, and persuade ourselves that the result is an index of the personality traits enumerated. There is a great temptation in that direction — to make the simple serve as *Ersatz* for the complex and think it's "just as good." That is admissible only if the fundamental essence is common to both. In most cases, it does not work out that way; and critics are not behindhand in bringing forth their pertinent objections when such royal roads are taken. No wonder that so few personality experiments have found support, as contrasted with the classical experiments on memory, perception, or even determining tendencies. Personality, as a study, is still in its swaddling clothes, but it is time that it took its first steps on level ground, and not on an artificially padded springboard.

We can understand why P. E. Vernon writes:

> In our opinion a major line of advance will consist in a more careful analysis of these complex subjective factors bearing on the interpretation of test questions and the psychological significance of test responses.

[177]

A useful start might be made with a thorough introspective study, in the German tradition, of the mental processes involved in rating, in answering Yes or No, like or Dislike, etc. The trend of thought in American investigations has always been opposed to such subjective approaches. Symonds (1931) is representative of the majority when he states, in effect, that subjective reactions to particular test items need not concern us because the significance or validity of the test as a whole should always be determined empirically; that the resistances and inhibitions aroused by many of the tests do not matter to the psychometrist, since the psychological variable which such tests measure should be established by objective correlational comparisons with other variables rather than by subjective speculations or "arm-chair" considerations. Yet it may be precisely this neglect of subjective analysis which is responsible for the poor empirical validity of so much of the work, and for the apparently slow speed of advance. Certainly "arm-chair" psychology alone will not solve our problems, but it is, and always has been, an essential precursor to the most fruitful experimental research. [3]

[3] P. E. Vernon: *The Assessment of Psychological Qualities by Verbal Methods* — p. 105.

This emphatic declaration has come from one who is not a dabbler but at least a journeyman in personality testing, one who is familiar with the technique and statistical treatment of the data: If the statement is to be qualified or moderated to some degree, the following distinction may be drawn between the "arm-chair" psychologist and the "intuitivist." The former simply spins out theories and views from his own meagre observations, which are not checked against the experiences of others, nor are they subjected to critical analysis in the framework of scientific requisites. The latter, i.e., the intuitivist, has come by his "art" only after cultivating the field of science for an adequate period. He has learned to go through the experimental procedure, as it were, in his mind, just as one learns to solve a problem in mental arithmetic.

Some of us sooner or later get to know a medical diagnostician who, without subjecting the patient to a long series of laboratory tests, can tell better what is the matter with him than the mechanical internists who spot minor defects and cannot construe the syndrome as a whole. And, the human body, let us remember, is a much simpler matter to explore than personality.

PERSONALITY

A Psychiatrist Takes Issue

A similar attitude is evinced by an American authority in medical psychology and neurology — the senior professor of neuropathology at the Harvard Medical School and psychiatrist-in-chief at the Massachusetts General Hospital; and the following straight-from-the-shoulder passage will doubtless cause a good deal of eyebrow-raising in the camp of experimentalists and testers, but there is a good dose of sound counsel in these words, even though the average psychologist will be taken aback at the opinion that the greatest contribution to our insights into human nature has been made by the inspired poets and prose writers. Coming from a scientist, it is certainly fraught with greater meaning.

A multitude of observations have been made on the behavior of man toward man. The greatest contribution is still that of the inspired poets and prose writers; intuition still plays a great part even with the most careful psychological investigator of human relationships. Social experiments are so complex that short cuts must be used and intuition (to my mind) is simply wide experience used as a short cut. The "psychologically minded" psychiatrist may get the right "feeling" of a situation and make an immediate contribution. The "scientifically minded" investigator makes up for the deficiency in control material and for the complexity of the problems by insisting on many cases and statistical evidence. To get ahead with the job of studying human nature, one must accept the observations of all honest workers and fit them together as well as possible. Only the intolerant worker who says that results "never can be obtained" by the other man's methods is to be ridiculed. There is plenty of work in medical psychology for more good Behaviorists, Gestaltists, Pavlovians, Sherringtonians, and Freudians. [4]

Two Types of Method — Empirical and Intuitive

From the conflicting issues it is possible to arrive at some workable compromise (as a matter of fact it had been suggested in the first edition of *The Psychology of Character*) by which both the intuitive methods developed and prized, on the other side of the Atlantic, and the quantitative techniques so sedulously devised in the United States would be combined; for it must be recognized that while one phalanx of workers, stimulated by the results in the intelligence-testing field, and encouraged by the practical demands of

[4] S. Cobb: *Borderlands of Psychiatry* (Harvard) 1943, p. 122.

applied (vocational, industrial, etc.) psychology, have been busying themselves with contriving batteries of tests galore, another movement, gathering its momentum in France and Germany, has concentrated on the *understanding* of personality, on the *interpretation* of character, and the method its leaders have adopted is that of *intuition*. Broadly speaking, the two methods contrasted would correspond to the inductive and the deductive. The latter, as is well known, always proceeds from general to particular, from principles or formulas to categorization; and that is just what the "understanders," or intuitionists, are following out. Their principles, or formulas in this case, are *schemata* of types, into which are to fit roughly all individuals.

CHAPTER X

INTUITIVE METHODS AND TYPOLOGY

FROM the day of Hippocrates, in the fourth century, B.C., there has existed a rough and ready chart for the classification of people. In fact, the sanguine — phlegmatic — melancholic — choleric scheme is still manipulated in books on temperament, and thus claims the honor of being the oldest theory to be treated by moderns with a fair degree of respect.

Introversion and Extraversion

Recently, however, other divisions have come into vogue. Jung's dichotomy into *introverts* and *extraverts* has been universally accepted as a convenient mode of separating the individualistic, more or less shut-in type from the social, talkative, and usually more superficial person. Parenthetically, it may be said that, although the Swiss psychiatrist is supposed to have coined the terms "introversion" and "extraversion" and invested them with their signification, I find Emerson in his *Representative Men* referring to Swedenborg as an "introverted mind;" and in a no longer accessible book, entitled *Love vs. Marriage,* by the now obscure Fourierist, M. E. Lazarus, I have come across the word *extroversion.* The inference we may gather even from such a minor bibliographical observation is that people were looked upon as introverted or extraverted long before these expressions became current or had even been introduced.

It is not necessary to explain the further subclasses of introvert and extravert types: the sensation and feeling types, the thinkers and "intuitives," as these are less serviceable in the everyday laboratory of life. Nor shall we mention other schemes which are practically identical, except in name, with Jung's, but one classification must claim our attention for a few minutes. It is that of Spranger.

Life Values

Eduard Spranger, primarily a philosopher and pedagogist, maintains that one's direction of life or life-pattern is the key to one's personality; and one's life-pattern is always revealed in the value one sets on certain things. The economic man will, of course, think only in terms of money. "How much is he worth?" will express his attitude toward any individual he meets. The preëminently social person needs no introduction here. The "man of power" exemplified, in our own day, by Stalin (although he is, by no means, the worst of the world's dictators) is also too well known to require description. The theoretician aims at fitting every experience of his into a system. The artist, who is bound by sensory images, on the other hand, isolates every experience, and contemplates it as if it were something apart from the world, thus creating the esthetic value. And finally there is the religious type of individual, who loses himself in mysticism, in other-worldliness, and is not anchored to the spatio-temporal moorings of the theoretical man or tied to the sensory images of the artist. It goes without saying that in this scale, the economic type is rated lowest and the religious type highest. There is the animalistic human creature who does not even think in economic terms, but food and drink and satisfying the other appetites are all he lives for. He need hardly be considered.

Simple and somewhat arbitrary as this arrangement appears, as we begin looking around, we shall see that our friendships and enmities are often formed on the basis of our value reactions, and also that a view of complementary affinities might explain a good deal that is remarkable about the communion of noted figures in history.

Our Build and Personality

Ernst Kretschmer, as a psychiatrist, like many before him of the same profession, takes his point of departure from the constitutional make-up of man. It is not by sheer chance that psychiatrists have evinced such a keen interest in the problems of character and personality. Through their contacts with the human *psyche* in all its divagations and distortions, they have access to recesses that are hidden from the view of the lay observer, even though he be a La Bruyère or La Rochefoucauld.

Essential Agreement Between Sigaud and Kretschmer

That our build has something to do with our disposition to disease, both physical and mental, has long ago been recognized. The apoplectic *habitus* and the phthisic *habitus* were differentiated centuries ago, allegedly as far back as Hippocrates. Statistical correlations with regard to the long-bodied and the squat have been made by the Italian school of Morphology (De-Giovanni, Pende, Viola, Ravà, Naccarati). The French authority on digestive disturbances, C. Sigaud, about fifty years ago worked out a scheme of types which came singularly near that of Kretschmer's much later. According to him, people were predominantly (1) cerebral, (2) muscular, (3) respiratory or (4) digestive, in their organismal functioning. Kretschmer's fourfold division includes the "muscular" and the "digestive" under the respective heads of "athletic" and "pyknic," while the "cerebral," in part at least, corresponds to the "leptosome" class, i.e., the slender. The fourth class, "dysplastic," is made up of those individuals of asymmetrical proportions, or deviating in their physique from a common standard (large heads with small bodies, infantile types of various sorts). When we take into consideration that there has been no comparing of notes between Kretschmer and Sigaud, that the former probably did not hear until very recently of his French unwitting coöperator, we must look upon the *rapprochement* as an auspicious sign.[1]

[1] In H. J. Eysenck's *Dimensions of Personality*, the "leptomorph" takes the place of Kretschmer's leptosome; the "eurymorph" corresponds to the "pyknic," while the more or less athletic or muscular is called the "mesomorph," in accordance with the Index of Body Build (I. B.) gained by the following formula

$$\text{I. B.} = \frac{\text{Stature} \times 100}{\text{Transverse Chest Diameter} \times 6}$$

The leptomorph (long-shaped) is slender; the eurymorph (wide-shaped) is broad, while the mesomorph is midway.

Constitutional Type and Insanity

The *pyknic* type, *i.e.,* the thick-set individual with a fullness usually about the abdomen, is one that would likely develop under adverse circumstances, a mental disturbance of the cyclic type, like manic-depressive insanity, where excitement and depression alternate. On the other hand, slim persons are given, under similar circumstances, to the split-off disorders (persecution complexes, religious mania, ideas of reference). We all have a tendency, affirms Kretschmer, to be either cyclothymic or schizothymic; that is to say, our mind belongs to the alternating and recurring kind, or to the split-off type, which harbors ideas and affects loosened from the centralized whole — in a sense, a stratified consciousness. Perhaps my own aversion to repetition and monotony is explicable on my remoteness in temperament and constitutional make-up from cyclothemia. Conversely, I have known pyknic people to tell a story as many as twenty-five times in the space of a month, without being in the least bored.

No Absolute Types but Tendencies

At least a hundred investigations, most of them in connection with institutional inmates, have been undertaken within the last 25 years to prove or disprove Kretschmer's contentions. The question has not been settled, but the testimony is largely favorable to Kretschmer. Ideal types are, to be sure, comparatively rare. Mixtures and combinations will be most frequent, but the combinations too are in the direction of one tendency or another; and the data, statistically treated, confirm not only Kretschmer's, but also his French predecessor's observations.

There is a Constitution which Shapes Our Choices

Whatever we may think about the adequacy or inadequacy of the various doctrines of human types, the fact remains that we do measure up people as belonging to one class or another; and the more *schemata* we have at our disposal, and the broader our knowledge of human behavior, the more competent are we in dealing with our own affairs. The salesman has been told for a whole generation to "size up" his potential customers; and without being aware of the theory of introverts and extraverts, he probably fits his prospects into one or the other of the two categories. Employers and foremen eye their applicants not only with a view to discovering their vocational aptitudes, but also with regard to their temperamental and personality qualities. Caesar, tall and slight, with pale complexion, the typical leptosome of Kretschmer's table, preferred to be surrounded by stout people of a jolly disposition. Falstaff may have liked his companions to be slim. *There is a constitution which shapes our choices;* and also different circumstances will prompt different preferences.

Masculine and Feminine Components

Although it is commonly held that men are men and women are women, and that is really why the twain do meet, the fact is that every male has, with rare exceptions, a more or less female element in him, and, conversely, nearly all females possess a tinge of the other sex. In numerous instances, the opposite component is so marked that we speak of "effeminate" men and "masculine" women, of whom the *virago* or *Amazon* would be a pronounced specimen. The hermaphrodite, who may even change sex periodically, belongs to the abnormal cases of morphology, but the duality of sex in most of us is being more and more recognized not only by psychoanalysts but even by anthropologists; and the Harvard Grant Study assigns a special niche to this feature of typology.

Primary and Secondary Function

A typological dichotomy which has received much attention in the more solid books is that of primary and secondary functions. Heymans in Holland, Jung in Switzerland, and others have regarded this division as basic, not only because its originator, Otto Gross, was a psychiatrist with a faculty for penetrating the core much like his father's keen insight into criminological categories, but because the classification has a physiological foundation. Gross believed, on good grounds (in keeping with the theory of perseveration in memory), that there is a tendency for every nerve process to reverberate; in other words, that the nerve function carries along in its wake, a sequel, but while that is true of many individuals, there are many more in whom that tendency misses fire or is abortive.

In the case of the former, the secondary-function type, we may expect serious, deliberate, logical closely-knit, long-nerved individuals, who will nurse grudges, hark back to the past, and who will readily follow a complicated argument because the past is present in their reasoning at any moment, while the primary function denotes almost a primitive reaction, momentary, one which does not look back to connect the threads of past and present experiences. People of the primary function are superficial, scatter-brained, unreflective, but at the same time, they are cheerful, forgiving, will not nag and will be free from the anxieties and depressions of their counterpart.

The primary function is representative of the child of nature. Grief in that particular type will express itself in wailing or lamenting, but shortly, thereafter, it may be followed by amusement or laughter. Not so the other type. There may be little demonstration shown, but whatever emotion does affect the individual will linger or rankle, and thus friends will often be deceived by the apparent apathy. There have been court instances in which a case had gone against the accused because of the deceptive indifference upon the death of a close relative, which, to a lay jury, could be interpreted as an indication of previous hostility.

Since the main effects of a leucotomy seem to be: easing the tension, reducing the sense of responsibility, lowering self-consciousness, and the level of aspiration, as well as making the patient happy-go-lucky, euphoric, tactless, and aggressive with poorer judgment, it strikes me that one of the differences between the primary and the secondary function may be due to the rigid or loose connection between the frontal lobe and the thalamus, since it is that particular operation which severs the communication between these two regions of the cerebrum. This hypothesis would not preclude the possibility of another cause, perhaps more fundamental, viz., the quality of the nerve tissue itself, its conductivity.

In American textbooks, these terms are rarely found, and the *Dictionary of Psychology* came close to omitting them, but, then, the average American psychologist takes no stock in the doctrine of types, and would rather regard each individual as the product of his environment and experiences. In brief, the individual might be "typed" according to his learned reflexes and habits, and since every individual would necessarily have a different pattern, which incidentally we should never be able to trace, we could never hope to classify people except according to some arbitrary scale or schema for practical purposes, like those who came from prosperous homes and the ones who were brought up in the slums; children from broken homes and normally brought up youths, etc.

Somatotype

Recognizing the objections to the doctrine of

types, W. H. Sheldon[1] has devised a method for combining various constitutional tendencies so that the end-product would include three different components in various proportions. First of all, it was his purpose to establish static classes of individuals, individuals who differed widely *morphologically,* i.e. in form, structure, build; in other words, in their physical constitution. He set out with the simple task of taking four thousand photographs of individuals, in a standardized posture, showing the front, side, and back views. The next step was to see whether all the photographs did not fall into a very limited number of variational categories. Three such categories were found upon which all the experimenters were agreed; and the somatotype of any individual consists of all three dimensions, combined in various proportions. To arrive at any one somatotype, 17 diameter measurements are necessary. To facilitate matters, a machine was constructed which, on receiving the measurements, could be manipulated by a series of switches so as to present the correct somatotype of any male youth between the age of 16 and 21.

The three physical components which enter into

[1] W. H. Sheldon: *The Varieties of Human Physique* (Harper) 1940.

the somatotype of any individual are (a) endomorphy, (b) mesomorphy, and (c) ectomorphy.
The terms make use of the Greek roots for
"inside," "midway" and "outside," and "form"
or "shape." The viscera are derived from the
endodermal (inner) embryonic layer; the meso-
dermal (middle) layer goes to shape the bones
and muscles, while the nervous system and skin
are largely the products of the ectodermal (outer)
embryonic layer. The fleshy, paunched, rounded,
pudgy-faced, short-fingered have an inner physique.
They are the digestive type of Sigaud, and sometimes we see a man whose whole frame makes us
think of entrails. The mesomorph (midway form)
is characterized by well-developed muscles, large
bones, firm connective tissue, large blood vessels,
tough skin, and erect posture. The hallmark of
mesomorphy is uprightness and sturdiness of
structure, as the hallmark of endomorphy is soft-
ness and sphericity. The "outside" form has to do
neither with fleshiness nor with muscle or bone
but with the nervous system, which is more or less
the outpost of the body connecting it with the
outside world. Here we have a fragile delicate
body poorly protected, since there is not the
fleshiness, nor the sinew or bone to lean on. Compared with the others, the ectomorph has much

more exposed surface. Just as the endomorph is usually round (except when emaciated in disease or through starvation) and the mesomorph appears rugged and taut, so the ectomorph is recognized without the aid of measurements by his slimness, long arms or legs, flat-chestedness, stoop, delicate texture.

Let us bear in mind that pure endomorphs, mesomorphs, and ectomorphs are rare. In other words, if the range is 1-7, with 7, 0, 0 indicating the absence of mesomorphy and ectomorphy, the individual is an extraordinary specimen. Hence Sheldon insists that since practically all have components of the three physical dimensions in one ratio or another, the type difficulty is done away with. The well-balanced individual would show a machine reading of 4,4,4, or 4,3,4, or 4,3,3 but we may have all sorts of combinations, even in decimal points, if we wish to obtain a fine discrimination.

Psychic Type or Temperament

The physical indexing is only a preliminary to the psychic pigeonholing of individuals. The question is: What do we do with our *static somatotypes* after satisfying ourselves that the machine "got their number?" Translated into dynamic psychological categories, we have endomorphy turned into *viscerotonia,* mesmomorphy into *somatotonia* (not to be confused with somatotype, which is the generic term for the physical classification) while ectomorphy corresponds to *cerebrotonia.* In short, the viscerotonic is a stomach man; the somatotonic is a muscle man and the cerebrotonic is a nerve and brain man (and, of course, man is used here to include the other sex). Like every simple formula, the above is too general, and may lead to misunderstandings, so a couple of explanatory remarks are in order.

A few of the characteristics for each type will bring out the essential differences. Let us take the viscerotonic. He is earthy, loves to eat, and particularly in company, is a sound sleeper, craves affection and praise, gets along well with others, and is self-complacent and self-indulgent.[2]

The somatotonic with his muscular frame is a glutton not for food so much as for power. He is energetic, aggressive, domineering, daring, and an adolescent (though not in appearance) even in mature age. Exercise is to him what food is to the viscerotonic.

One can always tell the cerebrotonic by his secretiveness, self-consciousness, inhibitions and

[2] W. H. Sheldon: *The Varieties of Temperament,* (Harper), 1942.

restraints, poor organizing and aversion to routine and noise, quick and often nervous movements, youthful or immature appearance, introversion, poor mixing, etc.

Exaggerated Products and Maladjustment

The *viscerotic* is one who is ill-adjusted because of a disproportionate amount of viscerotonia. Similarly the *somatorotic* has an excess of somatotonia; the *cerebrotic* shows personality difficulties for a like reason. Maladaptation because of deficiencies in any of the components is designated respectively by the terms *visceropenia, somatopenia,* and *cerebropenia.* Many of the neuroses are ascribed to conflicts among the components in the individual. Thus tics are the result of a clash between the mesomorphic and the ectomorphic parts, i.e., the muscular and the nervous systems.

In this anthropometric approach, which has been carried out on a large scale with all the facilities of a large university laboratory, we really have a revival of the constitutional typologies. True, Sheldon dismisses the type doctrine, but after all is said and done, the quantitative product of components is still a numerical *type,* deftly handled, it must be conceded. One of the curious features of Sheldon's system is that his viscerotonic, somatotonic, and cerebrotonic seem to be only other names for the vital, motive, and nervous temperaments as taught by — of all things — phrenology!

"Birds of a Feather"

I have noticed that most restaurant *chefs* are round-faced, make a pyknic appearance, and give evidence of feminine traits. Dish-washers are usually asthenic (weakly, slight) or dysplastic (disproportionate). As patrons, we choose neither the chef nor the dish-washer, but we are in a position to show our preference for certain waiters (the preference in the matter of waitresses on the part of men is, of course, on another level of discussion), and these individual differences throw no little light on our own personality.

At times the exigency of the occasion dictates a particular choice. Although masochism and sadism have been mentioned heretofore only in connection with psychopathic individuals, we know now that normal people show traces of the one tendency or the other, as I have been able to convince myself, at any rate, in the case of barbers. It may be surmised, then, that before approaching a vacant chair in a strange barber shop, I review the ready barbers most closely with the question in mind, which is the least sadistic of them, and, above all, which is most likely to follow instructions and just pass the razor over the face lightly instead of assuming that all skins are of the consistency of rubber.

What Determines Our Preferences?

Our judgments and estimates are naturally based on physiognomic and other bodily signs, interpreted in the light of past experiences. A barber with the bulging eyes and facial muscula-ture of a Bismarck would not, even in an emergency, stand the least chance of performing the tonsorial operation on my face, though I should not be so fastidious in the matter of a haircut. Physiognomy, one of the oldest arts, thus becomes somewhat of a guide — true, often a misleading one — of type discrimination. Personality testers, as scientists, pretend at least to keep aloof from such an instrument of information, but *the laws of uniformity of nature bespeak a correspondence between what a person is, what he does, and what appearance he presents,* in the broadest possible sense. That branch of personality study which may be called *psychodiagnostics* is slowly gaining ground, even though experimental psychologists are loath, as a class, to dignify it as a legitimate field of science.

CHAPTER XI

PSYCHODIAGNOSTICS

B Y PSYCHODIAGNOSTICS is meant the approach to personality from external symptoms, such as the features, facial expression, vocal inflection, gait, gesture, handwriting, and numerous other manifestations. There is as yet no full-fledged science of physiognomy or even graphology, but it would be futile to deny the great possibilities of such studies or to ignore, as regards the former branch, the large body of data that have been collected since the time of Porta [1] especially by Lavater, C. G. Carus, Duchenne, Bell, Darwin, and from a different angle, Piderit. Graphology, too, has been placed on a respectable footing through the scientific endeavors of Georg Meyer, Crépieux-Jamin, and Ludwig Klages.

[1] This philosopher, playwright, botanist and above all, observer of human nature, has not been duly appreciated by posterity, although his masterly work, *De humana physiognomonia* (1590) ran into many editions in a comparatively short period. This 600-page work, even if not its sequel on the nature of plants, should have found an English translator.

Probably the most critical of recent graphologists was Robert Saudek, whose work, over a quarter of a century, has raised this fascinating though obscure subject to an illuminated level. In his books, *The Psychology of Handwriting* and *Experiments with Handwriting,* he has given the results of thousands of individual experiments, and has succeeded in separating the environmental factors from the personal and, apparently inborn, elements.

Bias against Graphology

Conservative people of the educated class were wont to disregard the claims of graphology. Courts, to be sure, would allow handwriting experts, in cases of forgery, e.g., to testify as to the indentity of the writer under examination, but that is about as far as the service of these experts was invoked. Certainly they were never consulted officially as to the character of the accused or the mental condition of a witness.

That most books on graphology are worthless and savor of quackery does not invalidate the principles underlying that study. Every little movement, every gesture, no matter how slight, portends something to be interpreted. If we find ourselves unequal to the task of unraveling the mystery, if we are mistaken about our impressions, the fault lies not in the objective situation, but with us.

One of the chief sources of errors is the attempt to employ one method alone in evaluating personality. One puts all his faith in graphology; another in physiognomy; a third in the physique; a fourth in the mimetic qualities. Each of these endeavors is *monosymptomatic,* and can yield but partial results.

GRAPHOLOGY

Of all the individual or singular methods adopted to approach personality analysis, graphology seems to have fared best. Leaving aside the pseudo-sciences of palmistry, phrenology, and clairvoyance, we cannot even place physiognomy on a par with graphology, although the former has had such a distinguished and ancient following. Indeed, in some respects, graphology has shown itself to possess advantages not found among the latest scientific attempts to probe personality — I mean psychoanalysis and trait testing. Certainly this is a great recommendation for an art which in many circles is still regarded with snobbish contempt and looked upon as akin to quackery, because of its exploitation by the newspapers and "dumb Dora" journals.

Advantages over other Psychodiagnostic Methods

What graphology has to offer is significant because of the mechanism that it seeks to fathom. Let us consider that a smile is often "put on," a knowing glance is frequently lost sight of, that the features in general — the nose, the brow, the chin, etc., are stationary things and must be "sized up" intuitively, without checking up one against the other, while handwriting is the immediate stamp of the central nervous system in operation; it is not merely caught by the eye for a moment, but is recorded and is accessible at all times for study, so that any disguise or dissimulation can be eventually detected by the expert. Furthermore, it is the most complete expression of the nervous system at any given time because of the complicated habit-system built up through education around the discipline of writing, so that an ordinary letter might reveal many thousands of movements, and therefore many thousands of possible variations or deviations, say, from a perfect copy-book style, which constitute a key to one's personality.

A mere gesture or posture, or even the whole gait, is not sufficient to differentiate individuals in a detailed manner. In handwriting we find a thousand cues to personality, provided, of course, the purely technical and adventitious factors (material, circumstances of writing, fatigue, chirographic or calligraphic training) are separated from the endogenous elements. Certainly the old-type or dilettante graphologist cannot be expected to notice difficulties, pick out apparent discrepancies, or to enter into the subtleties of the various characteristics.

Methodological Requirements

The requirements of graphology are, first of all, that we make sure about the significance of a certain graphic deviation or element (*deductive phase* of the science) and, secondly, that after we have in hand our principle, e.g., that pronounced initial and final adjustments are indicative of the Babbitt high-power salesman, we must establish whether the handwriting under examination actually exhibits these adjustments (*inductive phase*), which is not easy to decide in some cases, and which must be judged, therefore, in combination with some other characteristic.

Is Graphology Purely Empirical?

Graphology is largely an empirical discipline; that is to say, the results are based on a comparison of the actual records, their styles and characteristics, twists and quirks, as corresponding with the same *personality* whorl or constellation in the writers.

But graphology must also produce the *rationale* of its findings. We must be able to grasp the *modus operandi* of its mechanisms. It may be readily understood that a sincere and fairly confident person will write a quick and natural hand, and that a *poseur* or schemer will reveal his inner weakness by his initial adjustments and irregular pressure, but why the *o,* open at the bottom, should be a sign of dishonesty, as is often contended on the strength of innumerable instances, must still be unraveled. Once the theoretical foundation of graphology is reconstructed, we shall have a direct means for tunneling out a passage to the *Struktur* mines of personality research.

The Two Schools

Ludwig Klages has been more intrigued by the theoretical approach to graphology, and has therefore laid himself open to the charge of being a metaphysician in this field. Perhaps it would be more reasonable to regard him as the leader of the intuitive school of graphology, and as such, he wields a great influence in Germany, especially in circles where there is an idealistic tradition. Robert Saudek, on the other hand, has dwelt mainly on the experimental aspects of graphology, and has devised methods for testing, measuring, collating, and evaluating the material. He is esteemed particularly in medical circles, in mental hygiene and psychiatric institutions, and more recently among psychologists.

According to Klages, the pivotal point in the interpretation of a handwriting seems to be the *Formniveau*, that is, the cultural level of the writer, as shown by the formation of the characters and their connection, but especially the rhythm of the writer. This *Formniveau* has to be perceived, it would seem, intuitively. Saudek, on the other hand, although he cannot altogether dispose of intuition, would prefer not to allude to it, and to rely wholly on objective methods. To him the matter of speed or slowness in writing is all-important, since specific traits and tendencies as well as conflicts and inconsistencies could be deduced from the interplay of quick spurts in a generally slow handwriting or slow spells in a generally quick hand.

American Skepticism

The attitude of the average American psychologist toward graphology is one of extreme skepticism, but as I have pointed out both in *The*

Psychology of Common Sense[2] and in the introduction to H. A. Rand's *Graphology; a Handbook,* the bias is traditional. Experimentalists and
testers with a statistical outlook insist on chopping
up the experience into minute cut-and-dried
chips which they must measure first, and then
count. Anything which resists this method must
be treated by the well-known formula "off with
its head." From psychiatry and clinical psychology
comes an encouraging note; for there, experiences
are studied in the raw, and it is recognized that
life is more extensive than the laboratory. Were
it not for outside influences of new blood,
psychology would have been stagnant, because
experimental psychologists would be loath to leave
their laboratory grooves, and the very "Mis-
sourians" and "you-show-me" psychologists are
the ones to be taken in by any old experiment, so
long as it was conducted at a reputable laboratory,
even if by an undergraduate.

It is a sad commentary on American psychology
that an undergraduate's negative results in a
supposedly graphological investigation of 17
scripts should be hailed as the classical experimental exposé of graphology as a method of
revealing personality traits. Some 25 - 30 years

[2] A. A. Roback: *"Psychology of Common Sense,"* Chapter 21.

ago, C. L. Hull, then directing research at the University of Wisconsin, parcelled out a few experimental problems to several undergraduates. Each dealt with a different psychodiagnostic claim. Thus, one would be assigned the task of investigating physiognomy; another the claims of phrenology; still another chirognomy (personality traits from the shape and characteristics of the hands), and the pioneer among these students, R. B. Montgomery, started off the series, in 1918, by examining the contentions of graphology.

Method and Technique

The experimenter asked 17 students of the same medical fraternity to copy about a dozen lines from a magazine. Then each was requested to rate the others on each of six traits. The so-called graphic signs for these traits, like sloping lines, heavy *t* bars, or closed *a's* and *o's,* were then measured to the 64th of an inch for width, or the nearest half-millimeter for length. The correlation between the ratings and the graphic signs, which presumably would indicate the traits was, in the main, less than negligible. On the basis of the conclusion, it is suggested that graphology has not a shred of value and should be consigned to the limbo of quackeries or superstitions.

That this experiment, probably more of a
student's exercise than an investigation, yet
calculated to decide a scientific issue, should be
taken seriously is in itself no tribute to American
psychology, but that this picayune bit of research,
in spite of its impressive technique, should be
regarded as the nemesis of graphology, making
gullible dolts of scientists like G. Meyer, W.
Preyer, G. Schneidemühl, A. Binet, or charlatans
of men like Ludwig Klages and Robert Saudek, is
almost a slur on our intelligence. Practically every
psychologist who, utterly unfamiliar with its methods, wishes to make light of graphology, cites
this article of 11½ pages by Hull and Montgomery [3]
of 30 years ago, as the final verdict.

The situation, however, is this: the postulated
graphic signs are not acceptable except through
some combination with others; the student ratings
are questionable; the measurements, in spite of
the excessive zeal, may not have been per-
tinently applied, so that the tables of figures
may have no weight. A sample of the bias
exhibited in this experiment may be seen in the
following sentence "It is probably significant, how-

[3] C. L. Hull and R. B. Montgomery: "An Experimental Investigation of Certain Alleged Relations between Character and Handwriting." *Psychol. Review,* 1919, vol. 26, pp. 63-74.

ever, that Binet's graphologists made very bad records on the only test of character he employed." In what way can we call it a "very bad record," when Crépieux-Jamin made 3 errors out of 11 judgments, which is equivalent to a 73% score, while the two others gave 6 correct answers out of 11, which again is above chance? Again, when Binet has shown conclusively that intelligence could be deduced from handwriting, one of his observers obtaining about 92% correct answers (even those with no special training hit it correctly in 66% - 73% of the cases) the writers imply that the handwriting may have been known to the observers, hence the success.

Reductio ad Absurdum

We might compare this whole procedure to the following: A man has purchased a suit of clothes in a first-class clothing store, and he is perfectly satisfied with the fit, but a friend of his expresses his doubts on this, and sends a surveying clerk with all his measuring instruments, in addition to other apprentices with T squares, slide rules, and calipers, and they measure both the man and the suit in every which way, and come to the conclusion that the suit should be returned as an ill-fitting garment.

There is no intention here to question the academic eminence of Clark Hull or the integrity of his student, but to call attention to the fact that there are scientific prejudices as well as those of creed and race, and that the first step toward an unbiased inquiry is to familiarize oneself with the subject to be "exposed." The best engineer will not be an adequate judge of medical claims, and the so-called "objective" scientific conditions, which so many experimenters, including our critics above, pride themselves on, are often "sicklied o'er with a pale cast" of rank subjectivism.

The Blind Spot in Experimental Psychology

The wonder is that after G. W. Allport[4] and G. W. Hartmann[5] have disclosed the inadequacies of this particular procedure, the Hull-Montgomery report should still be "enthusiastically cited," to use, Allport's phrase; and that investigations which have confirmed the postulates of graphology should be ignored, either through lack of knowledge, or intentionally, on the ground, presumably, that they were not conducted in accordance with scientific requirements. Even such

[4] G. W. Allport and P. E. Vernon: *Studies in Expressive Movement* (Macmillan) 1933, pp. 192-194.

[5] G. W. Hartmann: *Gestalt Psychology* (Ronald) 1935, pp. 253-255.

an excellent textbook as L. P. Thorpe's *Psychological Foundations of Personality* lays itself open to this charge, largely because the author supposes that all science consists of mechanics and minute measurement — a belief which is "inherited" from the behaviorists. Let us admit that most of the practising graphologists are not scientifically trained. Is that a good reason for ruling the subject out of court? There was a time when medicine was almost altogether in the hands of empirics, yet who would have thought of denying it scientific status?

Within the past twenty years, I have had an accumulation of overwhelming evidence in the form of analyses by graphologists, in support of the scientific art, for that is what graphology is, even if I were to disregard my own hundreds of readings, of which more than two hundred were validated by the staff of the Harvard Grant Study, consisting of highly trained specialists: a veteran psychologist, [6] two psychiatrists, an anthropologist, a medical man with assistants. Am I to discount all the corroborative testimony on the part of these men on the strength of a restricted experiment conducted by a student over a few weeks' period?

[6] F. L. Wells: "Personal History, Handwriting, and Specific Behavior." *Jour. of Personality,* 1946, vol. 14, pp. 295-314. The graphological results are discussed here as a preliminary report only.

Experimental Confirmation of Graphology from England

H. J. Eysenck, in a recent book, reports no less than 1350 comparisons of handwriting specimens and replies to questionnaires by 50 patients, in the Maudsley Hospital, in England, who were not seen by the psychologist. "In actual fact, 62% ± 1% agreed. Taking only those judgments on which the graphologist felt particularly sure, the number of agreements rises to 68% ± 3% . . . when it is remembered that the patients' answers to the questions may often have been false to fact . . . then we must surely conclude that graphology does to some extent at least succeed in correlating handwriting and personality traits." [7]

The matchings of the handwritings and the psychiatrist's personality sketch were carried out in groups of five. On a chance basis, one matching out of five ought to have been correct; as a matter of fact, 2.4 matchings were correct on the average. This figure is very significant statistically, and confirms our previous conclusion regarding the value of graphology. As a comparison, we may cite the attempts of non-graphologists to match writings and sketches; the average success

[7] H. J. Eysenck: *Dimensions of Personality,* (Routledge) 1947, pp. 240-241.

of twenty such matchings was 0.7., i.e. rather less than chance would allow.

If graphology is to be thrown overboard, then it could be decided on only in consequence of a long-term probing in which mature researchers in the psychological and social fields will participate together with one or two reputable graphologists — and there are such. Within the last decade, we have had serious, although limited, attempts to examine one phase or another of graphology through experimental controls, with a fair degree of success, but

The evil that men do lives after them;

and it will be long before graphology succeeds in living down the sins which have been committed in its name by tyros and commercializers who have had no professional standing nor scientific training.

Encouraging Prospect

The universities and colleges have lately become more interested in graphological problems, and *bona fide* graphologists are asked, on various occasions, to coöperate with investigators in psychological laboratories and to lecture before the students.

From my own experiences with graphology, I might say that I was impressed with the results. A certain amount of intuitive filling-in is, to be sure, nearly always to be found in the analyses, but the groundwork must be supplied first from the actual objective observations gained as a result of close investigation.

Aside, however, from the practical value of studying personality from outward characteristics, I maintain that there is a symbolism in every bit of behavior, normal and abnormal, which is as yet a *terra incognita,* and for that reason it behooves us to dwell on this point at some length.

Note:

Prof. Hull (Institute of Human Relations, Yale University) was kind enough to supply the following information in connection with the hand-writing experiment in which he participated more than thirty years ago, and which has figured so prominently in psychological textbooks:

Montgomery became interested in the study of handwriting from reading on the subject in popular magazines, coming to it with a strong expectation that it would prove sound. I was somewhat skeptical but agreed with him that it ought to be investigated, so the experiment was set up and completed with the results which appear in the article. Montgomery, at the time, was an undergraduate, and the study was performed out of a scientific interest on our parts. It was in no way connected with any degree at all. Montgomery subsequently took his B.A. degree at the University of Wisconsin, and then his M.D.

Apparently the youth, then, was not even a senior at college. The report was well worth printing, but it is evident that there is not enough substance contained in it to countervail a vast body of experimental data in favor of graphology; and both Prof. Hull and his erstwhile student at Wisconsin University must have been quite surprised that the article should have carried so much conviction in psychological circles.

That my surmise was correct may be gathered from a note just received, in which Dr. R. B. Montgomery (with a quarter-century medical practice behind him) informs us that "it was 'just another paper'," and concludes with the sentence, "My curiosity is aroused; may I ask why you are interested in this long forgotten article?" Little does he, apparently, realize that the oft-cited article has *not* been forgotten by psychologists!

Chapter XII

MEANING AND THE PERSONAL IDIOM

The Three Approaches

HITHERTO, much stress has been laid on the meaning of the term personality, but the manifestations of personality in habits and other forms of behavior have only recently begun to be interpreted in conjunction with the whole problem of motivation. There are three possible approaches to this study: the behavioristic, which sees no meanings in the individual differences exhibited by different people, except as actually intended by the subjects, or as representing the automatic effects of a pure conditioning to stimuli; the psycho-analytic, which derives all the significance from certain experiences of an emotional nature, undergone in early childhood; and what, for want of a better name, I might call the "constitutional" avenue.

Constitutional Conception

The stand taken in the constitutional method is

that we are all so constituted (not only because of organ inferiority) as to express our personality in everything we do which is at all a deviation from a rational standard. This is, by no means, to be interpreted, (as several editorial writers did, when they took me to task for such a "peculiar" view, after the account of the Yale International Congress in Psychology appeared in the press) that a high-grade personality consists in deviations from a rational standard. Quite the contrary, the nearly perfect personality is governed by such a standard. It is, nevertheless, true that through such deviations do we learn to discriminate between one personality and another and to characterize them in one way or another.

By a rational standard, I mean whatever type of behavior furthers the achievement of the end in view. If a thrifty individual, for example, spends a few hours looking for a one-cent stamp, when he could have used a two-cent stamp without any bother, he certainly deviates from a reasonable course of procedure. When some one uses unfair or undignified means in order to become a celebrity for the sake of the honor attached to the status and for nothing else, he has actually committed an Irish bull on a high level. A thousand and one illustrations may be cited of such irrational conduct in everyday life, both among the lowly and among the mighty, although it must be recognized that the truly great have been far less prone to lapse into such inconsistencies, at any rate within their special spheres of greatness.

Irrational Twists in Personality

Why should so many unwittingly do the very things or manifest the very behavior which interferes with their purpose in life? The answer is that, in their subconscious or unconscious depths, there are other sub-purposes tugging away at their central aspiration. Or, conflicts may arise between two sets of desires. The basis of these irrational twists and twitches is, in the last analysis congenital, although when questioned about the *modus operandi,* we must humbly answer, "We do not know." That experiential effects may graft themselves on, or modify, the original foundation, we cheerfully concede, but they are never the sole determining factors.

Rich Personalities not Neccesarily Integrated

Is it to be inferred, then, that personality consists in irrationality and that the more reasonable, the more balanced we are, the less personality do we have? That is what I am afraid has been gathered from a previous utterance of mine, but it is a misconstruction which requires correction. We are hardly justified in assuming that the temperamental Whistler possessed more personality than the serene Joshua Reynolds, or that the capricious Wagner had a higher personality coefficient than the correct Mendelssohn. Nevertheless, Wagner and Whistler, because of their greater divergences from a rational mode, revealed more upheavals in their make-up; and we may, for this reason, regard them as more interesting personalities. Although health is the goal of medicine, it nevertheless is concerned with the study and treatment of disease. If all individuals manifested absolutely rational behavior, there could be no differentiation whatever; and consequently it would be doubtful whether we could, under such circumstances, reasonably speak of personality. It is through our oddities and eccentricities that we are known, but the evaluation of our personality certainly does not depend on, much less is it enhanced by, the *number* of such individual deviations from a rational standard. At the very most, such people may be said to possess *rich* personalities, but very rarely can they be regarded as having *fine* personalities. Their varied experiences are engendered by the very difficulties in their *psyche,* but it is not likely that they would be sufficiently unified as *men* and *women* (not merely as artists) to offer an example of an integrated mental life.

Meaning in All Behavior

The meanings are to be sought not only in idiosyncrasies and eccentricities, but in gesture, posture, gait, vocal inflection and modulation, as well as in the higher personality syntheses, such as the recurring phrases or ideas in Shakespeare's plays or Beethoven's and Bach's compositions. It is here that new horizons promise to unfold themselves. The technical analysis of great masterpieces, to a large extent, has shunted the probing into the meanings of what I would call the *personal idiom* of the author, painter, or composer. Why did Wagner show a fondness for major sevenths? Why was Chopin in the habit of jumping octaves?

Beethoven's Personal Idiom

In the second part of his suggestive little book, *The Unconscious Beethoven,* the British music critic, Ernest Newman, traces a peculiar ascending succession of notes in many of Beethoven's symphonies, sonatas, and other works, which leads the author to believe that this progression is a reflection of the great composer's subconscious. This is undoubtedly true, but the discovery does not take us very far in our investigation. We must decipher the meaning of this musical curve in Beethoven, who gives evidence of a stratified personality. What makes his music so *interesting* — although Bach's is equally, if not more, beautiful — is the coming to the fore, in the shape of musical symbols, of his "split-off" ideas, of his conflicts, his temperamental limitations, his "two souls in one breast." He hardly ever begins without faltering, stumbling, and beginning again with greater gusto and growing ardor, until he triumphs in the finale — all his difficulties surmounted.

How different from Mozart, Haydn, or Mendelssohn. Mendelssohn would have been a much finer artist, had he a more corrugated temperament. Beethoven seems to have been the possessor of a peculiar constitutional make-up. At first blush, he appears to contradict Kretschmer's formula: for although of a "thick-set" physique, he presented the symptoms of a "split-off" personality, as if he were slim and Nordic in appearance. My solution to this problem is that Beethoven was a "thick-set" type, with extraverted tendencies and the circular diathesis, when *living on the lower plane,* with his boon companions, engaging in raucous laughter and sipping wine at the coffee-house; but the moment he was by himself, in the spiritual sphere, he was a true "split-off" type, and could now assemble the dissociated mental components (ideas, affects), which were up to now floating aimlessly, into a symbolic masterpiece.

Individuality of Chopin

The more individual a creative mind is, the more unique is his *"personal idiom."* Chopin stands in a niche all by himself as a composer of piano music, because no one could approach him in musical individuality, in the uniform character which runs through his numerous varieties of musical phraseology. When we hear Beethoven's twenty-eighth sonata, we exclaim, "How Chopin-esque!" And the inference may further be drawn that when writing this sonata, Beethoven must have been in a mood similar to Chopin's. Chopin was a true "split-off" type, with *occasional* outbursts of bravado, peculiar to the "thick-set" type.

Important Inferences for Critics

In Bach, the personal idiom is not so marked,

so clear-cut as in either Beethoven or Chopin. Händel and other contemporaries approach him sufficiently to lead to mistaken identity. Schubert's and Schumann's personal idioms were somewhat akin as regards the melody, but the skipping rhythm of the former (*Rosamunde,* some of the *Impromptus* and *Moments Musicaux,* the most popular *Military March, Symphony in C Major,* second and third movements) distinguishes him from his successor. In view of this essential, which is claimed here to be the carrier of the artist's personality, the recent talk of completing the *Unfinished Symphony* must strike one as fatuous.

Wagner's Musical Trade-Mark

It is my belief that Wagner stormed the musical world largely through his personal idiom, which was characteristically his own. Even the tyro could recognize a Wagnerian phrase, whether he hears it in *Parsifal,* in *Trisan,* in *Die Meistersinger,* or even in his *Albumblatt.* If Schubert is skipping, Wagner gives the impression of climbing, a perpetual Valkyrie rider, soaring into worlds of myth and fancy, where there is no resistance to his boundless self-confidence and pretentiousness, and yet revealing all the while his twain existence by

[225]

means of the double strain [1] that runs throughout his operas, a melody of poise, on the verge of pose, and dignity ever rearing itself against a turbulent background.

A more epochal and cultural illustration of this ideational conflict I have come across but once in the opposition chimes, sounded alternately by the bells of two different colleges at Oxford — one of the most enchanting experiences I can remember having — when the restless temper of progress in the Middle Ages seemed to be crying out through all these centuries against the easygoing placidity of Scholasticism. In a sense, I may say that I had caught, on that balmy September evening, the spirit, if not (because of our previous restriction in the use of this term) the personality of Oxford. The duet, although it continued in steady repetition, for about fifteen minutes or more, was all too brief.

---

[1] This is not to be likened to objective double motives required for descriptive purposes, such as to be heard in Honegger's *Pacific 231,* where the mechanical roaring and panting, against the self-complacency and leisure of the engineer, does not reflect the personality of the composer, but gives us an insight into his conception. In Tennyson's *Ulysses,* we have a similar objective antithesis which is not to be interpreted as a personal idiom of the poet, although Tennyson does not, by any means, lack the personal idiom in his poetry, as seen especially in his assonance and onomatopoeic effects.

The Idiom in Painting

Personal idioms may be readily discovered in masterpieces belonging to other arts. The personal idiom in Rembrandt's light and shade effects is unmistakable. Raphael's unique conceptions, Da Vinci's psychological expressions and Titian's elegant forms are all to be regarded as personal idioms in the light of the present discussion. The personal idioms of the literary giants are scarcely mentioned here, for the connection is too obvious. The very term "idiom" is borrowed from the sphere of language, and the relationship between words and meaning is a commonplace.

Meaning in Nervous Habits

Probably few psychologists will be willing to assent to the special thesis that nervous tricks, like blinking, heaving the shoulders, see-sawing the legs, or puffing up the cheeks and exhaling, after getting settled in a seat, are also to be invested with a personality meaning. Psychoanalysts will see in these symptoms merely the functioning of complexes, unfulfilled desires, repressions, and so on. They will link this behavior up with an experience in the past (as in conversion hysteria) while behaviorists and their sympathizers will say "Shucks, only a habit twist! Wrong conditioning!" My rejoinder is that if children of the same parents, but of different mental and physical make-up, present marked differences in their behavior, although reared in the same environment, and if persons that are apogeal to each other in every environmental respect but bear resemblances in other ways, manifest similar tendencies and behavior, even to the nervous habits — it is clear that we are dealing with laws of germ-plasm, not of environment, except in its modifying effect.

Symptomatic Behavior of a Would-be Executive

At one time, a young man came into my study and slightly annoyed me by his hemming and hawing and artificial nonchalance in flicking the ashes off his cigarette. He also fidgeted a good deal, making passes with his hands, as if he were an executive, giving orders. It was not long before I learned that this former student of mine was a petty official in a national concern where he was longing to be advanced to an executive position. His gestures told the story. It was not so much the salary that counted in his case as the command, the social prestige and self-esteem. The meaning does not have to be explicit. It is a psychophysiological fact, nevertheless.

Stereotype Phrases

In daily conversation, the personal idiom recurs in the constant use of some particular expression, "As the saying goes," "the short and the long of it," a habit of speech encountered more in the uneducated and illiterate, but by no means confined to them. The frequent interspersion of phrases like "so to speak" or "as it were" typifies the individual who is groping for analogies because he is not quite at home in the matter of accurate nomenclature. The phrase "you don't say," which registers surprise, is seldom on the lips of phlegmatics; and as for "after all," we sometimes can hear this uttered in relation to nothing in particular, simply as an interjection with nothing preceding or following it. A speech habit may be of environmental origin, but why did that specific phrase, of the many heard, make the effective impression, and why did it cling while others were discarded, if it didn't strike a responsive chord in the individual adopting it?

The Mute but Eloquent Language of Greeting

Of all the expressive modes of behavior, that of greeting somehow has been neglected in psychological discussions. We may be looking forward to a series of experimental investigations after one

[229]

enterprising psychologist will have broken the ice. There is much to be learned about a person from the way he greets another, aside from the fact that for the social psychologist, the attitude of the greeter toward the greeted is reconstructed, if not intuited in a flash, from the type of salutation. Greeting often consists of a very articulate exclamation, but it is just as frequently a gesture or a glance or a wink without words. We may really begin with the inclination or disinclination to greet altogether. A personal confession is pertinent here. In my early teens, I would balk at the usual salutation expected like "good morning" "good evening," and when taken to task would argue that it is meaningless, because my saying or wishing it would not decide whether the morning or evening would be good or bad. The scoldings and threats which followed the lapses would lead to compromise involving a good deal of ingenuity so as to satisfy the family and yet not violate the "principle" of refraining from mumbo-jumbo. Similarly, I could scarcely understand why my much older brother on meeting me on my way from school, as he was going to work, would pause to greet me, although I had seen him earlier and would see him again in the evening.

The disinclination to go through the motions

may have been an extreme case, symptomatic of a precocious adolescence, but it is typical of many people who would rather not look up lest they meet scores of people they knew and would, therefore, be expected to nod to them. They may be introverts, or they may have too many acquaintances, or students. I often wondered why Hugo Münsterberg would, in spite of his general alertness, direct his eyes downward, as he would be passing along at Harvard Square; and it only occurred to me much later that he was trying to save his energy and time. There was, however, no inner disinclination on his part to meet people. It is, of course, possible that the energy factor is instrumental in much of the aversion to this constant movement of head or hand in a small community.

Varieties of Salutations

Of the different forms of salutation — and their number is legion — only a few will be adverted to here. We may group them under national or ethnic tendencies, ideological or political outgrowths (Fascistic extension of the arm and the Nazi lifting it, the Communist raising the balled fist) the cringing, scraping, and bowing of Uriah Heep, and the offish and snobbish salutation of a British colonial administrator. There is the very perfunctory nod, when we meet people we do not particularly care for, or the serious mien may sometimes belie the plausible semblance of a smile. Again, the head may be raised briskly while the lips are separated as if to utter something, but the whole process is an abortive one. On the other hand the head may be raised very slowly and then lowered abruptly as if to say "Yes, I saw you" (often the greeting of a creditor). Whether the head is turned to the right or left, in the direction of the acquaintance or rarely away from him (the affection cannot be too great here to overcome the principle of ideo-motor action) or whether the nod is accompanied by a gesture and supplemented with a friendly smile, not a mechanical one that lasts a fraction of a second and seems to be electrically induced—does not tell the same story in our interpretation of the act, as well as of the personality of the greeter.

Greeting may be accomplished by a sudden thrust of the hand and a spreading of the fingers; in the more emotional, a lunge at the person may serve a special purpose. The military salute, which is a symbol of discipline, is most likely derived from the necessity of calling attention to the eyes and ears under compulsion to obey orders.

Verbal Greetings

Again, the *words* used in greeting an acquaintance, friend, or relative are of some consequence. Whether we use the formal "how do you do?" or "how are you?" shortened to "hy," or the more countrified "howdy," or whether we get into the habit of saying "how're you doin?" or stick to the natural "hello" or just emit a grunt or growl — will make a difference as to the type of individual we are — but thus far, we are on virgin territory. We may go still further and interpret the accent and the inflection. The "how-are-you today" greeting with the accent on the time typifies a certain individual, while the accenting of the verb or the pronoun is characteristic of another. It is all a matter of pose, ceremony, or pretense. Genuine concern transcends accents or frills upon stereotypes. If the person greeted has been ill or indisposed, the word "to-day" might be stressed, but the question would be framed differently. The inflection, too, and the facial expression would be more telling.

The Tone and Modulation

Inflection adds another angle to greeting. There is the genial, the matter-of-fact, the quizzical, the gruff, the perfunctory, the sympathetic and cordial inflection and many others. Let us take the word "Hello." Sometimes it is articulated in a gulp, at other times in a grunt, or again it may be in a monotone or in a cheery inflection, stressing equally each of the syllables, a sort of "I-am-so-glad-to-see-you-again" tone of voice. The *l* may even be softened, so that "Hello" will sound like *"Hel-lyo."*

The farewell or parting pattern similarly offers a rich variety of possibilities. Whether one says in leaving "Goodbye," or "Goodbye, now," or "Good-day" ("Good night") or "Bye-bye," or "So long," or "I'll be seein' you," or "Take it easy" discloses something about the personality of the speaker as well as his relation to the interlocutor.

The Handshake

The handshake is not quite the same index as the verbal greeting, because physical vigor and temperature may determine the extent of the grip or the clammy moisture experienced in the hand grasp, but even then, we can have varieties of approach and attack, almost in the physical sense, as when our hand is clutched as in a vice by the unconsciously "vicious" welcomer, or when some-one is chary of yielding all his fingers and will risk only two (as mid-Victorian women would

shake hands) or when your hand will be shaken in
minced and nervous movements as if it were a
pepper caster or on the other hand, it might be
made to bob up and down, or it might be swayed
or wiggled. The flabby handshake, as is well
known, is distinctly unpopular with salesmen and
politicians. Can there be any doubt about the
symbolic individuality of the handshake?

Gait

The gait is another psychodiagnostic avenue.
How many different manners of walking can we
observe in the street on an ordinary day! There
are those who sway from side to side, who swing
their hands pendulum fashion, who almost wad-
dle, those who affect a sideling walk, who move
about as if in military formation, or who try to
get into step by dragging the other foot half a
pace; there are those who get on their toes every
once in a while, or change their stride or pace,
those who stop to look back — and one can
enumerate possibly a hundred other deviations
from what may be considered the normal gait, if
there is such.

Certainly the gait is a complex expressive movement which may tell a good deal about an individual. A retiring person will not turn his body first
in one direction, then in the other, because that

would be exhibitionism, which is out of character. Similarly the extreme extravert would not tiptoe with arms resting motionless at the sides. Walking in company with another adds to the complexity and affords us a deeper clue. There are such as walk so close to the other that they bump into their partner, while others keep aloof as a general habit, regardless of their attitude toward their fellow-walker.

Possibly some of the idiosyncrasies in gait are due to variations in structure or the result of acquired defects (knock knees, bow legs, pigeon toes, flatfootedness) or imitation, or conditions imposed by the environment (sailors, horseback riders, and others are known because of their specific gait) but after discounting the circumstances, there is still an individual residue which hinges on the particular personality, partly because some can resist more than others the adventitious; others can even throw it off, while still others fall in line very readily with the environmental stimulus; and partly for the reason that the gait in question is in keeping with other aspects of the personality, so that correlations may be drawn up among groups between one set of movements or gestures and another.

The Voice

No less an index of personality is the voice. H. Cantril and G. W. Allport have posed the question whether the voice conveys "any correct information concerning inner characteristics of personality," and their experimental results have established an affirmative conclusion. "The results show that *the more highly organized and deepseated traits and dispositions are judged more* CONSISTENTLY *than the more specific features of physique and appearance,"* [2] and not only consistently but more correctly, which suggests in the authors' opinion, that expression is most closely associated with the highly organized qualities of the inner personality. Naturally a voice can be trained. It can be affected and sound cultured when its bearer is more of a philistine, it may become husky because of too much imbibing or smoking, or because of climatic conditions, but by and large, we do even anticipate the individual timbre of the voice (nasal, throaty, guttural, high-pitched, deep, aspirate, orotund, cackling, froglike, etc.) at the sight of the person. The experiments have only confirmed what was generally known, except that we now have quantitative

[2] H. Cantril and G. W. Allport: *The Psychology of Radio* (Harper) 1935, p. 123.

data. One of the common beliefs, viz., that the blind can judge personality by voice better than the seeing has been discredited, thanks to this investigation.

Other Sounds as Indexes

I should go so far as to say that even the laugh is characteristic of any individual. The vocalic structuration of the sound in laughter (*ha-ha; hi-hi; he-he; hu-hu*); the pitch (differing of course with age); the rhythm, speed; modulation, whether unrestrained or inhibited, tittery, giggly, guffawlike, rollicking, braying or neighing, etc. are not only differentiating but revealing. They do not amount to the same thing; each variant emanates from a specific personality organization, naturally modified by circumstances to some degree. We might also make a list of the different manners of sneezing or even coughing, and find a much larger variety than we had anticipated. Laboratory work on such phases has still to be done, and as usual, probably the first impetus will come from clinical and psychiatric quarters, where experience is of greater account than technique, and where the urgency of the situation calls for immediate attention.

So-called Habits Fraught with Significance

It is not a matter of mere habit, when one individual crosses his hands behind his back, another holds them in his pockets, a third folds them in front, and a fourth holds the right arm flexed while walking. Orientals are likely to cross their hands behind. Americans frequently find their hands in their trouser-pockets or, more deliberately, thrust their thumbs into clothing at either side of the chest. The meaning of this attitude on the part of the Babbitt salesman need hardly be explained as one of self-assurance, "cockiness."

Meaning in Posture

Even our various postures are not without significance. Turning to Sigaud's four types — the cerebral, the muscular, the respiratory, and the digestive — have we not noticed that the individuals representing each type seem to parade that part in which their prowess is evident? The intellectual person with the stoop; the soldier of fortune, with excellent breathing apparatus, throwing his chest forward; the athlete exhibiting his muscular tonus in the sinewy arms, or moderately taut manner, and finally the corpulent man with paunch protruded are all involuntarily drawing attention to their *forte*; and it would be nothing short of remiss to fail taking account of the mechanism which is responsible for these differences in posture. To be sure, these variations seem natural in view of the bodily changes which take place in these different types; but the meanings of the personalities, in each case, seem to speak through these mechanisms. As the Psalmist expressed it, "All my bones do speak."

It is easy enough to account for every bit of unwilled behavior by saying it is a habit, but when confronted with the question why we "fall into" a particular habit and not into another, we are in a quandary, unless we are willing to accept the circular explanation of frequency. We are also at a loss to understand why some habits may be broken easily, others only with great difficulty, by different individuals.

Peculiarities Requiring Study

I have had ample opportunity to test both others and myself in this regard. Sometimes I realize that certain words which I might employ aptly in writing escape me at crucial moments. I try to bear them in mind and promise myself to make use of them the next time. For once I may be successful, but again the words "don't seem to stick." Apparently, they do not fit into my personality-pattern. There are block phrases which are the stock-in-trade of many writers, (like "the climate of opinion," "a frame of reference"). They save time and energy; and, because of their currency, they are assimilated by even those who run and read. It always strikes me as a hardship to be compelled to construct a phrase out of the ideas that range themselves rather abstractly before the words come to concretize them.

Another type of illustration comes to mind. Some people have a "habit" of coming long before they are due, whether to the railroad depot or to a reception. Others, no matter how many times they had vowed, in consequence of unpleasant experiences, to come on time, still keep arriving late. Stekel, in his *Disguises of Love,* ascribes this tendency to the fact of being born the youngest in the family. The late-comer thus shows that he resents losing the opportunities that his older brothers and sisters may have had. This intuitive flash of Stekel's, because of its speculative nature and disagreement with the circumstances where the youngest has much to be thankful for, will not bear examination, although Stekel's attempt, at least to read a meaning into such a habit, deserves our commendation.

From one of the cases personally known to me, I should attribute this fault to a constitutional "time complex," forming, in a slight degree, a sort of clinical syndrome; for the individual in question is always grappling with the impositions of time, never could work out the tormenting clock problems of grammar-school arithmetic, could not distinguish between morning and afternoon hours, would be surprised if told that it was late, would often overstay in making social calls and would allow visitors to take many hours of his time without being aware of the lapse, is almost afraid of consulting a timepiece, and finally could never learn the proper use of tenses, although this is a comparatively simple matter.

A Central Factor!

Do these deviations not point to a central factor? Or are they to be left as so many *disjecta membra,* without rhyme or reason? If a physician were to ignore the symptoms of a case in the same way as the behavioristic psychologist does in dealing with personality, medicine would, indeed, find itself in a sorry plight.

The symbolic meaning of any movement is difficult, of course, to interpret offhand, but to pigeonhole them all into the various stage-categories of genital development, such as oral, anal, genital and to add fantasy and motor groups seems neither reasonable nor practical; and yet M. H. Krout,[a] on the basis of the psychoanalytic doctrine of displacement, catalogues about 150 of such gestures and acts in this wise; and we wonder why "swaying buttock" should belong to the genital rather than to the anal group, or why "grinding teeth" should be listed in both the oral and the fantasy groups, or why smiling, "belching," "hiccuping," "yawning," or "crying" should be called symbolic and carry a sexual significance. Purely physiological processes, the result of fatigue, indigestion, or emotional outbursts need hardly be accounted for in esoteric or highly speculative terms.

First of all, it is necessary to establish whether a certain act, say coughing, is the result of a cold, or something that has gone down the wrong way, or is of a "nervous" origin. If it is the latter, as can easily be detected from its artificial nature in the presence of others, there can scarcely be any doubt that it is related to a sense of insecurity, embarrassment, temporizing, or a stuffed-shirt attitude to subordinates — all really manifestations

[a] M. H. Krout: "A Preliminary Note on Some Obscure Symbolic Muscular Responses of Diagnostic Value in the Study of Normal Subjects." *Amer. Jour. of Psychiat.* 1931, vol. 11, pp. 29-71

of the same ego involvement. Here we have at least a foundation for further study.) [4]

Or let us take teeth grinding. Has it to do with the mouth? Anatomically, yes, but symbolically it connotes again an attitude of a deeper nature. Gritting the teeth is commonly associated with great determination. Grinding the teeth is only a more intense gritting, and therefore suggests a more violent or tenser emotional reaction. When it arrives at that stage, mere determination to reach a goal is superseded by a personal attitude of resentment or hatred for someone. Displaying the teeth in ordinary social intercourse, and when not engaged in spontaneous laughter, especially while curling the lips, has always been symbolic of a fighting spirit or attitude, harking back, according to Darwinian theory, to the prehistoric days when the teeth were a formidable weapon. During the Nazi atrocities, some of the victims, more especially women in the clutches of the brute, reverted to that type of warfare, since all else was denied them.

In attempting to explain symbolic gestures, let us ask ourselves: What is that organism trying to

[4] A. A. Roback: "Meaning in Personality Manifestations." *Ninth International Congress of Psychology* (Proceedings and Papers), 1930, pp. 362-363.

say in spite of the inhibitions imposed upon it by the realistic ego? When a man blows up his cheeks and puffs out air, is he not actually then acting the turkey-cock or thinking, perhaps, of "talking turkey" in the slang sense? When an individual is going through the motions of some act, then that substitute should be examined in the light of the general situation, and if the gesture brings to mind some animal, a dog, cat, bird, or mouse, then rather than looking for a conditioned reflex in the distant past or a repressed experience during early childhood, it is meet for us to search for that trait in the person which is characteristic of the particular animal. It will certainly be more fruitful than groping in the stack of environmental conditions to find the needle of a motive.

Many of the elaborate explanations offered in the literature of what used to be behaviorism (and now its more respectable offspring) and psychoanalysis have a fine rolling sound, but after a careful analysis of the so-called reasons, we find nothing but a Pelion upon Ossa of assumptions and declarations.

The Future of Personality Research

We have seen that the study of personality is

in the very forefront of several sciences: psychology, sociology and social ethics, psychiatry and even ordinary medicine. Personality testing, which is largely a product of American initiative and ingenuity, examines, figuratively speaking, the bricks of the great structure, weighs each one separately, and puts it back again, or sometimes lines it up differently. The interpretative school of personality, as established in Europe, adopts methods by which individuals may be rated as they are, without their reactions being subjected to piecemeal analysis. In the absence of such detail treatment, the personality, however, is studied as if it were a tri-dimensional structure, with a façade and sides. The experimental approach must of necessity be restricted to linear measurement. Depth is not recognized. Nor is there any possibility of discerning layers of different material in a personality (stratification): physique, emotional make-up, character level.

The investigation of personality in the future will exploit all methods. Not only the physique, the "chemique" (the influence of the glands, of which we know next to nothing as yet except in the case of the thyroid and sex glands), the "mimique," expression as exhibited in handwriting, gestures, vocalization, intonation, creative and non-creative productions and so on, — our whole psychodynamique — but also the *meaning* of our reactions, tendencies, postures, and *personal idioms* will have to be gone into both extensively and intensively.

Chapter XIII

PROJECTIVE METHODS AND TECHNIQUES

PERSONALITY testing has naturally followed in the wake of intelligence testing. The tests have been not only varied but voluminous. As far back as 1927, [1] the present writer has written a lengthy critique exposing the scant harvest, amidst great pretensions. The tests have since multiplied, but experimental procedures like Kurt Lewin's have deflected some of the interest into dynamic channels. The test does not have the same function as the experiment. The former attempts to place the individual, with regard to some capacity or trait, on a scale so as to be compared with others. The norms are taken for granted. In the experiment, some new result is to be established through the reactions of the subjects or observers. Under such and such conditions, it may be said, the individual will become frustrated, or irritated, or indifferent.

[1] A. A. Roback: *The Psychology of Character*, pp. 354-384.

Function of the Test

The test sets out to *measure* the degree of a particular quality, hence the testing of all mental characteristics comes under the head of psychometry. Correlations between one quality and another have been set up by noting to what extent one set of measurements agrees with another. The factor schools (University of London and University of Chicago) have distilled all sorts of information regarding abilities, skills, interests, attitudes, and traits — out of the statistical computations of results gained with divers batteries of tests.

But even intelligence tests can afford us glimpses into the personality of the testee, if we are only on the alert and turn, for the moment, away from the quantitation in order to explore some general tendencies. While scoring the *Roback Superior Adult Tests,* e.g., I was surprised at the number of sidelights that loomed up. Thus, in some instances, the examinee would show a pedantic streak by stressing petty irrelevancies. Another would show a tendency to criticize the test ("No case, abuse the plaintiff"). Some would exhibit an aversion for a whole test, like the Directions test, and leave it undone. There were cases of intermittent good and poor results (the whole examination requires about three hours, with a brief recess). Some of the misunderstanding of questions is apparently also due not so much to lack of intelligence as to affective tuggings, thus providing an insight into the subjective self of the individual. Mere scoring will only bring out the rank of the examinees, but something more crucial may be obtained, if their personality is not lost sight of in the evaluation as a whole.

Measuring vs. Interpreting

Lately, however, another type of test has come into the foreground. Its objective is not to measure so much as to *interpret,* and it comes under the head of *projective methods* — projective because the subject probed is bound to project his own inner life when the materials are presented to him. Of course, we always project ourselves in reading or listening to anything. The personal equation has long since been accepted as a snag in objective or factual perception, but the more definite the situation, the less scope for subjective interpretation, and *vice versa.* At this point, someone may wonder why we should wish to deal with the indefinite. Surely our goal is to obtain uniformity; and our endeavors should be bent in the direction of seizing the facts of reality in as specific a sense as possible. Would a physicist or a chemist waste any time in experimenting on diffuse and hazy particles, if he could help it? (Perhaps he would, at that, because the haziness might reveal something deeper, if sufficiently tapped).

The answer lies in the difference between man and matter. If man were only a machine as all mechanists would fain believe, psychology would be non-existent as a science, and most of the problems we are confronted with would have been avoided, but the responses in man are fraught with unexpected idiosyncrasies, where each is a world by himself (*microcosm*), and in order to ferret out these private quirks, the situations must be irregular, so that the subject might be caught unawares, (which is not the case with the ordinary test, involving conscious selection and rejection); since the universal tendency is to answer so as to appear in a favorable light, concealing a thought or modifying it, etc. True, all testers make an attempt to elicit objective responses by frequently disguising the purpose of the test, but seldom with any success. The projective tester tries to catch the subject "when he's not looking," so as to find out more about him.

A New Name for An Old Method

The projective method, in one form or another,

may be found in antiquity. L. K. Frank points out that "trial by ordeal involved the exposure of the accused to stressful situations in which, as eating dry rice, he would respond in an individualized manner, indicative of his guilt, however he denied it or attempted to conceal his participation in the crime."[2] One might allude to the "evidence" wrested by means of the bitter water which the woman accused of adultery was to drink, according to Biblical usage. The popular mind has fashioned many proverbs in which the criminal's guilt feeling or anxiety seeks him out, in other words, is projected through some neuromuscular or glandular outlet.

In one of the older German psychological books, it is related that two people were sitting on a bench in a park, when a stranger came along and began to admire the tree that was sheltering them against the sun. He spoke of the foliage, the color of the leaves, the branches. Soon another came and talked only about the timber, while a third examined the bark. They each represented different interests and points of view, each projecting his own outlook; and what is an outlook but a reflection of the person's inwardness? There is no reason why we should not be able to include,

[2] L. K. Frank: *Projective Methods,* p. 46.

among projection materials, the many ambiguous figures, like the duck-rabbit, or black and white cubes, or the so-called Zöllner illusion, even though there are only alternative reactions here, both of which are obtainable at will. The question might be, nevertheless: which is seen first? Or, which takes a longer period to present itself to the mind, or which has more staying power or which is apt to perseverate?

All free, and even controlled, association tests, may be looked upon as projection techniques. G. Aschaffenburg employed them in order to detect guilt, while C. G. Jung introduced them into psychoanalysis and psychiatry for the purpose of discovering unconscious elements, complexes, archetypes. Even dreams may be considered projections of the unconscious, as all genuine projection is fundamentally. None of the products are measurable, although norms have been found for a great many words on the basis of response frequency. Also the time factor is very important. The true picture, however, does not consist in the number of right or wrong responses, but in the over-all diagnosis gained through interpretation.

Pioneers of Projection Methods

It was not until the ink-blot was thought of as

a test that the technique became an independent instrument. Curiously enough, a book, of which the title, translated into English, might read "Blottographies" (*Kleksographien*) appeared close to a century ago.[2] Its author, J. Kerner, was struck with the imaginative possibilities of the ink-blot, which tends to take on its own fortuitous shape.

In 1895, A. Binet, the most original psychologist France has produced, in collaboration with V. Henry, made the ink-blot the basis of a long experimental article on individual psychology, and a few years afterwards, a fad broke out with the ink-blot covering, not only white paper, but a multitude of whimsies. One of the pages in a little book by John P. Carmel, called *"Blottentots and How to Make Them,"* published, in 1907, by Paul Elder Co. is herewith reproduced. In the newspapers, it had at one time almost the vogue of the cross-word puzzle.

As may readily be imagined, all these efforts were intended for youngsters; but, as usual, adults too, found them entertaining, and perhaps even exciting. Personally, I think the perfect symmetry in a weird, or even hideous-looking, figure had much to do with the fascination and popularity of the fad nearly fifty years ago.

[2] B. Klopfer and D. M. Kelly: *The Rorschach Technique*, p. 1.

HOW TO MAKE BLOTTENTOTS

To make a funny Blottentot,
  First take a piece of paper,
Splash on some ink, a single spot,
  Crease, press, but cut no caper.

Don't crease exactly at the blot—
  You'll have a fearful muddle ;
Press gently, too, and not a lot,
  Unless you want a puddle.

With everything we humans do,
  Practice makes us apter:
So start at once, you'll find it true
  At the end of your first chapter.

The Rorschach Method

It was not, however, until the Swiss psychiatrist, Hermann Rorschach, published his monograph, *Psychodiagnostik*, in 1921, that the messy ink-blot became the foundation of a new scientific structure, which has expanded so as to include many other devices to help us *interpret* a given individual's inner life. Again the moral may be drawn that no nuisance but what some good may come of it, if properly exploited.

That a single book, more or less incomplete at that, should inaugurate a new movement is remarkable indeed, especially as the method had already been known to others. In fact, C. J. Parson, in 1917, published a monograph entitled *"Children's Interpretations of Ink-blots,"* but even a cursory examination of Rorschach's book will impress one with the methodicalness, the systematic development of the subject, the clear-cut observations from many angles and the critical attitude toward the problems involved, aside from the evident patience and painstakingness with which the mass of data had been worked up.

We may, at times, be disposed to question Rorschach's individual conclusions, with which the book is replete, but at no time would the trained reader be inclined to doubt the scientific spirit of the author, who was certainly gifted with an intuitive and synthetic mind which could pick out the significant features of the various relationships the ink-blots brought out. Almost on every page, there is a challenging or, at least, suggestive statement. Even if we are skeptical of the Rorschach method as an effective diagnostic approach, we can still profit by the astute psychological aperçus contained in the exposition.

Shortly after the book was published, Rorschach died, at the age of 37. He was fortunate, however, in his devoted friend and colleague, G. Oberholzer, who not only carried on the work of his superior, but trained a number of workers from abroad, including the United States. The Rorschach movement grew as more researchers appeared in print and more institutions made use of the method, until today well over a thousand publications in the form of books, monographs, and articles may be listed, although I know of no complete up-to-date bibliography. The most comprehensive treatment of the Rorschach Method, in English, is contained in S. J. Beck's two volumes, published in 1944 and 1945.[4]

---

[4] S. J. Beck: *Rorschach's Test,* vol. I. *Elementary Principles,* vol. II. *A Variety of Personality Pictures.* The accounts of sex maladjustments and schizophrenia are particularly illuminating.

The method itself seems very simple. First, Rorschach produced a number of ink-blot figures, some in color, and presented them to a number of mental patients to describe. He found a variety of reactions as to color, form, movement (which was often read into the pictures), space, shading, the matter of detail, etc. Moreover, Rorschach perceived a definite consistency or relationship between reaction to the cards and type of disorder. After a good deal of experimentation, the cards were standardized, some of the ten featuring shape or form; others emphasizing greys or red, some more harmonious or pleasing to look at than others. The common denominator was the fact that the design was vague, so that it would mean all things to all people. W. Mons, in his clear-cut exposition tells us that "the fact that 'no two people see alike' is strikingly illustrated by results, for among the records of two thousand people, no two are identical." [5] This, in itself, is a significant datum which should make us pause ere we insist on being right in our observations.

Other Methods

The Rorschach, with its ramified technique,

[5] W. Mons: *Principles and Practice of the Rorschach Personality Test*, p. 18.

which has led to divisions and institutional biases of one kind or another, is only one of many projective methods. L. K. Frank lists five categories: (a) We begin with the constitutive, like the Rorschach test or William Stern's cloud pictures, where interpretation of the unstructured figure will bring out many reactions of a dynamic kind, revealing unconscious motives and traits without special probing. Hearing can also be utilized in a similar manner. Youngsters used to play a game of transmitting several unfamiliar words to one another, in a large group, just to see what the last perceiver would make of the sounds. There are those who are constantly mishearing, and that is symptomatic, when the ear apparatus is not impaired.

(b) The constructive methods make use of materials to arrange into a unit — say, furnishings and furniture of a doll house, or pegs to construct into a model. This is a method adopted for testing children. That even toddlers manifest their interests, attitudes and inclinations can be gleaned from the investigations of Alschuler and Hattwick. [6]

(c) Among the interpretative methods, the

[6] R. H. Alschuler and La Berta W. Hattwick: *Painting and Personality*, vol. 1.

Thematic Apperception Test stands out as the best known. Taking their cue probably from one of the Binet-Simon tests, C. T. Morgan and H. A. Murray have compiled a series of pictures about which the subjects are asked to tell a story, going into as much detail as possible with reference to the characters in the picture. It is a test which plays up the imagination of the individual, but it is not imagination alone; it discloses wishes and longings, aversions and complexes, provided we know how to locate them in the descriptions. This is true of all creative work that is not strictly scientific. When Goethe, in a widely quoted couplet, brought out the point that if we want to understand the poet, we must study him in his habitat, [7] he was simply giving us the obverse of the medal. The interpretation of a tune may come into the same category; and we are doing this all the time at concerts. Filling in gaps in a series of incomplete sentences, e.g. "We must . . . for we live but once" can be treated as a projective method, inasmuch as it brings to light particular attitudes (serious, cynical, happy-go-lucky etc.).

(d) The cathartic methods are those which allow the subject or patient to "emote" with some-

[7] *Willst den Dichter du verstehen*
Musst du ins Dichters Land gehen

one else, like an actor or actress, on the stage, and thus easing chronic tension. While the purpose of such catharsis is of a therapeutic nature, it is also true that the mode in which the movie addict reacts is a specific projection of his personality. According to Frank, (e) the refractive methods include the manipulation of all conventionalized activities, like speaking or writing. "Almost all conventionalized patterns may be examined for the way the personality is transmitted, as through a lens which, like the eye, refracts the light combining, distorting, warping, bending, even eliminating, some parts of the pattern of light waves." [8]

Projection or Ejection?

Perhaps Frank is extending projection to embrace too many spheres. It is true that an individual projects his personality in everything he does, but there is quite a difference between interpreting a vague and unstructured cloud and writing or copying a few lines, or answering an explicit question. If we take the position that whatever is diagnostic is also projective, then hardly any reaction can be eliminated from this purview, simply because our personality is reflected in the way we eat, drink, sleep, cough, or sneeze. Pro-

[8] L. K. Frank: *Projective Methods,* p. 60.

jection, to my mind, entails different possibilities and adjustments in dealing with the situation in hand. Handwriting involves a neuromuscular mechanism, with little lattitude. When an individual sees in ink-blots all sorts of animals or human shapes, he is projecting something *from within*. Handwriting and speaking are, if anything, *ejective*. Our integrated nervous system is transferred, through movements, to the paper, where it becomes a frozen record, like a fossil. Similarly our voice and diction, inflection or modulation is one index of our personality, but the process is too spontaneous and smooth or regular to permit of projection. Drawing and painting, or modelling, on the other hand, is by no means mechanized even for artists. *One does project something of himself in every thing which is creative.*

Not Rivals but Complementary

It is not necessary, however, to go into such nice distinctions. What concerns us is the fact that the quantitative application of tests is not superior to the interpretative evaluation of human responses. They are complementary to one another. Measurements in terms of scores have their place, and so have the projective techniques. It is a mistake for the statistician to turn up his nose at the projective tester, who is dealing with *qualities* rather than quantities. The figures may be absolutely correct, and yet the information gained may be negligible or even worthless, depending upon what postulates were taken for granted in the original investigation, even assuming that the statistical formulas are unexceptionable.

Danger to Guard Against

Eventually the projective technician must resort to scoring, correlating, and computing, but it is to his credit that we are enlightened on a definite relationship between a condition and a response. Even if he does not actually provide us with the key to unlock the secret, he, at least, lets us peer into the keyhole for a fraction of a second. As time goes on, perhaps the aperture will widen. For the present, it is not so much the rivalry between the two types of testing, the quantitative and the interpretative, which is troublesome. The stumbling block consists, rather, in the schisms and factions in the movement itself; for as it expands and absorbs new workers, differences of opinion are bound to crop up; and, both, terms and techniques are apt to be misused, as the large issues are slanted to suit the individual leaders. Secessions which subsequently take place are detrimental to the movement as a whole, as we have seen it happen in psychoanalysis, in spite of the dominating personality of its founder. The projective methods have not the same adhesive power; and there, one must be especially careful lest the original purpose, which avowedly must be an objective goal, itself is turned into a projective test unveiling the subjective tendencies of the experimenter. This eventuality can be averted only if each scientific worker, while evolving some fresh construct, technique, or idea, nevertheless takes cognizance of the results of his predecessors, who, alas, are often too soon forgotten, and his contemporaries. He then becomes a collaborator in a vast field, a co-cultivator, and not a rival or, what is worse still, a pseudo-pioneer. The sciences are so interrelated in the present age that no one, not even an Aristotle, could master the whole of his own science, whether it be sociology, psychology, biology, or physics. A complex science like psychology or sociology is far more difficult to encompass. The average scientist is now a specialist in a small area, but it need not be the mere narrow strip in which he happens to be interested.

CHAPTER XIV

THE ADEQUACY VALENCE OF
PERSONALITY

ONE OF THE most popular terms in the general
sphere of psychology about twenty-five years
ago was "the inferiority complex." It still is used,
although not quite so frequently, by the semi-
educated to express either their own lack of self-
confidence or, more commonly, some attitude
toward a friend or acquaintance whom they would
like to take down a peg.

The inferiority complex, in spite of its being
bandied about by school children, is a useful term
and describes a condition, regardless of Adlerian
or Freudian involvements. It is more comprehensive than a feeling, because it includes many
manifestations of a seemingly opposite character
to inferiority feeling, which are, in addition,
unknown, or at least unrecognized by the person
involved.

Correlate of the Inferiority Complex

The wonder is, however, that we do not find in the whole literature the correlate of "inferiority complex." No doubt many will at once point to "superiority complex" as proving the opposite, but there is no such thing as a "superiority complex," for any overt signs of a superiority attitude would be indicative of the inferiority complex, in an altered pattern. Nor is a *superiority feeling* the term we are looking for. A superiority feeling *in general* and toward everyone else is still rooted in the old inferiority complex, while a feeling of superiority toward a moron or a simpleton represents just a specific attitude at a particular time. It is not an aspect or a full-blown dimension of personality such as an inferiority complex is. Obviously we need a term for that rare combination which spells completeness, not merely "at-one-ness" which religio-ethical writers sometimes talk about, nor "integration" which affords efficiency, but a personality-nucleus which, when found, represents an ideal relationship between the individual and society. This particular nucleus might be called the "valence of adequacy."

The term has appeared first in my account of William James,[1] but since it was not amplified

[1] A. A. Roback: *William James,* etc., pp. 209-210.

some readers might have thought that it had been commonly employed in the literature, while others may have passed it by as a casual reference. In the *Albert Schweitzer Jubilee Book*,[2] there was a lengthy explanation of the phrase, which was applied to the great man of the jungle, but to date, perhaps because of the lack of diagrams, the concept appears to be still unrecognized.

Justification of Phrase

The word "adequacy" requires no interpretation. It is to be understood in the fullest sense, both subjective and objective. A smug, self-complacent person is no more adequate than a timid or disgruntled individual. "Adequacy" carries a social connotation as well as a psychological. It may be lacking in genius (Ruskin, Chopin, Carlyle, Rousseau, Voltaire, Strindberg are corroborations of the statement) while some of the mediocre may possess it in a fair degree. Naturally like everything else, it is a relative matter, and, in the strict sense, it may be said that the valence of adequacy is to be found only in those who are entirely free from an inferiority complex, which means: in mighty few, but those few would be *mighty* for that reason alone.

[2] A. A. Roback: (ed.) *The Albert Schweitzer Jubilee Book,* pp. 57-58.

What does the word "valence" mean in this connection? Although this term has its special sense in chemistry and in topological psychology, which bears a certain relation to that employed here, it is not so much the "mingling" or "evocative' quality that is uppermost in our mind, as the *worth* constituent. In other words we are to ask ourselves the following question: Which are the ingredients of our personality which together constitute human worth? In other words, which are the elements or qualities that go to make up this synthesis, and why have we selected them?

Derivation of the Blend

To begin with, it must be apparent that although personality consists of hundreds of ingredients, its essence or nucleus, like a carefully arranged bouquet of flowers, would contain but very few items. The peak of the pyramid does not allow too much space, even though "there is always room for one more." It is not necessary to fix the number at this juncture. We might reason as follows: personality is made up of four departments of characteristics: (a) the physical, (b) the cognitive, (c) the affective, and (d) the conative or volitional. Each of these large divisions (artificial, to be sure, from an operational angle, nevertheless analytically indispensable) must yield its quota to the composition of a human personality. It stands to reason, then, that the core of personality, in its highest form, will also be represented by each of these divisions. Our task is now to discover the most important or *basic* element in each of these classes and group them together as constituting the *adequacy valence.*

A Significant Triad

For the moment, the physical will be put aside; and we shall deal with the other three departments. Let us take the cognitive side first. This embraces intelligence, intellect, insight, and the sense of humor. All four kinds are of value, no doubt. There may even be a certain amount of overlapping between some of them, but of the four enumerated, the most outstanding quality for our purpose, i.e., to ascertain the valence of adequacy, is neither intelligence nor intellect, but *insight,* or the ability to size up our relation to others, to see ourselves as others see us, whether we agree with them or not.

From the affective range of qualities, it is not emotion as such nor temperament which counts most but sentiment (certainly not sentimentality) which has an emotional root upon which there grow cultural branches. Sentiments like friendship, loyalty, etc., can overflow into a sort of universal sympathy and love (*amor intellectualis*) which is somewhat remote from the ordinary love of kin or sex.

In the volitional or characterial sphere there are also a great many traits to examine: persistence, honesty, reliability, initiative, bravery, etc., but it seems to me that the one which is most representative of character is *independence* or *courage*. It is the one quality which counts in the preservation of liberty. It covers both the individual and the social virtue; and even when society is flouted, if in the right direction, it is only for the sake of ameliorating social conditions. Naturally an independence which is born of eccentricity or egotism or stubbornness will display a woeful lack of insight, or sentiment, or both.

Complete and Incomplete Personalities

Independence of character embraces many situations. Thus to a votary of the Wagner cult, there was no one so courageous or adamant in purpose, indomitable in spirit, as the composer who achieved his triumph at Bayreuth, but there was more of the *idée fixe* and aggressiveness in the attitude than real independence. Anyone who demands loans or expects others to maintain him lacks a vital component of the adequacy valence. Genius, as Wagner may have been, he belongs to the class of "shortcomers," not so much because of Goethe's reason — the uneven ratio of ability and accomplishment, but for making demands and flaunting his pretensions upon friends and acquaintances unduly.

The following passage from the *Maxims and Reflections* might easily have been written by a twentieth-century psychologist. "The botanists," Goethe tells us, "have a department of plants which they call *Incompletae*. One may say that there are also incomplete people. They are the ones whose longings and strivings are not in proportion with their accomplishments." Here Goethe has put his finger on the "frustration feelings" that we hear so much about nowadays, but is it not true that even a Goethe felt that he had not fully realized all he had striven for? On the other hand, with all his opportunities and appointments, he did not seek sinecures or aid from influential friends. He really worked for a living and engaged in creative work at the same time.

Karl Marx was undoubtedly a colossus of intellect. Hundreds of millions have fallen under his spell as a thinker, or theorist, in the historical and economic spheres, yet a man who expects to live off another, even though the other, Friedrich Engels, was quite willing to support him, cannot rate as an independent personality.[3] In that connection, Spinoza, the lenses grinder, would have to be our model. The excuse "I have a great work to accomplish, therefore the world owes me a living" is inadmissible, because there would be no way of drawing the line between self-appointed stipendiary and parasite. Whether or not we attach blame to such celebrities for seeking Maecenases, the fact is that we cannot give them the high credit which a truly independent person merits.

Nor would it help their cause to point to the royal patronage of others or to the awards of fellowships and grants today. It is probably the importunacy or opportunism, or even rapaciousness, which is at fault, in the first place. If we make a thorough search of history, we shall find that the finest personalities, not necessarily the most adjusted, made little use of other people's favors, or to put it another way, the rich and the powerful were not attracted to them, no matter

[3] Rühle's *Karl Marx; His Life and Work* revolves around the view that the founder of the socialistic system was definitely a victim of the inferiority complex; and the case is well documented.

WILLIAM JAMES
(A portrait hitherto unreproduced)

how well-deserving they were because of their endowments.

Examples of Adequacy Valence

Picking up our three basic components, viz., *insight, sentiment,* and *independence,* we may now recognize in them the triad of the adequacy valence constellation.

The picture which Aristotle draws in his *Nicomachean Ethics* may well be of the personality blessed with a high coefficient of the adequacy valence, and the individual, in our time, who may be regarded as the paragon in this regard is Albert Schweitzer. A remarkable balance which a tremendously active life under trying conditions cannot shake, let alone dislodge, characterizes this world-acclaimed personality. William James also stands relatively high in adequacy valence, although his *inner* adjustments were not as well-knit.

Sometimes a single incident related about an unknown person is sufficient to determine the index of his or her adequacy valence.

Among many noble deeds which helped to keep our faith in humanity alive during the dark period of the twentieth century when bestiality and fiendishness were rampant in Europe is the one related about an unnamed lady soon after the and sent them the following message: "I shall not receive the gentlemen — not because they made me scrub the street, but because they and those in their command have insulted the women of Vienna. I am happy that it has been possible for me to demonstrate my sympathy and unity with these unfortunate women."

Evolution and Personality

As far as the physical component of the adequacy valence is concerned, we may regard an animated expression as the most essential. This involves the play of muscles of the eyes and around the mouth. Since the physical is only secondary, however, as compared with the three other departments, the choice may call for more latitude.

In our selection of qualities for the valence of adequacy, it will occur to the reader that the difference between man and animal would be discerned in each of these components. It is possible to attribute intelligence to a dog, horse, or monkey, but not insight, in our sense. (Köhler's use of the word, in regard to the perception of a practical situation such as placing one box on top of another in order to reach food, is still a matter of *ordinary* intelligence). Sentiment is a problematic item in animals — certainly very debatable, unless we can call loyalty, friendship, and coöperativeness, as manifested through their behavior, sentiment. It would seem that man's sentiment is of a *reflective* order: The independence of character, required for our purpose, is not to be compared with the courage and bravery of certain dogs, for instance, while animation or vivaciousness is something hardly to be found on the infra-human level.

This argument is not intended to stress the superiority of *homo sapiens,* but to indicate the high degree of development and self-control which is required to reach the stage of adequacy valence.

pare a well-adjusted Babbit or bounder with a poorly-adjusted saint. (2) The full meaning of adjustment has long been in question. Is it possible to be inwardly adjusted without being outwardly adjusted, and *vice versa?* (3) Should a well-adjusted individual, for some reason, perhaps in another milieu, become maladjusted, would that argue for a complete drop in the evaluation?

Adjustment is no more a criterion of personality than adaptability is of intelligence, although that appears to be the standard definition. The keen mind of Alfred Binet took a different position when he made self-criticism and a purposeful attitude pivotal in his own definition. His outlook was functional with a social implication; for self-criticism, (not necessarily criticism of oneself but a critical oversight of one's work) involves putting ourself in the place of another, adopting the stand of an outsider.

A Functional View of Personality

I propose a functional and social approach here too. Personality is an individual entity but the criterion, like the fulcrum, is outside of the object handled. The question, now is: How are we to go about deriving this criterion? Will it be found in our definition? Hardly, the criterion must comport with the definition, but the criterion is a further consideration, and may be deduced either transcendentally, as Kant might have said, or discovered empirically, as is more in keeping with the temper of psychology nowadays.

Let us, then, take instances of personality from actual life, either historical or contemporary figures, and ask ourselves what it is that singles them out from the rest of mankind? Is it their intelligence, their achievement, their will-power, or the integration, the happy blend of the various qualities, even in a moderate degree? If we have at all a smattering of biography, we shall at once think of many men or women who were admired for their acumen, zeal, artistry, organizing ability, professional skill, and because of these single virtues, they may have been rated as outstanding personalities, but we know very well that Samuel Johnson, Alexander Pope, John Ruskin, Otto Bismarck, Thomas Carlyle, and hundreds of others who have distinguished themselves and who have been practically worshipped in their generation, did not possess personality of a high order, and the halo around them was placed there by *admirers of their work*. That character is not the criterion here, as many of my readers who are acquainted with *The Psychology of Character* might have the influence is deleterious, no matter how agreeable and jolly the individual might rate in his coterie. The time factor must enter in; for a particular type of influence might be just a flash in the pan, of ephemeral duration. A great personality will beneficially affect not only his contemporaries but succeeding generations, as well.

There is one codicil which ought to be added: mass influence carries much less weight than individual influence. A speaker who sways many thousands at one sitting, or a writer who influences the thoughts of millions (perhaps by the publication of a best seller) may, in addition, to being a powerful orator or a dynamic writer, or even a bold and clear thinker, rate as a personality of distinction, but the latter reputation should not, although it, as a rule, does, follow from the fact of his ability.

At this juncture, someone may hark back to the definition of personality adopted in this book, and will wonder how the elements will dovetail into the main criterion. A moment of reflection will, I believe, convince the puzzled that the more pronounced the components of personality, and the better integrated they are; the greater valence of adequacy *via* insight, sentiment, and independence, enhanced by a radiating expression, one possesses — the *greater the disposition to affect others beneficially,* and the more extensive the opportunities. Naturally, because of certain personal anomalies, quirks, inconsistencies, and paradoxes, allowance will have to be made in our evaluations, and a system of pluses and minuses could be developed whereby the personality index might be computed and established for each individual of note. Regrettably, the halo of an individual's achievement, or his colorfulness, is often confused with his personality, a fallacy which must be guarded against.

Applications of Our Criterion

A criterion is valid only if it works out in practice, hence it would be the reader's turn to apply it to well-known instances. Let us take as an example Francis Bacon. One of the most acute minds of the century, astute as few can claim to have been since his time, a man who has influenced the course of philosophy (perhaps the *courses* in philosophy would be more accurate) for perhaps two centuries, through his emphasis on inductive methods, he nevertheless is, on our criterion, a shabby personality, not to speak of his character. Voltaire exercised a much greater influence over his countrymen and the course of events in the world at large, and possessed a temperament and mind of great vivacity, but as a personality he falls below the less known Diderot. Rousseau, who revolutionized education and was one of the most striking personalities of the age, neverthless is far from reaching the pinnacle, according to our criterion. He lacked stability, insight, and in a considerable degree, independence. His personal influence was spasmodic and not always beneficial.

In point of creative genius, Goethe far surpasses Schiller and Lessing, but their personality index is superior to his. As between Ignatius Loyola and Francis of Assisi, who will ascribe a greater index to the Jesuit-Order founder, except an incorrigible partisan? That there are strange judgments and preferences even among the giants is a commonplace. With what amazement I read that the rebel of rebels, August Strindberg, looked up to Bernard of Clairvaux, the fanatic preacher of the twelfth century and arch-foe of Abelard, as his ideal in history; but then anyone who has read *The Fool's Confession* will know enough to take some of the author's views, colored by a strong affect, with more than a grain of salt.

Food for Reflection

The subject is vast and offers new vistas, disclosing unlimited possibilities in reflection and evaluation. What is the nature of human influences, for example? How can we tell whether the influence is for good or for evil? Here we are moving in historical and sociological domains. No doubt Lenin's influence will be a matter for debate, but Peter Kropotkin's beneficial and personal influence will never be questioned, no matter what course world events will take.

There are noted men whose work is much greater than their personality, and *vice versa*. William James, e.g. was undoubtedly the most beloved philosopher of his time, just as Moses Mendelssohn, as Beate Berwin [2] has proven conclusively from expressions of celebrated contemporaries, including Immanuel Kant, was easily the most esteemed man in his generation. Even bitter adversaries, like Hamann (who might have had a complex about his name in relation to the exalted Jew, reminiscent of the Biblical chronicle) paid moving tributes to the man's personality as reflected in his works and deeds. And yet a greater gulf between James and Mendelssohn in antecedents and appearance could hardly be imagined. The grandfather of the idolized composer (who inherited much from his

[2] B. Berwin: *Moses Mendelssohn im Urteil seiner Zeitgenossen* (Kantstudien, Ergänzungshefte, 1919)

grandparent) was handicapped by virtue of his
creed, which made it illegal for him to reside in
Berlin without a special permit from the King; he
belonged to an ethnic group which was reviled
and mistreated, only to have been all but extermi-
nated in that country two centuries later; he came
of humble birth, and, in addition, he was afflicted
with a spinal deformity, while his facial features
were anything but prepossessing. This man, nevertheless, became the prototype of Lessing's *Nathan
the Wise,* the mentor of German literati, the
glamorous lecturer whose discourses attracted the
nobility and cabinet ministers of Frederick the
Great; he rated as the arbiter of elegance and
one of the creators of German literary style,
although his native tongue was what later came to
be known as Yiddish. His influence reached far
and wide; and his contacts were so numerous that
his health broke down from overstrain. Mendelssohn's works cannot begin to compare with Kant's
but the man himself, his personality was far
superior to that of the author of the three critiques.
As to character, they were probably both on an
equal level.

Examples from American History

Illustrations may be drawn aplenty on American

Peter A. Kropotkin

Born a prince, and serving as a page in the Imperial Court at St. Petersburg, he chose to fight the cause of the people and courted imprisonment in Russia and France rather than give up his revolutionary ideas. His geographical works brought him fame, and his books on ethics, anarchism, and literature have been translated into many languages.

"He was an authority on agriculture, as well as on geographical subjects, and put forward many practical suggestions for its development. Kropotkin had a singularly gentle and attractive personality and was much loved and respected in England. He desired the minimum of government, and the development of a system of human coöperation which should render government from above superfluous." *Encyclopedia Britannica,* vol. 13.

After several arrests, and expulsion, he settled in London, where he, in addition to writing, engaged in bookbinding, living very modestly in a proletarian section.

literature and politics for our distinction between personality and character. Thoreau was a character; Emerson — a personality. The character of Thomas Jefferson stands out, but Benjamin Franklin shines, aside from his versatile attainments, by virtue of his personality. Both Roosevelts, Theodore and Franklin, were outstanding personalities rather than characters; and even an inefficient president like Harding would, had he remained a senator, have been long remembered for his attractive personality (physical, emotional, and social phases).

Characters and Personalities

For one thing, characters are fastidious, discriminating; characters will despise and even hate; personalities are inclined to level differences, and even in their indignation, they will not forget their function as conciliator, arbitrator, comforter, healer. The man of character deals with principles; the personality is concerned with feelings, hence to the personality, the man of character is a bit harsh or dour; while the latter regards the other as somewhat weak and undiscerning as to over-all values. In this connection, the fable of the sun and the wind may be thought of; but it is not my purpose to take sides, but rather to point out that there *are* these two sides, and for human progress both are a blessing. Moreover, in many cases, there is some overlapping; for a Benvenuto Cellini, a Casanova, or Villon, whatever their success or fame, could not be admitted to the sanctum of great personality, simply because one of its ingredients is character.

Readers will observe that various adjectives have been used with personality: attractive, striking, outstanding, rich, colorful, fine, great. The attributes vary with the preponderance of this or that component. A great personality is rare, rarer than genius, because it entails so much more, and presupposes a combination that is close to perfection in the blend of traits, so as to influence human beings (often even affecting animals) for better, and never for worse.

Paradox of Personality

By what means is the influence achieved? I am not referring to the manner in which a person may be helped; for that is but a detail to be decided on as occasion presents itself. Something quite paradoxical is necessary for the optimal functioning of a personality — paradoxical, because when we consider that a great personality is, first of all, a highly integrated organization, bespeaking a definite and significant consciousness of oneself as a personality, it seems strange that the *self must become selfless* in order to realize its purpose. In ministering to others, there is no thought of oneself. There is a depersonalization, not in the sense of psychiatry or clinical psychology, where the patient experiences a dissociation and his mental functions become detached, with lapses in memory, etc., but *a transference of self-ends to others,* a merging of interests. *Adaptability of a very high order* is a prerequisite for this type of depersonalization, quite apart from other essentials, like a sound intelligence, boundless sympathy, and a minimum of self-aggression. Men and women of character, for one thing, lack this adaptability.

Analogous to the personality paradox, which discovers the highest personality in a depersonalization, the truest self in selflessness—is the *hedonistic* paradox, according to which, we are prone to enjoy more fully an experience, if we do not think of the enjoyment or ourselves, but concentrate on the material (opera, concert, play, or even the food or sex object) since the outgoing energy in attention or muscular contraction is a determining factor in the affective (emotional) intensity, while concentration on the *thought* of the enjoyment only interferes with the function itself, just as thinking

[291]

about the emotion experienced tends to stifle it in process.

Self-Sacrifice in Personality

As exemplars of great personalities who have evinced complete selflessness, and, in consequence, have affected the lives of many thousands, the illustrious Albert Schweitzer and the late Elsa Brändström (Mrs. Ulich) may be cited. The former has given up a cultural career which has made his name familiar in philosophical, theological, and musical circles throughout the world, in order to treat, as a physician and surgeon, the unfortunate natives of French Equatorial Africa; the latter, in her capacity as a nurse during the First World War in frigid Siberia, literally saved the lives of tens of thousands of wounded men, by dint of her efficient organization and persistence. Self-sacrifice is the common denominator of the two, but Albert Schweitzer has attained eminence as a thinker and artist as well; and is often referred to as the "great man's great man." More books and articles have appeared on Dr. Schweitzer than on any other figure during his lifetime; and he is easily the foremost living personality. If we knew nothing about him, and only saw him among others of world fame, his striking appearance would still set him off as apart and above. He takes his place with the mightiest and the lowliest, rising to every occasion with extraordinary presence of mind; and even the animals find in him a genuine friend, who is willing to forego his own comfort so as to alleviate their distress or reduce their privation.

It was after the above was written, that an inspired interview appeared in The *Reader's Digest*. The man interviewed was Albert Schweitzer, and the following extract is a more personal and direct statement of the view outlined in this chapter.

As I look back upon my youth, I realize how important to me were the help, understanding, and courage, the gentleness and wisdom so many people gave me. These men and women entered into my life and became powers within me. But they never knew it. Nor did I perceive the real significance of their help at the time.

We all owe so much to others; and we may well ask ourselves, what will others owe to us? The complete answer must remain hidden from us, although we are often allowed to see some little fraction of it so that we may not lose courage. You may be sure, however, that the effect of

your own life on those around you is — or
can be — great indeed. [3]

Just as Albert Schweitzer had earned the title
"the greatest man of our generation" so Elsa
Brändström has deserved the sobriquet, by which
she was known throughout Europe, "The Angel
of Siberia," after spending five and a half years
in Russian war camps as delegate of the Swedish
Red Cross, which brought her in touch with some
700,000 prisoners of war. But she was not merely
a delegate; she served as a nurse performing the
most menial duties, e.g. emptying the buckets of
excrement, in order to set an example to the rest
of the personnel, just as Dr. Schweitzer has
engaged in rolling logs, masonry, tending trees,
because, as he explained to me on his recent visit
to America, he would never delegate work to
others in which he did not participate himself.
Democracy of the deepest grain constitutes apparently the warp and woof of personality. Elsa
Brändström's work has also called forth books, a
biography and a novel which were inspired,
although not even remotely suggested, by her.

In the Foreword to her book *Among Prisoners*

[3] Albert Schweitzer: "Your Second Job" (as told in an interview
to Fulton Oursler). *Reader's Digest,* October, 1949.

Courtesy of Mr. Gilbert Loveland,
Vice-President Henry Holt and Co.

Albert Schweitzer

of War in Russia and Siberia, which appeared in Sweden, in 1929, the then Archbishop of Upsala, Dr. Nathan Söderblom, paid the following tribute to her — and we must remember that she was then a young woman of 31 only —

> The regrettable shortcoming of her book is that she tells too little about herself. Where men could not stand the spectacle of the horrors and atrocities of misery and suffering, she stood sometimes alone, delivered *sans merci,* as it were, to the fancies of wild and uncontrolled men of the roughest kind, but she always was master of the situation, and when she tells about it in her unaffected way, it becomes quite natural to her.
>
> Sister Elsa Brändström has continued her calling in taking care of former prisoners of war, who are prevented from earning their living by loss of limbs. She takes care of counts and tramps, men from the most opposite social spheres and with the most different ideas, from nationalism to communism. She considers them all as beings belonging to the same Humanity. She very often succeeds in teaching the same lesson to her friends that difference in worldly position and ideas does not matter. The only thing that matters is faithfulness in

the endeavor to make life more bearable
and to create joy for our fellow-men.[4]

It was while she was serving at a restaurant
conducted by refugees from Nazi Germany and
Austria that I first observed her. She certainly did
not look like a waitress, and I was a bit puzzled,
and embarrassed to ask her to bring me another
glass of water. Only later did I learn that she
was the wife of a Harvard professor; but her
work in Siberia, and her nickname "The Angel of
Siberia" were unknown to me until after her
death, in 1948, but although I was ignorant of
her achievement, her high-grade personality was
unmistakable in her energetic movement, in her
benign and yet confident expression, radiating
countenance, and invariable good humor, blending
with an air of decision and determination. These
qualities, perhaps in a more pronounced degree,
are observable in Albert Schweitzer's personal
appearance and robust physique.

It is somewhat unusual to dwell on actual personalities in a textbook. For this reason, it may
be well to introduce a deviation which, by right,
should have been the norm. There may come a

[4] Elsa Brändström: *Among Prisoners of War in Russia and
Siberia,* (Foreword by N. Söderblom), pp. 10-11.

time when the conditioned-reflex experiments on dogs and other animals will find little space in a text on personality and when our deeper insights and illuminations will come not only from mazes and psychiatric wards, but from watching the behavior of paragons of mankind, inasfar as we are privileged to meet such. One hour in the presence of Albert Schweitzer, I contend, is worth more for an understanding of personality than a dozen, or even a score of, mice experiments, important though they are in their own sphere.

PART TWO

CHAPTER XVI

APPLIED PERSONALITY

I T DOES not seem to be realized by the psychologist who writes a textbook on personality that
the theoretical discussions, no matter how enlight-
ening to the student, are not the whole story, that
personality is an applied field as well, and that it
is high time for the student to learn a few things
that would be to his benefit other than terms and
theories. It is not a question of exhortation or
sermonizing, but pointing to some everyday
defects and faults which should be corrected.
Possibly some instructors introduce a few hints
orally as *obiter dicta,* so that the scientific tone of
the text might not suffer from so popular an
approach which they may associate with the pep
dispensers who tell us how to advance in the
world by following 7½ rules, but the fact is that
those who are taking courses in personality, even
in the best university, have had and will have
certain problems, some of which are only hazy to

themselves. Sometimes the problems are visible to the naked eye of others, but not to themselves.

Theory and Practice

The theory of personality is one thing, the practice quite another. All theory eventually ends in application; and the study of personality assuredly leads to such a goal; for what boots it if anyone knows all about the various hypotheses of motivation, the various doctrines of reflexes, the *pros* and *cons* of instincts and drives, and yet repels people by obnoxious habits, disgusting bits of behavior which, true enough, should have been pointed out at home or in school, but unfortunately these objectionable acts continue unhampered and uninhibited, and the loser is the individual, be he ever so brilliant and conversant with theoretical personality.

Some of the reviewers of my little book *Personality: the Crux of Social Intercourse,* not accustomed to the applied treatment in the framework of a text, were distinctly puzzled that certain types of behavior should be dwelt on or even mentioned. My reply is that every intelligent person should aim to improve his or her personality. Were this attitude put into language, it would be formulated in some such words as these: "What means might I adopt in order to further my own interests *in a genuine manner?*" It will be noticed that the last phrase sets the method off from the attempts to make capital out of foibles and follies. The wholesale dealers in personality fodder are thus eliminated by such a qualifier.

Three Planes of Dispensation

There are three general approaches to the dispensation and absorption of personality material: (a) the academic (b) the applied, based on common sense as well as on theoretical conclusions which, in the last analysis, require common sense to select, and (c) the meretriciously practical, derived from the "way of the world," and encouraging a cynical outlook. It is clear that we should have no truck with that approach, but the second one is not only sound but salutary.

Young people particularly are often in a quandary. They are told one thing and yet in actual life the opposite appears to be the case. The letter, reproduced here, from a young woman attending a large university extension course in the psychology of personality may serve as one of many illustrations.

A Perplexing Letter

When I started working about ten years ago, I did it with the understanding that hard work, honest effort, further study pertaining to the work, and such qualities were what made a person successful. The text of this assignment seems to follow out the belief I had and still wish to have. Yet in the last five or six years the reverse has appeared to be true, and those who know little and bluff and bustle seem to get the raises and get ahead.

Without any idea of contradiction or complaint, I would like to ask you if this is the general trend during depression, or why these years of actual experience have been shaking the illusions of young people. I am looking at the experience of those about me as well as of myself.

Ingenuous and unseasoned as this student is, she naturally did not make allowance for the part personality plays in getting ahead; and whether it contributed 85% of success or failure, as N. L. Hoopingarner maintains, there is no doubt that the personal element looms large in every sort of human contact, and even in scientific and academic circles, as we shall have occasion to see in the Appendix.

It may not generally be known that studies made a few years ago under the auspices of the Carnegie Foundation brought out the fact, later confirmed by studies at Carnegie Institute of Technology, that success, even in such technical lines as engineering, was due approximately 15% to the technical knowledge of the particular field and about 85% to those human qualities necessary to successful performance — primarily those qualities which have to do with successfully dealing with people. Schools and colleges were training in only about 15% of the essentials of the job — that is, in knowledge and facts — leaving practically untouched any training in the larger part of the requisites of success. The point of view was that, having the facts—the technique,— the student would make good *if he had it in him;* it was up to him! [1]

Wrong Stress

Let us take another angle. Various undesirable habits have often been regarded as symbolic. There is no question about many of them actually speaking, although not too eloquently, the unconscious mind, but to lump them all together under genital categories, and refer to grinding the teeth

[1] N. L. Hoopingarner: *Personality and Business Ability Analysis.* (1927) p. 1.

as oral and picking them as anal, or seeing in leaning against the wall a fantasy symbol or in touching things a motor symbol, and so on *ad libitum,* is futile, if not fatuous. In the chapter on "The Personal Idiom," we have already seen that many of these acts are fraught with meanings, but picking one's nose, like scratching, needs no explanation of a psychoanalytic character. When performed in the presence of others, it is just disgusting, and that part should be stressed. The interpretation, along typological, physiological, or other lines may be undertaken as a *specific* investigation, carefully handled. There are hundreds of gestures, habits, tics, etc., that are purposeless and even annoying. There is the grimace, wheezing, grunting, puffing, staring, puckering the lips, snapping the fingers or the clip of the pen, jingling a coin or keys in one's pocket, making a suction sound by swishing the tongue against the teeth — but of what benefit is it to know that they represent different genital levels of development and to treat them all in the same fashion? Is swinging or rocking the legs under a table, scarcely perceptible to anyone except the inquisitive, as objectionable as picking one's nose and afterwards handling food or shaking hands, or as burping constantly, or as blowing the nose without benefit of handkerchief? Can a hiccup be taken as seriously as a belch *alla bravura?*

Is there something symbolic about these acts? Yes, symbolic of a type of constitution, symbolic of what we have eaten and indicative that adults have still to learn to control themselves, and that this lack of control is definitely a personality flaw, not only on the volitional side but probably also on the cognitive; for it betrays want of insight in an individual who has been moving in civilized society.

Not Symbolic but Symptomatic

In fact, all self-indulgence is symbolic or, perhaps better, symptomatic; and so is the *milieu* which tolerates it. When a student in a university library, instead of keeping his feet on the floor where they belong, insists on placing them on the table right under the nose of the person sitting opposite, then it is not symbolic but symptomatic of a shabby personality, not merely bad manners. It shows not only want of refinement (the shoes have been in all sorts of messes on the street) not only lack of sensibility, but downright inconsiderateness. No matter how much knowledge and theory he has assimilated in the personality classes, he has not learned enough; and he will be judged by his behavior rather than by his fund of information.

The average university student is often suffering from a displaced problem i.e., he refers the handicap to some other sphere. He is blind to the beam but is bothered about the mote, which is especially natural in the young. Since college and knowledge go together, it is on that side that the immature student develops his concern about himself. As no other course is expected to develop anything other than the intellect, it surely devolves upon the instructor in a personality class, or the author of a textbook in that subject, to make it clear that there are other sides to one's personality, and they are not restricted to the craving for sports.

Task of Education

The question now arises, in the light of what had been set forth earlier in the book, viz., that we are constitutionally determined and are like loaded dice, whether we can throw off these objectionable features. To an environmentalist, of course, there is not a single idiosyncrasy which has not been conditioned in childhood days, and to the psychoanalyst, such behavior is ascribable to repressed experiences. We may concede that

most of these "habits" are learned or acquired
rather than congenital, although even here I should
contend that some individuals are so built as to
acquire special habits.

Many are hangovers from infancy when the
"cute mannerisms" of the baby would delight the
parents and visitors who would encourage these
displays of "personality;" but even so, since the
specific reactions differ in children of even a few
weeks, and certainly months, there is still a constitutional disposition to pick up certain reactions,
like wrinkling the skin of the nose, oggling,
"chewing the cud," lolling the tongue, instead of
others. This is not a case of instinct, but of
structure, like inanimate materials so constituted
as to give off certain sounds. The environment
plays an important part in touching off these
reactions, or in modifying, if not inhibiting them
altogether; and that is exactly the task of education,
not merely to mention, describe, or even to make
an attempt at explaining the *modus operandi* in
some speculative manner, but to point out the
damaging effects of such questionable and annoying behavior with the purpose in view of stopping
it. Some of the movements are either tics or of
the type of nervous manifestations which may call
for treatment, but the large majority of such acts

are controllable, if the attention of the agents is drawn to them; and if the former, again, are sufficiently interested in improving.

Improvement vs. Adjustment

The word "improvement" is here used advisedly. There seems to be an aversion to employ this term except with reference to learning (memory or skill), where quantitative measures clinch the issue. One might suppose that everywhere else, more particularly in the realm of personality, the mark to be attained is adjustment, but that exactly constitutes my quarrel with the adjustment psychologist, mental hygienist, clinicians, and allies, who imagine that to talk of adjustment implies objectivity. It does not. It implies only that we are thinking not in terms of *standards* but in the framework of an environmental *status quo*. *Paramecium* adjusts; a personality either improves or retrogresses. All that is necessary in the one is behavior. The other measure requires conscious effort as well as some idea of an unseen goal or ideal.

ELSA BRANDSTROM
As a young woman

ELSA BRANDSTROM *(Mrs. Ulich)*
Prior to her death in 1948

CHAPTER XVII

THE AROMA OF PERSONALITY

THERE is one trait not mentioned in textbooks; yet if all other qualities should be discounted in an individual, and this alone rating high, it would invest the bearer with something that might compensate for a great deal else. It is not the halo that was thought to surround saints with its peculiar effulgence, but it comes close to it, except that it is more realistic, more factual, even though the designation "aroma" is, of course, a metaphor — a metaphor, however, which enjoys a solid basis. I am referring to refinement — a word often heard in everyday conversation, but shunned in academic textbooks, as if it did not exist, or else as if it bore no relation to personality. Psychologists treat the subject as if the less said about it the better. I feel certain that they will come around to it; and tests will, in the near future, be devised to probe this trait too, which is now regarded as a conglomeration of habits, some good and some bad (especially in a "red-blooded" man), and which environmentalists will ascribe to education, upbringing; and psychoanalysts will trace to fixations and the superego which was built up in the individual, thanks to paternal rigor and the awe it has inspired, while sociologists will keep telling us that refinement is simply a function of the culture we live in, and that what is regarded as refined in China, Japan, or the Fiji Islands will strike us as coarse, and vice versa.

Relativity — No Proof of Absence

Such comparisons and relativistic conclusions are irrelevant, for they might apply to ethics too, as indeed the descriptive writers on ethics, (particularly Herbert Spencer,[1] who cited mendacity as a virtue in some primitive tribe, or the ancient Egyptians, and murder, as an honored custom among the Fijians) never tire of stressing. It applies equally to aesthetics and other fields. The matter is, of course, to be determined in the light of the more highly developed societies and organisms. It is quite possible that there are degrees of refinement among primitive races, although anthropologists, who usually set out with a different purpose in view, do not commit themselves. They are interested in the mores, the

[1] H. Spencer: *The Data of Ethics,* Chapter 3, § 14.

ethos, the folkways and folklore of a certain group, hence refinement as an individual quality would not be alluded to, but in spite of the tribal law and custom which dominates the life of the primitive, there must be individual differences encountered, although not as frequently as in a highly civilized milieu.

Essence of Refinement and Civilization

Sometimes one wonders what refinement, of which we hear so much, consists in. I, too, have been at a loss to frame an adequate definition of the term, although the existence of the trait in a minority of mankind is incontestable; and it is just as certain that the majority lacks it. Of this majority, the men are in the lead; and that is a natural consequence, since women are endowed with finer sensibilities.

Refinement, it strikes me, comprises several sub-traits. It includes cleanliness, with stress on the social phase, delicacy of expression and of reference, especially in regard to personal relations, but above all it consists in refraining from drawing attention, whether knowingly or unwittingly, to the organic functions; in other words, in making the bodily machinery felt as little as possible in company, at least. This view is not a Plotinian reaction against the body. Let us review a few types of behavior that we have all observed, and the meaning of the above formulation will be clear.

There are innumerable individuals who, the moment you are in their presence, make you keenly aware of their body, perhaps not so much because of the odors which some bodies emit more than others, but largely on account of the sights and sounds they occasion. They either pant or sigh or sniffle or grunt, or by means of the tongue, teeth and lips they utter a variety of suction, gurgling, clicking and sibilant sounds, worthy of a savage. In fact the description of Batouala's morning routine, in Maran's novel by that name, almost fits the deportment of many a European and American.

When he had rubbed his eyes with the back of his hand and blown his nose through his fingers, he got up and scratched himself. He scratched his armpits, he scratched his thighs, his head, his buttocks, his arms.

Scratching is a splendid exercise. It sets the blood in circulation. It is a pleasure, and it also points to something. One only needed to look about. All living creatures scratched themselves on waking. It was a

good example to follow, since a natural one.
It is a bad waking up for a man who
doesn't scratch himself.

But, if scratching was good, yawning was
still better. It was a means of chasing sleep
away through the mouth.

*   *   *   *   *   *

Here a yawn, there a scratch — movements of only trivial importance. Contin-
uing to yawn and scratch, Batouala belched
noisily, an old custom that had come to him
from his parents, who, in turn, had inherited
it from their parents. [1]

Have we not been in the company of educated
and intelligent individuals, with some standing in
the community, who will show how much they
are enjoying their food by smacking their lips
and gulping down air with a whistle when about
to put the spoon of soup into their mouth? After
the meal, they will begin exploring their teeth
with a toothpick, or sometimes with their fingers.
Then they will hiccup and belch or emit peculiar
abdominal rumblings. Later they will yawn
audibly, sniffle, expectorate, wheeze, choke, or blow
their nose with considerable *éclat,* or at least cough
— as if all this were necessary to show that they
are active — up and about.

[1] Maran: *Batouala,* pp. 33-35.

While it is true that all these objectionable habits are very seldom to be found in the same individual, there is the presumption, based on observation and the principles of constitutional make-up (physiological organization), that the disposition to indulge in the one type of behavior will be coupled with a tendency to particpate in like behavior. The common denominator is a vulgar exhibition of bodily processes, which should be hidden from view, an exhibition which a little effort and understanding will dispense with.

Demarcation of Terms

In large centres, it is difficult to encounter people who will admit that they are unrefined. This is true especially of women, among whom the trait is more commonly found, but even in outlying regions, mining districts, on ranches and farms, some surprising specimens of this article turn up, simply because the environment is not everything in the determination of a trait. There are inner sensibilities which, at times, rebel against conditions in a given milieu; and these sensibilities are probably of hereditary origin, either derived from a combination of congenital qualities, or developing in conjunction with other traits — cognitive, affective, and conative — like reflectiveness, sympathy, or considerateness, which influence each other reciprocally. The term "sensibilities" is perhaps too much of a blanket term, as used in the plural, reminiscent of a word like "risibilities," yet "sensitivity" or "sensibility," because of other connotations, renders itself open to ambiguity. We may discover, however, a correlation between "sensitivity," in the sense of "touchiness," and "sensibility," in the sense of refinement, both flourishing predominantly in the cerebrotonic, while the *cerebrotic* is, as a rule, overrefined and finicky, which is an indication that excessive fastidiousness is the faulty extreme of refinement.

The framing of a definition to include all phases of refinement is not easy. The specificity school of traits may deny that there is such a trait or cluster altogether, or, at least, they will maintain that there are as many kinds of refinement as there are situations, and that an individual may be refined in one respect and coarse in another. The same type of fallacy would be committed by the school as in chopping up honesty or dishonesty into tablets without *considering* the *motives of the individual* (either conscious or unconscious) who is being tested or experimented on.

Profanity

Let us take another facet of refinement, the use of profane or obscene language. I have heard that the environment or upbringing has had much to do with it, and once a habit is formed, it stays. Experience, however, has taught us that there are those who do not succumb to the milieu, and *select their environment.* Imitation, certainly, plays a part in the use of objectionable expressions of which the very popular "lousy" was among the moderate ones, but surely the behavior that is imitated counts for something too. It is the belief of many adolescents in their teens — although this belief persists often through life — that unprintable words only can convey their emphatic feelings on a certain subject or individual. The British parliamentarian wins his point through the use of the most dignified language with a distinctive turn; for it takes little intelligence to perceive that the vulgar will not be impressed by coarse expressions, and the refined will only be offended and distracted, so that the force of the epithet will be lost either way. Any one who supposes that the hundreds of nuances found in polite diction are commonplace and ineffectual whereas the few scurrilous or scatological phrases which tend to reverse the functions of the speech organs and other parts of the body are expressive of one's personality must, having had some education, be lacking in common sense as well as in refinement.

Too many college students think that it is smart to say to one another in jest "Aw, you're a stinker" at some slight grievance. Granted that the word has lost much of its maladorousness in the mouth of members of fraternities and fraternal orders, the association is still putrid; and such apostrophes can only examplify the old saw "Familiarity breeds contempt" with the result that the personal relation breaks out in personalities, or simply breaks up. We rush into friendships prematurely by discarding the surname at the second or third meeting, and the road to familiarity is clear and smooth. Ernest Renan, in his auto-biographic fragments, tells us that at the Séminaire St.-Sulpice, his priestly instructors might have been teaching at the same institution for a quarter of a century or more, and would yet address one another as "Monsieur." Such an attitude is calculated to maintain an even keel and prevent ill-considered sallies. We know how annoying it is to talk to any one who can scarcely bring out a word without using an imprecation or obscene adjective as an expletive, as if that clarified the sense. It may be a compensation for a lack of vocabulary, or it may be a speech habit picked up in imitation, but the individual himself has much to do with it.

The Place of Environment

Two boys I know well have been brought up in a family where there was constant marital discord. The air was thick with a luxuriant variety of maledictions and execrations such as might be expected only in the Orient or Levant. The boys, widely differing in age, although exposed to scurrility for years, during their formative period, nevertheless rarely uttered a coarse word, let alone a "curse word." They seemed to have been able to transport themselves mentally whenever they did not succeed in leaving the scene of the fracas. The parents had no education, but the boys had tasted of civilization. One of the parents was refined enough, but could not refrain from matching profanity with profanity. This apparently was the only outlet for the resentment felt, while the sons, more enlightened, could cope more effectively with such situations as they were placed in, without resorting to imprecations, which would have violated their sense of refinement.

I am not pleading the case of dignity, which is often another name for pompousness and snobbishness, nor of decorum, which is not in our province, for it is no trait, but a condition. There is nothing more ludicrous than when a ward politician appears at a public function, let us say at a college commencement, because the incongruity is so glaring. Inner refinement does not take on a formal aspect. It is natural, spontaneous, and individualistic. To say "Oh glory" or "Mercy!" instead of "Oh hell" [2] is not necessarily the hallmark of true refinement, but to use ------- in airing one's grievances is certainly, to put it mildly, a symptom of unrefinement.

Even a disbeliever can hardly quarrel with the Radio Commission for upholding the action of a radio station in shutting General Smedley Butler off the air, in 1931, after he used a phrase like "What the hell." Since the radio is an environmental influence to which children are constantly exposed, the example set by radio orators should not conflict with the precept taught in school and at home, or education, in a sorry plight as it is, becomes virtually a farce. "Bloody" is merely the

---

[2] To many people, the word "hell" is nothing but a sound which means no more than *Utopia,* but since probably the majority believe there is such a place, and the association is disagreeable, it is no more than fair to consider the other fellow's feelings. But even a meaningless word can become a nuisance when repeated dozens of times a day as an expletive.

adjective of "Blood," in itself a harmless enough word, but in Canada, its utterance was regarded as an insult. To call someone a "bloody fool" used to be considered serious enough to start litigation or to create a sanguinary battle (not to use the phrase "bloody fight").[2]

Vulgarity

Not only the profane or obscene is unrefined, when thrust upon unreceptive ears, but any common expression which has lost whatever usefulness it once had. Thus "like nobody's business" is vulgar not because of the word it euphemistically purports to cover, but because it is mob (*vulgus*) usage and inane, although the simile may have had the sound of novelty the first few weeks it went from mouth to mouth. When the poet said, *"Vulgus profanum odi,"* he could not but have referred to the humorless banality of the unreflective herd. Such phrases as "ya betcha," "He's got what it takes," "I'll tell the cockeyed world" are hardly more than meaningless vulgarisms.

The same trait crops up in the telling of Rabelaisian stories because of the obscenity alone.

---

[3] H. L. Mencken, in *The American Language* remarks on the inexplicable taboo, among the British, in the case of the word "bloody".

Smut is often mistaken for wit by the unrefined. References to sex or the excretory functions may be unavoidable in some decent jokes, but such are few. The unrefined laugh at the references more than at the humor which is based on them. The coprophilic tendency of young children takes this somewhat sublimated form with many adults in regard to the appreciation of wit. It is the senselessness, along with the more unpleasant asso-associations, that constitutes the symbol of unrefinement in this case.

Overrefinement

On the other hand, since obscenity may serve as a sexual stimulus, it is, on occasion, not inconsistent with refinement, provided there is an implicit understanding so as not to cause offence to the listener. Actually this is the test of any act as regards refinement — the useful purpose it serves and inoffensiveness to those in the perceptive orbit. Even so, the refined person would have to overcome a certain aversion, so as to be brought to the point of uttering or listening complacently to an obscene expression. Recent literature has become so naturalistic that one cannot avoid the scatological, at least in print; and the mid-Victorian attitude would be regarded now

as utterly anachronistic and squeamish in culti-
vated society, unless it be dominated by religious
dogma. It is not the locution which counts so
much as the context, mental set, and the situation.

There can be such a thing as overrefinement, as
when the consummation of marriage is repugnant
to one of the partners (the woman), which
defeats the matrimonial purpose. The philosopher,
Plotinus, (who lived in the third century) seemed
to have had an obsessional neurosis in connection
with the process of conception, which, to him,
meant a deep humiliation. A man who was
engaged for some time, jilted his fiancée, it was
told me, because she asked him to get her a
glass of water, saying she didn't "have the guts"
to go into the kitchen. That is one case where
love was not blind or deaf, but perhaps the request
was one of many which irked him; and the
harmless use of the word "guts" was only the
last straw. Refinement to such an extreme degree
might lead to complete isolation, apart from the
hardship it works all around.

The Self-Indulgent Abandon of Lovers and Parents

To take other samples of unrefinement, the
fondling of couples in public places is indelicate
not because of the suggestive love-making, or

because the couples are not married or even affianced to one another, but because of the utter disregard of others. In certain types of society, the complete abandon goes unheeded, but in a civilization where there is some restraint, passersby or casual onlookers will wonder why the beach or park must be turned into a chamber in broad daylight. Any excessive demonstration of affection in public, except under unusual conditions, is to be considered in the same category. When a parent, oblivious of other parents, who may have lost their child, or children who are orphans, unduly caresses his or her own child in public, we may look upon it as a want of refinement, unless the child had been hurt or is ill and requires special attention or comforting as compensation.

It is to be seen that there is no Puritanism involved here, but a certain regard for the feelings of others, to which the majority, in their preoccupation with their own interests, are insensible. What has here been dubbed "refinement" will, without doubt go by the name of bad manners, poor form, lack of *bon ton,* poor taste, etc., but the fact is that if there is a trait which encompasses those and other modes of behavior to be further illustrated, then refinement is that trait, and although it reaches out in so many directions, it is still the generic term which subsumes the various activities.

A Cleansing Exhibition at the Wrong Time

Sometimes, refinement is associated with cleanliness, purity, chastity, but there is only an overlapping; and occasionally unrefinement stands out like a sore thumb in the midst of ablutions. When a woman caller — at most an acquaintance — during conversation takes out her nail file and proceeds to clean her nails before filing them, and becoming aware of the *faux pas,* wishes to ease the situation by saying "I know this is not polite, but I must have my nails clean," is she not proclaiming her want of refinement from the house-tops? And yet she pretends to flaunt her love of cleanliness at her host. Psychoanalysis may interpret this as a displacement, a symbolic act, but whatever the unconscious motivation, the negative trait is there and is a personal handicap. It may or may not be displaced, but of one thing we are certain, it is *out of place.* Let us, by all means, try to establish the motives, but let us first of all, for practical reasons, call attention in general, to the observed fact. The normal individual who realizes the impression such behavior induces would seek to make the proper adjustments; for surely this takes less effort and requires less endurance than plastic surgery or electrolysis for hypertrichinosis.

Banter

"Joshing" or indulging in persiflage is another manifestation of unrefinement, although one must here, take into account age and circumstances. It is the chronic chaffer and banterer who comes under that head. It would seem as if the three psychotypes assail their fellows, each according to his own nature. The unrefined viscerotonic through the digestive system, the unrefined somatotonic through horseplay, nudging, elbowing and touching his companion, or taking hold of his lapel or sleeve, while in the cerebrotonic of the same class this negative trait expresses itself in sarcasm, banter, or ridicule. Thus without actually wishing to become obnoxious, their pre-dominant systemic component (viscera, muscula-ture, grey matter) contrives to do its part, each in its own style. In some cases, where two components may be almost equally pronounced, we may even have a double-barreled offence.

Interrelation

Refinement is, as may be expected, interrelated

with other traits in all departments of personality.

It can scarcely function without a fair amount of intelligence; it involves sympathy (feeling with and for others) and even if we do consider its development on the basis of an innate disposition, effort is essential in combatting the so-called natural impulses. Infants are anything but refined, but some have the making of refinement, and the environment is a great factor in shaping this trait, but it is the *individual* who allows himself to be moulded by one force or another.

A genteel person need not be a mollycoddle or a Caspar Milquetoast. During the Nazi war, many of those who distinguished themselves in combat, both in the British and American armed forces, were youths of refined sensibilities, although, to be sure, the class of conscientious objectors would contain a much larger number, and some of these conscientious objectors, in their medical duties at the front, acquitted themselves splendidly.

There are effective personalities and striking personalities, as well as rich and fully integrated personalities, but if they are minus refinement, they lack the aroma which flavors the blend of qualities that go to make up the truly desirable personality.

CHAPTER XVIII

CAN PERSONALITY BE CHANGED?

WHEN I was about to leave the auditorium after my first lecture in the course on the psychology of personality at the State House in Boston, I remember two young ladies approaching me diffidently, the one nudging the other to speak. Finally one of them mustered up some courage and haltingly asked the question whether they "would learn in this class how to change one's personality."

It was a question which surprised me; and still steeped in the academic atmosphere, I was not very encouraging or accommodating, giving the students to understand that a course was given for the purpose of imparting knowledge and not in order to effect cures or remedy defects.

That evening, however, the "dumb" question, as it struck me, perhaps because of the overawed and faltering manner in which it was put, stirred up something in my mind. Of course these girls, even though their cultural outlook was restricted, were within their rights to interest themselves in this practical question. My slight displeasure was occasioned simply by the fact that one might gather that unless the course was to modify their personality, they would not take it, as if the information and the training did not count.

Popularity and Capability

I had then decided to veer from the academic position and adapt the material to suit the practical needs of the many hundreds who would attend this course for the sake of bettering their lot in life. Information about types of personality, about theories of temperament and the growth of character is, of course, essential, but men and women not of the student class are ever confronted with the problem why they always remain in the background when others who are less capable are made much of among their friends. The old solution: there is no accounting for human tastes, or the mental reference to the Oxford epigram:

> *I do not love thee, Dr. Fell;*
> *The reason why, I cannot tell,*
> *But one thing I know full well,*
> *I do not love thee, Dr. Fell,*

can hardly be a consolation when one feels that

other people are definitely liked and are not subject to the whim and caprice of human taste.

Exploitation by Charlatans

There are charlatans who are aware of the poignancy of this feeling experienced by hundreds upon thousands, and are ready to trade upon their misfortune and *naïveté*, selling them books and lessons which purport to enable them to change their defective personality in five days. Of course, for the most part, these books are the most outlandish balderdash. The so-called exercises prescribed are worse than useless; they are apt to make out of an inferior personality a psychopathic case.

Are Personalities Born or Made?

We must first of all ask the question whether there is at all a possibility of changing our personality before we attempt to suggest ways and means. There may be some fatalists who take it that once born with such and such characteristics, we can do nothing more than abide by them or make the best of it. It were sad indeed if the situation were as hopeless as all that. While it is true, in a sense, that personalities are born, it cannot be denied that there is a possibility of modification and improvement, and that as we look back upon the personalities of certain of our acquaintances we knew in the teens, we are often surprised at the progress they had made. Can it have been the result of circumstances? But it is my contention here that even circumstances are frequently made by us. It would take too much space to analyze illustrations in corroboration of this somewhat novel claim, and we shall defer such documentation to a more leisurely bit of writing. Suffice it at present to allude *en gros* to the captains of industry, the leaders of finance, the pilots of statecraft who started out with what would not be regarded as a prepossessing personality by the man in the street. If physique and personal appearance are stressed, then in their boyhood days, many of these celebrities were anything but attractive. They arrived, however, where others could not, because of their self-discipline, and with every new notch in their staff, their personality would take on a brighter tint.

Mental Cosmetics Not an Aid to Personality

These people did not go about looking for the secret of personal magnetism, did not buy, borrow, or steal books on instantaneous success, nor did they deck themselves out with mental cosmetics.

They found in themselves an inclination toward some definite goal in life; and in the course of their strivings to make good, they kept adjusting themselves when they found something in their personality was wanting. There was not, as some think, a set plan to study and experiment with themselves. The latter was just the natural outcome of the exigencies of the moment — one step leading to another, until people coming in contact with them, both their subordinates and associates, would not only attribute personality to them but would refer to them as personalities. They had realized the Latin saying

Per aspera ad astra.

Again, however, we must come back to our definition of personality before the statements made here could be accepted. Personality has been defined as an integrative blend of all the cognitive, affective, conative, and physical elements in man. But it is evident that sometimes the one set of elements is stressed, at other times, another. There are different conceptions of personality. That quality spoken of as personal magnetism pleases the majority. Other people prefer to possess the commanding presence, though devoid of charm. The combination of both in one person is such a rarity that it is practically a fiction. In my own contacts, I have met but two or three that might have possessed this blessed blend.

Personality Differences in Men and Women

In spite of the melting-pot nature of personality, there can be no doubt that the heart or crux of it is that which appeals to most people and which affects social relationships; *viz.*, the physical and the affective sides. Furthermore, men and women may be said to diverge as regards personality requirements. The former express their personality most fully in the cognitive (intellectual) and conative (character) elements; the latter would be quite satisfied to forego these two elements, if they could be guaranteed the affective and the physical factors. In other words, a woman would much prefer to *have* personality than to *be* a personality. The man is not quite complete until he is something of a personality. (I have heard it said about a popular matinee idol that "he is all personality." This does not mean that the actor *is* a personality, but is another way of saying that he *has* a great deal of personality, affective and physical).

It is not to be understood that we are dealing here with different materials, but simply that these same materials for men and women are mixed in different proportions and require a different standard of judgment for the two sexes. A charming man is usually ineffectual; a woman of commanding presence, even when not awe-inspiring, is nearly always atypical — more masculine than feminine — in either case, defeating the purpose of nature, in its evolutionary course.

Personality More Modifiable Than Character

Reverting now to the problem in hand: whether and how we can change our personality, it is encouraging to note that personality is more pliable than character. A man given to dishonesty is not likely to become more honest with age because of his relationships with his fellow-men. If he is a coward by nature, he will perhaps curb his behavior, but not his dread; and he will even find means to escape the slightest danger, unless he belongs to the handful who can remake themselves. When Schopenhauer and others spoke of the fixity of character, they were referring, and with justice, to the ethical phase of behavior.

In the matter of personality, however, not only can we modify our original tendencies, but we actually do change our personality in the course of time. Many a morose person becomes sociable and communicative, and some there are who toward old age, as a result of bitter experiences, become shut-in, perhaps even murky personalities. There is a greater stimulus to change personality than to change character. It costs less pains and, in the popular view, at least, brings greater returns. The vital question, however, is where to start and what means to take in order to accomplish that end.

The Trifles That Become Momentous

We may all know that there is room for improvement, but to pick out the specific flaws is quite a different matter. There are not a few whose sensibilities are so dull that they cannot become aware of their shortcomings until these are brought to their attention; and even then, will they not admit them but suppose that the objector is too finicky, if not impudent. There are others who recognize their weak points but suppose that no one minds them, any more than they do, but they forget that while they are prone to make allowance for themselves, and what is more, have become habituated to their objectionable behavior, their fellow-beings are not likely to be so tolerant and cannot become inured to the faults; for that is not the practice which makes perfect. What one considers a trifle, others regard as a severe and inexcusable piece of vulgarity; and it is not ourselves who are judges of our own conduct, but those we come in contact with.

Insight a Prerequisite

We thus perceive that the improvement of personality hinges on an intelligence factor, viz., *insight*. People with little insight cannot have an attractive or desirable personality to begin with, nor can they improve themselves except at a snail's pace. Such, if they are conscious of their deficiency, can at best put themselves in the hands of a wise mentor who would point out specific errors and advise what steps to take to correct them. After a while, they might "catch on" themselves to what is required, and will acquire a certain amount of *savoir-faire*.

The Will to Change

There is left then the large class of those people who are on the alert for cues and suggestions from the circumstances themselves, but they lack method, and are never quite certain as to what is wrong, or else they are loath to leave the grooves of their personal routine. This is a case where the conative (will, effort) factor in personality must be invoked. Not only insight is essential, but the attitude, the stamina to break down the natural inertia, e.g., for a sullen introvert to open up and become expansive, or for a flighty and forward extravert to become self-controlled and consider the privacy or individualistic leanings of his newly-made acquaintance.

To be sure, there are very few people who will please everybody, since "so many people, so many minds," but just as with genuine beauty there is a consensus of opinion, in spite of the subjective nature of taste, so when we have before us a personality on a high plane, we may be certain that the individual in question will call forth approbation on all hands. If we cannot please all, we can at least impress the majority favorably.

CHAPTER XIX

REMEDYING CERTAIN DEFECTS

THAT some defects are beyond our control will not be denied. Homely features, disfigurements, a sottish or comical expression, a tic, chorea, and many other unfortunate characteristics are the bane, the silent tragedy of thousands, but even these personality impediments may, to some degree, be mitigated, if not removed. Dressing the hair in a certain manner will often hide an eye defect. Most moles and warts can effectively be handled by a competent surgeon. The skillful use of cosmetics is another consideration which does not escape the women in France, at least.

It is fortunate that physical disagreeableness, when not insistent as, in the case of a foul odor, for instance, wears off, especially where other qualities enter into the situation by way of compensation. President Eliot of Harvard University was handicapped by a birthmark which disfigured his whole face, yet he was honored in ripe old age as no American citizen has been in his time.

A person with, say, Kalmuck eyes and a typical Mongolian grin will not be likely to rate high on the personality scale, yet should he happen to have acquired culture and to have made the interests of his fellow-men his own, he probably would have also effected a change in his outward personality. I am fully aware that there are puzzling exceptions, e.g., the great Hindu leader, Gandhi, whose appearance belied his extraordinary qualities of mind and character, but those who have seen an early photograph of him will realize that he had an attractive outward appearance, but his self-imposed rigorous discipline and hard struggles to free his country from British domination had much to do with his unprepossessing cast later on. Those who knew him saw only a shining light in his eyes and a saintly expression nevertheless. The very title of V. Sheean's recent book on Gandhi is a corroboration in this regard. It may also be remarked that Gandhi belonged to the class of characters rather than to the personalities, as the distinction was made on pages 282-289.

A Fundamental Law in Personality Change

The thesis laid down here is that the inner personality must be modified first before the outward appearance assumes a different aspect. A man who is ill-natured cannot, with all his artfulness, put on a gracious or agreeable mien. The villain who "smiles and smiles and is a villain," after all, cannot deceive many. The inconsistency will glare out, if carefully watched. A friendly soul will radiate friendliness, sincerity, and devotion. An unsociable individual will appear dour, sulky, peevish, or morose. Only the injection of a little sympathy for others would change the personality of that individual.

It is the same inner attitude which will help to soften hardened features or what is spoken of as "hard lines." Intellectual interests and exchange of ideas with intelligent persons will do much to reduce the "dumb" expression around the mouth and the eyes that the totally uncultured often exhibit in the presence of the intellectual.

A face lighted up with enthusiasm will always atone for asymmetry, disproportionateness, a poor complexion, a too large nose, a too wide mouth, or too small eyes. Because of their mobile and dynamic functions, the eyes and the mouth (lips) are probably the carriers of facial expression more than any other features, although none are to be disregarded. They all support one another in order to produce the total effect, but *the eyes and the mouth are the centers of expression.* There is something to be thankful for, then, in that we have greater control over these features, because of their muscles, than over any others. (The wrinkling of the forehead, the dilation of the nostrils, or the movements of other parts of the face are either artificially induced or the results of emotional or nervous disturbances, not to be identified with, let us say, the knitting of the brow while frowning, which is a consequence of the eye movements.)

Expression Must Possess Content

The artificial practice of smiling, simply to be pleasant, cannot achieve its purpose when there is not a genuine disposition underlying it, for the smile, then, becomes a smirk or a grin. A naturally pleasant person will not need to practice smiling, and a sincere and self-reliant person will have a frank and open look, without taking exercises for it, as some of our personality dispensers would urge us to do. It is not always that eyes are "the mirrors of the soul," as is commonly believed, but they are a fair index of an agreeable or disagreeable personality. The so-called magnetic (not hypnotic) eyes draw *only because they go out to people first.* They always seem to be looking at, or with, someone. Even when alone they are in a social milieu. The cold steel--like eyes are always alone even when in a crowd. They look beyond or within, and their aloofness sets up a barrier between themselves and others.

Where Practice Is of Advantage

We can now see that there is an inner relation between the physical appearance and the social and affective make-up of man. Bearing, posture, gait, modulation of voice, intonation, and even articulation enter into the total personality picture, but here practice and exercise can accomplish a great deal; and it is not the purpose of this chapter to suggest practical exercises, which of course must be adapted to individual needs, but merely to point out that such endeavors are beneficial when properly directed.

THE POPULAR APPEAL AND ITS SECRET

If we ask a number of our friends to pick out specific qualities in people accounting for their popularity, there will, in all probability, be one outstanding factor, and that is agreeableness or pleasantness of manner. Numerous other items will be mentioned, such as the "winning smile," the "strong" face; even the dimpled cheeks will not be lacking, but good-naturedness, sweetness of disposition, will top the list. The grouchy person, the constant grumbler, will be left severely alone except by chums who have become attached for one reason or another; and it is a curious fact that grumpy people will occasionally be surrounded with devoted friends who have peered beneath the rough surface and found a kind-hearted foundation.

Naturally, since the social success of the jolly and pleasant is so well known, it is surprising that there is still such a large class of cold and reserved individuals who give the impression that you cannot approach them on equal ground, and who are generally regarded as offish, if not cranks. The answer is, of course, in the first instance, "They are built that way," which is only another way of saying that their constitutional make-up (nervous organization, glandular and muscular structure, etc.) is such; but had they sufficient insight and were they to take a different attitude, it would be possible for them in time to grow more cheerful and sympathetic.

Exaggerated Sociability

Again, there is the fault of exaggeration, when really sociable people become gushing and forward, handing out advice that is unsolicited and

making many a *faux pas* because of their indis-
cretion, engaging in gossip, not out of real malice,
but "just to be sociable," or out of *Schadenfreude*
(literally, taking pleasure in someone's discomfi-
ture, which is a refined substitute for malice).
Such persons are liked when you are with them
but disliked the moment you think about them,
when their agreeable presence does not make up
for the importunate and not very pleasant under-
current. Toward such people there will be an
ambivalent reaction, even on the part of those,
or perhaps especially on the part of those, who
are like themselves. They will be liked and disliked, or more strictly speaking, they will be liked
but not respected; and in the appreciation of a
personality, respect has a part to play as well.

We must bear in mind, too, that personality
is made up not alone of positive qualities but
also of negative characteristics. It is the minus
features which perhaps count for more than we
think in the final estimate. Let us make a list
of those things which we dislike in people of our
acquaintance and which repel us in strangers. A
thousand and one kinds of behavior can be enumerated. There is the braggart, the liar, the "bounder,"
the "bester," and so on, but here our reaction
smacks of the ethical judgment. In the last analy-

sis, probably, everything we do which is a nuisance to others, even smoking the usual foul-smelling cigar or puffing columns of bitter tobacco fumes out of a pipe into someone's face at dinner, reduces to a question of ethics, but there are definite lapses of taste, good breeding, and refinement which are forced upon us at almost every step we take, especially in an environment of a low form of civilization.

Why Some People Are Disliked at First Sight

It is the objectionable feature or behavior about a person that thrusts itself upon one on first acquaintance. When an individual who partakes of garlic wonders why people turn away when he speaks to them, he shows a lack of insight. He may tell you after being apprised of the cause that, in France and Italy, a garlic breath is not taken amiss, he may find half a dozen plausible reasons for indulging his taste, but offensive sensations cannot be argued. Similarly the barber who belches with gusto while shaving a customer will not be sought after by the clientèle of the shop. No matter how agreeable the personality otherwise, an exhibition of nose-picking, with its disgusting sequel, or ear-drilling is bound to lower its value in the eyes of the onlookers. Such liabilities as general fidgetiness, sputtering, boister-ousness, and the making of noise in handling things (some people can never sit down without drumming on the table, desk, or arm of the chair they sit in, or cannot refrain from beating time with their feet while listening to a concert, never considering for a moment that they are annoying their neighbors) may cost more than one valuable friendship in the course of a lifetime.

Truly worth-while people are supposed to be immune from such tendencies or to have overcome them. Lack of integration, incompleteness, or in-feriority is at the root of such so-called habits, and lack of consideration or want of insight is the cause of their continuance.

In a word, we may repeat the words put into the mouth of Cassius:

> *"It's not in the stars, dear Brutus, that the*
> *fault lies,*
> *But in ourselves."*

APPENDICES

APPENDIX A

THE ROLE OF PERSONALITY IN THE PROMOTION OF IDEAS

SCIENCE is the most objective of human endeavors. In its most representative form it is demonstrable, and, therefore, its progress or success should not depend on human whims or foibles, although a measure of chance cannot be avoided, since science is the creation or, better perhaps, the organization effected by human agencies.

We must make allowance, then, for all the casual discoveries and inventions made since antiquity from the legendary bathtub observation of Archimedes to the many instances of archeological finds in excavated territory, but we can scarcely make room for the forcefulness or attractiveness of a personality as a means of promoting a particular doctrine or school in either science or philosophy. Yet that very personal equation — not the personal equation which originally referred to the speed of the astronomer's reaction in noting the transit of a stellar body through the ocular of a telescope — I contend, is responsible for the growth of science in a particular direction, at times for its stagnation, and occasionally even for its distortion.

To the ordinary layman it is almost inconceivable that a universal truth should require certain amenities to render it acceptable or that a doubtful theory should make headway because of the social status or personality traits of the proponent. I shall make no secret of it that in all my nine years at the university it had never occurred to me that such could be the case. It was not until I had attended the counsel halls of the mighty savants and also peered behind the scenes that I too made the discovery that science and politics are not disparate from each other.

Cynical? No, on the contrary, *they* are cynical who will tell you they knew it all along and that it is only natural. There are probably enough people to harbor such a thought, although few scholars and scientists, if any, will express it. As a matter of fact I have never come across any discussion of this topic, one of the most fundamental issues in the fabric of our civilization. When I picked up some years ago a book by Dr. William Brown of Oxford, entitled *Science and Personality*, I was almost certain that at last someone has approached the subject which had been perplexing me for a decade at least, but the volume turned out to be a sort of *apologia* for psychical research. Since then the conjuncture of science and personality, in its social phase, seems to have grown closer; and the problem offers to assume a sociological significance, second to none in that particular sector.

In a short chapter one can only cull a few instances here and there. A book of sizeable dimensions should disclose this phase of personalized science through hundreds of illustrations. After all it is the general rule that concerns us. The factors which promote the spread of an intellectual system are not unlike those which induce acceptance of the gospel.

We are still at a loss to understand how of all the illustrious minds who have both preceded and followed him, Albert of Bollstadt (born about 1200) should have to be the one to receive the honorific title "The Great" (*Albertus Magnus*) [1] an epithet reserved only for the few monarchs whose industry and initiative had set them off from and above the average nincompoop idler and wencher.

That Albert was an erudite and prolific man, steeped in the philosophy of the day — Scholasticism — is an incontestable fact, but his pupil Thomas Aquinas was a giant in thought compared

[1] It is a curious coincidence that the two greatest men of our own age are both named Albert — Albert Einstein and Albert Schweitzer.

with him; and even the Scotch Englishman, John Duns Scotus, stood high above him as a subtle reasoner and follower of scientific method, yet Scotus was rewarded by being allowed to serve as the prototype of our "dunce" (which is derived from his middle name). Albert the Great might have acquired the augmentative by virtue of his presence and sensational effects, after the fashion of Herman "the Great," in magic and illusionism. He seems to have been looked up to as a mystic healer by the masses, but his name in the history of philosophy is merely mentioned now, in spite of his medieval glory.

The relative fortunes of the two Bacons in the history of thought have been dwelt on in various connections. It would be natural for the works of Roger Bacon, the Franciscan monk, to remain obscure while less consequential productions of the famous Lord Chancellor found an admiring world upon which to impress themselves.

It is fortunately true that posterity, through the medium of critical and enlightened investigators, has a way of reversing the verdict of contemporary devotees, but were it possible to isolate the true scientific element of a creative mind, such delays, pernicious influences and revisions would be unnecessary. We need only reflect on the persistent stand that the phlogiston theory made, not to speak of the many chimerical beliefs that were current in every century, yes, even to this day.

* * * * * *

With the increase of education and instruments for testing truth one would expect the value of a doctrine to be determined more promptly and definitively, but the distribution of intelligence is apparently a constant, while education is doled out in the colleges to hundreds of thousands. The regard for teachers on the part of students is quite well known. Those professors who happen to be teaching in large universities and lay down the law to hundreds, if not thousands, of students a year will become the celebrities of their age. If their classes include many foreign students, their fame will spread to the remotest parts of the earth.

Little boots it that these leaders may be palming off commonplaces in technical language or else relieving themselves of obscurities in scholastic terminology. The students must read their books and the doctrines contained therein become part of their intellectual organization in its formative stage.

The next generation or century may scarcely devote a reference to these leaders except in histories of that subject for that particular period, just as posterity has slurred the hundreds of

professors who had once dominated
at Oxford, Cambridge, Halle, Pari
large centers.

What presence does may be gather
illustration. Only about 40 years ago,
was a name to be conjured with
References to his philosophy were hea
in the philosophy department where th
were in the habit of discussing one an
in mild opposition, but in other cour
His books were so much in demand
assigned to students, more than one
go out of the library without bein
Today I doubt whether 50 students
have heard of him; and were it n
large painting over the staircase in Em
portraying the illustrious trio, James, P
Royce, probably only a handful of stud
history of philosophy could be said
bowing acquaintance with his philos
students, professors in various small co
cherish his idealistic philosophy, and
letters often speak of his gigantic mi
philosophic circles, generally, his na
evoke the reaction "Oh, yes, it seems to
heard this name before." I am not bel
philosophical acumen and tremendous
of Josiah Royce — on the contrary, I thi
been undeservedly forgotten — but a

speak of the many chimerical beliefs that were current in every century, yes, even to this day.

* * * * * *

With the increase of education and instruments for testing truth one would expect the value of a doctrine to be determined more promptly and definitively, but the distribution of intelligence is apparently a constant, while education is doled out in the colleges to hundreds of thousands. The regard for teachers on the part of students is quite well known. Those professors who happen to be teaching in large universities and lay down the law to hundreds, if not thousands, of students a year will become the celebrities of their age. If their classes include many foreign students, their fame will spread to the remotest parts of the earth.

Little boots it that these leaders may be palming off commonplaces in technical language or else relieving themselves of obscurities in scholastic terminology. The students must read their books and the doctrines contained therein become part of their intellectual organization in its formative stage.

The next generation or century may scarcely devote a reference to these leaders except in histories of that subject for that particular period, just as posterity has slurred the hundreds of professors who had once dominated their circles at Oxford, Cambridge, Halle, Paris and other large centers.

What presence does may be gathered from this illustration. Only about 40 years ago, Josiah Royce was a name to be conjured with at Harvard. References to his philosophy were heard not only in the philosophy department where the professors were in the habit of discussing one another's views in mild opposition, but in other courses as well. His books were so much in demand that when assigned to students, more than one copy would go out of the library without being charged. Today I doubt whether 50 students at Harvard have heard of him; and were it not for the large painting over the staircase in Emerson Hall, portraying the illustrious trio, James, Palmer, and Royce, probably only a handful of students in the history of philosophy could be said to have a bowing acquaintance with his philosophy. His students, professors in various small colleges, still cherish his idealistic philosophy, and in their letters often speak of his gigantic mind; but in philosophic circles, generally, his name might evoke the reaction "Oh, yes, it seems to me I have heard this name before." I am not belittling the philosophical acumen and tremendous scholarship of Josiah Royce — on the contrary, I think he has been undeservedly forgotten — but am rather illuminating a phenomenon in our intellectual fabric.

Perhaps the case of William James and Charles S. Peirce is more striking. The former was voted as the greatest name in American science by his contemporaries. He still is ranked as the foremost philosopher America ever produced (with the possible exception of John Dewey), but gradually a name that had been obscure until recently is beginning to vie for the honor with that of William James, who, incidentally, himself was instrumental in making the name more familiar to philosophical readers. The man I have in mind is Charles Sanders Peirce, whose seven volumes, out of many which may never see the light of day, have disclosed him to be a mind of the first order, in sweep and depth, perhaps, too, outweighing the author of the *Principles of Psychology*. What has been responsible for Peirce's dimness as compared with James' effulgence? The answer will be found in the difference of their personality traits and circumstances.

James was a well-poised educator. Peirce was a typical bohemian, an individualist with erratic tendencies. James, as professor of psychology, and subsequently philosophy, at Harvard University, lectured to hundreds of students, attended congresses, entertained colleagues from abroad, who were charmed with his hospitality and good breeding. Students wrote dissertations on his philosophy; foreign colleagues translated his works; and, of course, his inimitable literary style was a great help, indeed, in disseminating his ideas. William James had received his just recognition, but had he been transplanted to a small college in the south with but few students, and those, too, of mediocre calibre, the name of William James would not have resounded so universally in philosophical circles.

Peirce, on the other hand, had no students, was not the incumbent of an academic chair, and did not mingle much with the moguls and pundits of science. Hence, his voluminous manuscripts were accumulating dust until, long after his death, the legacy of a namesake (except for the transposition of *e* and *i*) had made it possible for the Harvard Philosophy Department to bring out these all but forgotten gems.

* * * * * *

The fortunes of entire intellectual movements are bound up with the non-intellectual qualities of their leaders. The history of Behaviorism, the standing of *Gestalt* psychology attests our thesis. Max Meyer gave us the groundwork of Behaviorism. It made little stir. John Watson *advertised* his particular brand, and immediately it created a furore. People craned their necks to see what he was selling. He challenged, he condemned and made guarantees. He would have none of the musty past. He was heralded in the press as a psychological Messiah. He traveled extensively, propagating his views and engaging foreign psychologists in debates. Behaviorism was *made*. If it were human, the American phrase, "a self-made man," could be applied to it.

Gestalt psychology too owes much of its success to the enterprising proclivities of its leaders. The movement was hatched in the University of Berlin, where there was a great deal of contact with American students in pre-war days, students who later became influential professors in large American universities. Representatives of this new school in psychology visited America and were naturally invited to speak on various occasions. They made an excellent impression intellectually, and even more so socially. Result: *Gestalt* psychology became intrenched in American citadels of learning, and the five pillars of *Gestalt* psychology soon found themselves permanently domiciled in the United States bolstering up their cause. They have been a great asset to American psychology, to be sure, but their personal qualities have had much to do with advancing the claims of their doctrines.

The Germans have been the world's greatest intellectual go-getters. Not only the Wagner cult has been fanned by German propaganda in musical circles throughout the world, but even their lesser philosophers and psychologists have found a market through agents, emissaries, apostles, ambassadors, converts, etc. Witness the imposition of the Eidetic school on psychological thought in America and elsewhere. The Jaensch brothers (E. R. and Walther) had made some interesting experiments to show the conditions under which images of objects removed from sight may arise in children particularly, but also in adults, enabling them to describe the absent object as if they had been looking at it. These experiments were not sufficient for the brothers. They developed a series of human types on flimsy evidence, and as if this were not enough, they proceeded to evolve a philosophy of life based on the constitutional differences which they posited in the first place. And shortly after, E. R. Jaensch, who became a sort of Hitler representative for psychology, began to promulgate the doctrine that there is an S type, which is the symbol of decline, degeneration, hybridism, etc., while the Nazi type, its diametrically opposed counterpart, also constitutional in origin, is the embodiment of all that is noble, pure, sublime, etc.

This only by way of introduction. Some years ago, a German lawyer (*Assessor*) arrived in America and was making a trip, it would seem, around the world, at least calling at the most important centers. During this trip, he was selling eidetic imagery, *i.e.,* not the concrete article but the theory. He was moving heaven and earth to have conferences, lectures, colloquia and even had gone to the expense of having certain of his masters' articles translated and printed as pamphlets. True enough, he knew nothing about psychology. For his part, the mental sciences began and ended with eidetic imagery, but he apparently had the wherewithal to spread his gospel even to far-off Japan.

If science is to degenerate into a ballyhoo reminiscent of the election bedlam, then might we not expect some day a situation in which the buying of votes will become an instrument of the progress of science?

It will probably be rejoined in certain quarters that every proponent or exponent has the right to make himself heard, that unless he does so deliberately, his views have a slim chance of surviving, even if they are correct. I have heard this argument advanced by ambitious scientists and philosophers, who keep repeating their results in periodical after periodical only in slightly changed form. Their aim is "to make the world sit up and take notice," and they succeed in gaining their objective by drumming it in.

The true pioneers and leaders of thought, it

must be said, did not resort to such methods. They published their conclusions, and allowed others to take up the cudgels. A grand array of names might be cited in this connection. Socrates never wrote anything. Spinoza left his most important work for posterity to publish. When Hume found that his philosophy was not being treated seriously, he turned to history. Kant needed no propagandists. Mendel's results in genetics had to be rediscovered. Scientists like Galileo, Newton, Laplace, Darwin, or Pasteur did not have to depend on their personality, students, or friends.

In conclusion, it must not be supposed that I am belittling the value of modern trends in philosophy and psychology. A doctrine, method, or system may be extremely important and significant even if salesmanship was used in "putting it across," but certainly critical minds should not allow the mere circumstance of publicity to stand in the way of properly appraising another school or trend of thought. In other words, *scientific perspective* is necessary for every educated person, let alone professors. We ought not to be guided like the Ph. D. candidate whose doctor's dissertation is an anthology of his professors' lectures and books (and some even publish works which are in essence extended seminar papers dealing with the utterances of their past instructors). Let us not wholly neglect those results and conclusions which lacked the advantage of personality and favorable conjunctures; and again, let us not accept uncritically the teachings, or take for granted the superiority, of someone who had risen to fame because of the devotion of friends and pupils.

APPENDIX B

Analysis of a Case Study

Several years ago, a request came to the author from a member of the Department of Sociology at the University of Chicago for an analysis of an unpublished case study "in order to see how much is gained through pooling the wisdom of a number of outstanding experts."

The case was that of a delinquent boy, at the time a youth, Karl Hunze, who had begun by playing truant in school, pilfering the pantry and running up the family bill at the bakery for cake, without the knowledge of his mother, who was a widow. He joined gangs, and became involved in thieving expeditions, one of which ended in ransacking a public-school lunch room. Although he and his confederates were discovered and taken by the police, "my teacher and several others, though, talked to the principal and he, in turn, had things fixed so we would be discharged."

So he took to stealing bicycles, together with one of his associates; and that seemed quite easy. "I was still stealing anything I wanted and knew how to steal." Coal off the coal cars was a lucrative business for Karl and three or four others. "Well I kept right on doing what I had been; missing school, stealing, staying away from home, and all the rest." When the police saw him riding a bicycle in an alley, after midnight, and chased him for an hour, through lane and alley, until they caught up with him, he was able to convince them that "my people weren't home at the time they chased me but that they had just come home, and I didn't know they were coppers when they chased me . . . so they stopped and let me out, and you can be sure that I was glad to go home that night."

Pocket-book snatching was the next enterprise for Karl. "It was simple, all you had to do was to grab the purse and run." A neighbor, whose purse was snatched, recognized Karl's pal, with the result that they were both apprehended "And we had a regular little showup by ourselves, and everyone of the 25 to 35 identified us." They were then sent to the Juvenile Detention Home. At the trial, one of the boys, who had his people in court, was put on probation; another received 6 months, while Karl was sentenced to 30 days in the Cook County School for Boys. "I laughed when he said 30 days and said 'Thank you, judge,' and as I started out of the courtroom, I could hear the women saying 'Gee, ain't it too bad, and ain't it a shame' meaning they were sorry to see me sent away.

"Well in a few days I felt like an old timer — all I had to do was to go to school, eat, and play; work there was very little, outside of keeping the cottage clean and that was divided up between about 45 of us. I learned how to get my smokes and all the rest, and all of the things they do in a place like that."

After a week and 4 days, the superintendent paroled him. "All the way home I was thinking what a big shot I'd be now. In reaching home, I seen the gang playing ball on Princeton Avenue, and when they saw me the game broke up. They all crowded around me as though I was the Prince of Wales and I had to tell them all about the place." After being freed, he did not report back to school. Two months later, a truant officer, direct from the Detention Home, "called at my home and wanted to know why I wasn't in school. I didn't have any excuse, but she said for me to report to school in the morning and she would fix everything up, but I never showed up, so she put my probation officer, Mr. Reynoldman, on my trail. It was a month after before he finally got me one day."

He was taken back to the Boys School where he was handling the keys more often than the house officer was. After a five weeks' period he was paroled again. There were now difficulties getting into school again, as Karl's record made him a risk, but his mother thought of a ruse which enabled him to enroll in a far-off district. Gang fights with those in a neighboring school followed, and once, Karl and a few others threw a boy off a bridge into the lagoon, and just as he was, face down, going under, Karl dove off the bridge, swam to him, and pulled him to shore. "What made me do this I don't know, for I'm sure as I looked at him I had no intention of going in after him." The job of pumping out the water was left to passers-by. This incident led to an investigation, which brought out that Karl did not belong to the district and as the various schools were refusing to admit him "I was having a wonderful time," but one morning, he was returned to the Boys School, where he was paroled after three weeks.

After that I talked to the priest of St. George's school, gave him a big line about reforming, etc. and after two hours got him to take me back. I had promised to stay away from my old gang, go to school regularly and let the kids alone.

In two months' time, I was again without a school, the priest took me into his office with the intention of thrashing me, but I had different ideas and fought him when we got in there, and while we were going strong, someone rapped on the door, and as he went to answer it, I left by the window and stood outside calling him all of the names I could think of and that was that.

It would scarcely be necessary to recount the series of returns to, and escapes from, the Cook County Boys School and Juvenile Detention Home, his "luck," his easy jobs, etc. "I served as a cottage boy for about 3 weeks, then I was given the best job in the institution, in the Administration building, running the switchboard. My duties were few and easy, as I was working with one of the officer's wife, and all I had to do would be to relieve her once in a while and deliver such packages as came in to the boys."

"Sleeving drunks" and burglaries were only stepping stones to hold-ups. "After that, we used to pull hoists pretty regularly. At this time, we were running around with a bunch of girls from the neighborhood, and we used to see them nearly every night. All this kept up for about two months and we never got more than a little chase from some flivver squad, which we could lose at leisure."

We must remember that all these episodes had happened before the boy was 15, for at that age, he was returned to the institution. We shall not pursue his career any further, and the story does not go beyond his commitment to Joliet Prison at the age of 19, but by that time he had managed to live a gay and merry life, "playing two broads" as he called his mistresses, and living on the scale of a small-time racketeer, after abandoning the hospitality of one of the girls' parents and taking their daughter with him. It was this girl who, according to his own testimony, was a virgin until he met her, that he blames for his fate, but he is strangely reticent about the details, which is characteristic of his whole narrative, in that he stresses what is favorable and glosses over much else.

REPLIES TO THE QUESTIONNAIRE

1—In your judgment, why did the boy enter into and continue in a life of crime?

1. Heredity is probably the chief factor, even if both parents were known to be law-abiding. The father and one of the brothers had a temper; the mother was easygoing and indulgent, particularly with the subject of this case. "On the whole I was pretty much pampered especially after dad's death." His older brother, who was "hot-headed," would bully him a bit, nevertheless, there was no stigma attached to him. Nothing has been said about the grandparents.

There is no intention, in attributing the chief cause of the trouble to heredity, to derive it all from some criminal taint that came at birth. Criminality may just be the product of a number of traits, in themselves not vicious, but the combination of positive and negative factors under a given conjuncture of circumstances would be sufficient to create the criminal pattern. Some of the undesirable features of his father's make-up, blending with certain crucial characteristics inherited from the mother or a grandparent, may have conspired to predispose the boy to a life of crime, even if he had not gone to the limit, before commitment to prison.

Not only atavism could be a possible reason for the deviation from the general family pattern, but mutation might account for it, if we knew more about the family tree and could collate common characteristics, as well as put to one side the isolated knots.

There is one thing here which throws some reflection on the superego theory of Freud, and his school, which claims the superego to have been produced by parental awe and rigorous methods of discipline. The father died when the boy was 10. The formation should have taken place, if the theory is correct, nor can it be said that the boy turned criminal as an unconscious reaction to his father whom, according to the theory, he hated; for during his whole childhood, mischief had been rife. I accept the division of mind into the *id, ego,* and the *superego,* but question the Freudian explanation as to the genesis of the *superego.*

Circumstances, of course, have been of some importance. The chief circumstantial reasons were: (a) social contacts and milieu, (b) glibness and presence of mind on the part of the boy in averting punishment, (c) the extraordinary ease of committing crime and evading the law. In fact, this was what impressed me most. Policemen were eager to let the boy go. In penal institutions, he would be given jobs of trust, even after he showed his incorrigibility. Personal interest in him and advanced reform ideas seem to have been responsible for continued and progressive delinquency.

The question "Why did the boy enter into a life of crime?" may refer to the motivation of the boy. This will be taken up in the answer to question 2.

2—List the outstanding personality traits of the boy.

2. After one reading, I gained the following impression of the boy's traits; (*a*) rebelliousness and restlessness, (*b*) adventurousness and emulation of "big shots" (possibly seen in the movies or

talked about among the gangs), (*c*) ideas of grandeur, (*d*) force and courageousness, probably the result of a robust constitution and high vitality, (*e*) inadequate inhibitions (*f*) powerful instinctive drives (acquisitiveness without working, precocious sensuality (*g*) unusual presence of mind, *sang-froid* and glibness, coupled with (*h*) resourcefulness, German efficiency in organization and (*i*) comparative shrewdness in sizing up people and practical situations. Older people would probably be attracted to his spunk, or nerve, and mistake it for strength of character. His appearance was most likely in his favor, and that, as well as his youth, would stand him in good stead. "Moral insanity" would be the term which the older writers would apply to this sort of character, but he could not be called a psychopathic personality. He was too "regular" for that, but his egoism was boundless.

He was definitely extraverted and sanguine in temperament, with a choleric shift, possessed a good deal of social intelligence (e.g. in replies like "you can cook good enough for a king, but I'm so full," etc.,) yet lacked insight. He was hyperkinetic, dynamic, and purposeful. His chief defect was an utter insensibleness to the values. His attitude shows gross cynicism and his slang expressions unrefinement.

It is clear that even in childhood, he wished to

be considered an adult with adult privileges, and had already formed some plans to realize his ambitions in a sphere which to him seemed accessible. Every time he was let off, he would conclude that the world was just one big pushover. That he had certain traits of leadership could not be denied. This is evident from the very fact that he would rapidly rise to the top in his circle or among the inmates of the institution.

3—We are interested in comparing the picture we have of the subject as a child with the picture we have at the end of the case study. For example, as a child we find him doing minor stealing and mischievous deeds, and at the end of the case study we find him a hold-up man and gunman. As another illustration, we can note a change in his attitude toward his home. What do you consider to be the most significant lines of development? How do you explain such lines of development?

(3) I see no difference except in degree between his delinquency as a child and that as an adolescent. It is what one would expect under the circumstances. As he became more experienced, and as his chances would grow more favorable, he would rationalize his acts. Luck seems to have favored him. The question crops up: What would have happened had one of his hold-up victims fought? Would he have used the gun? Much

hinges on the answer, which, of course, is unavailable.

4—Certain traits of the subject seem to have persisted throughout his life. For example, throughout, he seems sociable and adventuresome. What do you consider to be the most significant traits which have so persisted? How do you explain the persistence of such traits?

4. According to my view of character, persistence is what we might expect. His instinctive traits were most persistent (adventure, satiation of appetites, and aggressiveness). The ego instincts and the pleasure "principle" were his leading motives. He did have a few "lapses," occasional and ephemeral, e.g., when he does not run away from the reformatory, although he had a chance to, or when he stays with his brother for a while and is looking for a job, but these are merely brief spells. It must be borne in mind that many of the *beaux gestes* were performed in a spirit of braggadocio, typical of many gangsters, which is supposed to be a sure sign of big-heartedness.

5—We are also interested in the analysis of specific instances of the subject's behavior:

a) On page 14, why does he jump into the lagoon to save the boy of the other gang?

b) On pp. 26 and 28, why does he include in his story this discussion of whether Caroline is a virgin?

c) On p. 39, why does he give Caroline the gun and tell her to shoot?

5. (a) In spite of his inadequate inhibitions and disregard of consequences, he possessed a factual sobriety and realized that he might be tried for murder, if the fellow he threw from the bridge were drowned.

(b) To him the virginity of Caroline was an important matter. There may have been a little chivalry in this, but also it would titillate his vanity to have a virgin "fall" for him so completely. From what followed further, especially the indifference of her parents and even the cynicism of her father on the subject, as well as the bragging about her on the part of Karl's chums who knew her first, we may surmise she was a *demi-vierge*.

(c) He gave her the gun only after he "started to make up and square things. I told her I was sorry and a lot more mush and top it off, but not before I could see she was weakening" that he unlocked the safety catch and gave her the gun. It was in keeping with his air of bravado.

6—If the data of the case are not sufficient to enable you to answer the above questions as completely as you would wish, what kind of additional information do you regard as necessary for each question? By what means do you think such information should be secured? (For example, questionnaires, further interviewing, clinical examination, tests, study of the boy's family, etc.) What is your judgment as to the values and limitations of the kinds of data presented in the case?

6. From my acquaintance with autobiographies and diaries of criminals, I know enough to take many statements with a grain of salt. Often a mere *beau geste* is dwelt on to offset the callousness of confessed acts. The whitewashing urge is inherent in all recidivists.

In the present story, we have a rambling account that conceals more than reveals. Relatively unimportant particulars are gone into and significant details are omitted. Throughout, we wonder how old the boy was. Only once does he give the date, so that we figure out that he might have been 15 to 16 then. He blamed Caroline for his imprisonment at Joliet, but did not tell us how it all happened. He speaks of quarrels with her, her nagging, but does not give us the faintest idea what it was all about.

His kindness to the "cat woman" was a redeeming feature, but then she had mothered him and his companion, giving them "her last few pennies." His good behavior when under the influence of Mrs. Brandon, at the Cook County School, was also a ray of sunshine, but perhaps only a flash in the pan. He *could* be humored *for a time,* and had a spark of gratitude in him, but it would not turn the scale. He apparently liked to be independent in money matters, but can we praise him for giving the "cat woman" money, when he held up people to obtain it?

One of the most significant items in the story is his fight with the priest and calling him all sorts of names after he escaped through the window. Few catholic youngsters, even of the toughest sort, would be so devoid of respect. He nowhere speaks of any religious sentiments.

There is much more information that we need before venturing a final opinion. We don't know enough about the family. He seems to speak well of the father, and says he was a good provider, as well as a hard taskmaster. What would he have done with the boy, had he lived to see him in his teens?

Yes, questionnaires, clinical examinations, and especially ratings by those who knew the boy: his relatives, his brothers and sisters and chums. His photograph and handwriting would be interesting and probably revealing.

7—Do you believe that the analyses you have made are based on some particular theories of the nature of human conduct? If so, could you briefly indicate what they are?

7. Yes, I have a definite view as presented in my *Psychology of Character,* and *Personality, the Crux of Social Intercourse* as well as in many articles on the subject.

8—What does the case suggest along the line of
   a) research problems and
   b) experimental problems?

8. Research could be instituted along psychoanalytic lines, also through various expressive and projective methods (graphology, Rorschach test) but principally through a long series of experimental procedures, which the jail authorities would probably not allow.

9—Are there other comments you would like to make about the case study?

9. To my mind, the boy would have gotten into less mischief, if he had not found it so easy to commit crimes. It was difficult to catch him, and when caught, he could easily get his parole,

or make his getaway. In the reformatory, all he had to do was to go to school, eat and play, work very little outside of keeping the cottage clean — a task divided among 45 boys.

The boy supplies the clue when he says "I was you might say particular. I didn't want an errand boy's job, and wanted a man's job and also a man's wages. It's hard as hell for me to walk into an office and ask for a job. I just hate to do it. If I ask and the guy says 'nothing doing', I feel sorry as hell that I asked."

In other words, as a youngster, he wanted a man's wages so that he could indulge his appetites. Then he complains that as a thief, he could get no job. He might of course use an alias and not fear the consequences of Jean Valjean, but that doesn't appeal to him.

The most striking passage in this connection proving amply that crime is made easy for youngsters is the following quotation: "All the way home I was thinking what a big shot I'd be now (after having been in detention a little over a week). In reaching home, I seen the gang playing ball on Princeton Avenue, and when they saw me the game broke up. They all crowded around me as though I was the Prince of Wales and I had to tell them all about the place."

His philosophy of life — and that was scarcely picked up from the environment — is contained in the following statement which is typical of the desperado.

> Whenever I did anything, I never gave a thought to whether it was right or wrong, and never thought of the consequences. I knew what would happen if I was caught, but I let that take care of itself and figured ways whereas I wouldn't get caught. Ail I thought of was to pull what I was going to do, without getting caught myself and getting away from the place.

GLOSSARY

In order to avoid unnecessary repetition, only such terms as are not fully explained in the text will be found in the glossary.

ACCULTURATION: The adaptation of a mode of behavior or cultural element, on the part of one belonging to a definite culture, to that in a new environment, as the adoption of Stanley, as a name for a boy, in an American Polish family where he would have been christened Stanislaus, or Sydney, in the case of a Jewish boy named after his grandfather, Samuel.

ADEQUACY VALENCE: The particular constellation of traits from the different components of personality which constitute the worth of the individual (*insight, sentiment,* and *independence of character*).

AFFECT: Not to be confused with "effect"—is an emotion of considerable strength, brewed in the unconscious but without reference to the organic counterpart, so far as psychoanalysis is concerned.

ALLELOMORPH: Either of a pair of correlative Mendelian characters, e. g. stippled or black markings in an animal.

ALTERATION OF SELF: The complete change of a personality, so that an individual thus afflicted is unable to identify himself or herself during the period; condition of double or multiple personality.

AMBIVALENCE: An attitude consisting of contradictory emotions, such as love and hate, good wishes and malevolence, *toward the same person.*

[381]

ANTHROPOGEOGRAPHY: A term coined by Dr. Ellsworth Huntington as signifying the strip of territory between geography and anthropology, dealing especially with the influence of climate and seasons on man.

BEHAVIORISM: The school which either denies or discards consciousness as scientific subject matter and concentrates on the study of behavior as shown in muscular and glandular responses to stimuli as the only method of building up a science of psychology.

CYTOPLASM: The protoplasm of the cell, exclusive of the nucleus, which contains the chromosomes and genes.

COPROPHILIC: Literally "dirt-loving," inclined to handle or even taste refuse and excrement, as in the case of infants.

DIALECTICAL MATERIALISM: See *Historical Determinism*.

DIPHASIC PERSONALITY: A personality which reveals a different side to people of different classes or categories.

DISSOCIATION: Split-off states of consciousness found in abnormal individuals leading to double or multiple personality.

EGO: In psychoanalysis, not to be identified with conceit or self-aggrandizement, or domination, but representing the realistic side of our mental make-up, and coinciding with the ambitious, or professional, or esteem-seeking part of us; the governing control in us which usually aims to steer a middle course between the *Id* and the *Superego*.

ETHOS: The outlook of an ethnic group, which determines its social and ethical attitudes.

EUPHORIA: The state of heightened or exaggerated buoyancy and well-being, often found in the psychotic and in other deviates from the normal.

FACTOR THEORY: The view that there is, in intelligence and personality traits, a general reservoir with specific tributaries emanting from it, to explain the relationship of abilities and characteristics. The multimodal theory, which groups abilities, interests, and traits differently — and largely as specific — may also be spoken of as a *multi-factor theory.*

FRUSTRATION: The sense of failing in one's efforts, with a feeling of getting nowhere, expressing itself often in hostility toward others or a guilt complex ("taking it out" on oneself or others).

GAMETE: A biological term for any mature generative cell, which, when uniting with another like cell, forms the Zygote.

GESTALT PSYCHOLOGY: The psychological school which rejects the view that mental phenomena are built up of parts or elements, asserting, as it does, that the configuration or pattern as a whole is an indivisible unit.

GENOTYPICAL: Pertaining to or indicative of the inherited, but often latent, fundamentals of a personality, as contrasted with the phenotypical.

HISTORICAL DETERMINISM: The conception that everything which happens is determined by natural forces operating fortuitously. Dialectical materialism professes to introduce personal initiative and will as a factor in this process.

HABITUS: A bodily constitution or general appearance, as an apoplectic habitus.

HORMIC THEORY: The view, as taught by Wm. McDougall, that mental life is governed by a striving toward a goal, and implying an instinctive urge or thrust (horme).

ID: The reservoir of primitive and unorganized impulses (in the mind) which society frowns upon, and which the *Ego,* with the help of the *Superego,* as the individual develops, tames and checks.

IDIO-EMPIRICAL OCCURRENCE: An experience of a peculiarly personal nature (unlike the ordinary conditions of growing up which have a similar pattern) that exercises a potent influence on the outlook of the individual. (sight of murder, being kidnapped or raped)

INTRA-UTERINE: Within the uterus, as the phrase "intra-uterine experiences" of the fetus.

LEVEL OF ASPIRATION: A goal or standard one sets himself to attain, and which will be increased or reduced in accordance with given circumstances and the nature of the individual, thus giving us an insight into his personality.

MONOSYMPTOMATIC: Indicative of the presence of some quality or trait through one form of probing only, as in diagnosing a person's character from the facial features alone.

MONOZYGOTIC: Of one fertilized egg (as in identical twins).

PERSERVERATION: The tendency of any mental state or act to recur without any associative aid, based on the theory of the reverberation of a former nerve process.

PERSONALISM: A philosophical conception according to which the person is the foundation or core to be considered in all explanations and theories.

PHENOTYPICAL: *Manifest,* as contrasted with the fundamental ingredients of a personality, which do not come to the surface in social contacts.

"POLITBIOL": An assumed biological department which is dominated by the political ideology of a dictatorship, proletarian or otherwise.

PSYCHOGENIC: Of psychological origin (as contrasted with some thing of physical or organic origin) as in most mental ills.

REACTION FORMATION: The appearance of a trait in an individual in contrast with something which was hitherto characteristic of him/her, and which serves to cover up the repressed remnants of infantile development: thus a sloppy boy may become immaculate or a bully at some stage turns into a protective youth, etc.

RIGIDITY: The extent to which one organ or bodily region or system articulates with another. The concept is originally of *Gestalt* provenance, but has found a place in slightly differing connections in factorial theory as in Cattell's view of *rigidity disposition,* which is supposed to be a constitutional defect preventing the ego from shaping the id in accordance with environmental requirements.

SYNDROME: A group of signs or symptoms which, occurring together, point to the existence of a specific condition or ailment.

STRUCTURED: Divided or separated into distinguishable forms or attributes, as contrasted with *unstructured,* where the unit allows of no specific division except by means of the imagination and projection.

THALAMUS: A small chamber in the between-brain, where (especially in the hypothalamus) the emotional experience first develops.

TELEOLOGICAL: Pertaining to the theory that the world is ordered according to some plan or purpose in the mind of the creator.

TOPOLOGICAL: Pertaining to topology — a mathematical concept which deals with spatial relations, as part and whole, and the condition of being included within a space. K. Lewin has introduced the concept into psychology to designate the position of being inside or outside a particular region ("life space"). "Topological tools allow us to determine which events are possible in a given life space and which are not possible." K. Lewin: *Principles of Topological Psychology*.

VALENCE: The provocative character, either attracting or repelling, of an object or activity, as taught by *Gestalt* psychologists. The term was borrowed from chemistry where it relates to the degree in which one element can combine with another.

VECTOR: A directed magnitude as of a force or velocity. A concept introduced into psychology both by Kurt Lewin and L. L. Thurstone, but used in different connections.

XENOPHOBIC: Fearful of strangers, newcomers, immigrants, and thus exhibiting a complex of insecurity.

ZUKUNFTMUSIK: Literally "music of the future" — a matter, as yet, for time to decide or to bring to maturation.

ZYGOTE: The fertilized egg, formed by the union of two gametes.

BIBLIOGRAPHY

BIBLIOGRAPHY OF THE LITERATURE ON
PERSONALITY SINCE 1930

This Bibliography may be regarded as the second supplement of the present author's *A Bibliography of Character and Personality* published in 1927. The Bibliography in his *Personality; The Crux of Social Intercourse,* which appeared in 1931, was the first supplement. Most of the titles in the present Bibliography are recent. A few titles, which go back to an earlier date than 1931, were included because they were missing in the other two bibliographies.

It was thought best to exclude titles which are not directly concerned with the general subject of personality, but about a dozen *important* books and articles on the fundamentals of personality study, as in the case of the Rorschach and other methods, were thought of special relevance, particularly because of the discussion of the organization of traits contained therein.

A number of books and articles cited in the present book, either in the text or footnotes, are not listed here, since the bibliography is strictly on personality, while the quotations, though they apply to subject-matter in the book, are not out of literature dealing directly with personality.

Together with the titles in the previous bibliographies, the author has collected over 4000 titles on personality, including character and temperament. Many of the foreign titles are still on index cards.

1. ABEL, T. M.: "Free Designs of Limited Scope as a Personality Index." *Character & Pers.,* 1938, vol. 7, pp. 50-62.

2. ABELSON, H. H., and ELLIS, A.: "Other Devices for Investigating Personality." *Rev. of Educ. Res'ch.,* 1947, vol. 17.

3. ABRAMSON, H. A. & collaborators: *Non-projective Personality Tests.* N. Y.: Academy of Sciences, 1946.

4. ADAMS, H. F.: "The Good Judge of Personality." *Jour. of Abnorm. & Soc. Psychol.,* 1927, vol. 22.

5. ALBINO, R. C.: "The Stable and Labile Personality Types of Luriá in Clinically Normal Individuals." *British Jour. of Psychol.,* 1948, vol. 34, pp. 54-60.

6. ALLAN, D. M.: *The Realm of Personality.* N. Y.: Abingdon-Cokesbury, 1947.

7. ALLEN, A.: *The Self in Psychology; a Study in the Foundations of Personality.* London: Kegan Paul, 1935.

8. ALLPORT, G. W.: *Personality; a Psychological Interpretation.* N. Y.: H. Holt, 1937.

9. ALLPORT, G. W., and Cantril. H.: "Judging Personality from Voice." *Jour. of Soc. Psychol.,* 1934, vol. 5.

10. ALLPORT, G. W., and VERNON, P. E., *Studies in Expressive Movement* etc. N. Y.: Macmillan, 1933, pp. xiii + 269.

11. ALSCHULER, R. H., and HATTWICK, L. B. W.: "Easel Painting as an Index of Personality in Pre-school Children." *Am. Jour. of Orthopsychiat.,* 1943, vol. 13, pp. 616-625.

12. ALSCHULER, R. H., and HATTWICK, L. B. W.: *Painting and Personality. A Study of Young Children.* (vols. 1 & 2) Chicago: Univ. Chicago Press, 1947.

13. AMATORA, M.: "Some Elements in Teachers' and Pupils' Personalities." *Amer. Psychologist,* 1947, vol. 2.

14. ANASTASI, A.: "The Nature of Psychological 'Traits.' " *Psychol. Rev.* 1948, vol. 55, pp. 127-142.

15. ANDERSON, A. L.: "Personality Changes Folloing Prefrontal Lobotomy." *Jour. of Consult. Psychol.,* 1949, vol. 13, pp. 105-107.

16. ANDERSON, W. E.: "The Personality Characteristics of 153 Negro Pupils, Dunbar High School, Okmulgee, Oklahoma." *Jour. of Negro. Educ.,* 1947, vol. 16.

17. ANGYAL, A., *Foundations for a Science of Personality.* N. Y.: The Commonwealth Fund, 1941.

18. ARGELANDER, A.: "The Personal Factor in Judging Human Character." *Character and Pers.,* 1937, vol. 5.

19. ARLUCK, E. W.: *A Study of Some Personality Characteristics of Epileptics.* (Arch. of Psychol., 1941, No. 263, pp. 77).

20. ATREYA, B. L.: "Supernormal Factors in Human Personality." *Indian Jour. Psychol.,* 1943, vol. 18.

21. AVELING, F.: *Personality and Will.* N. Y.: Appleton, 1931.

22. AX, A. E.: "A Validation Study of the Rotter-Jensen Level of Aspiration Test." *Jour. of Personality,* 1946, vol. 15.

23. BALKEN, E. R.: "Projective Techniques for the Study of Personality." A Critique. *Psychol. Bull.,* 1941, vol. 38, p. 596—

24. BARNES, T. C., & AMOROSO, M. D.: "Electroencephalograms Correlated with Scores of the Bell Adjustment Inventory for Personality." *Fed. Proc.,* 1947, vol. 6.

25. BARR, A. A.: "Personnel, Teacher," in *Encyclopedia of Psychology,* (ed. by P. L. Harriman) N. Y. Philosophical Library, 1946, pp. 497-511.

26. BARRETT, DOROTHY M., & EATON, ELIZABETH B.: "Preference for Color or Tint and some Related Personality Data." *Jour. of Personality,* 1947, vol. 15.

27. BATESON, G.: "Cultural Determinants of Personality" in *Personality and Behavior Disorders,* vol. 2, (ed. by J. McV. Hunt,) N. Y.: Ronald, 1944, pp. 714-735.

28. BAUD, F.: *Physionomie et Caractère.* Paris: Presses Univ. de France, 1947.

29. BAUD, F.: *La Science des Caractères dans ses Rélations avec le Progrès Social.* Paris: Hermann, 1940.

30. BAUMGARTEN, F.: "Zur Psychologie der Agression." *Gesundh. u. Wohlfart,* 1947, vol. 27.

31. BAYET, A.: "Note sur L'Histoire du Mot 'Personne' " *Jour. de Psychologie,* etc. 1948, vol. 41.

32. BECK, S. J.: *Rorschach's Test,*
    vol. I. *Elementary Principles.* 1944.
    vol. II. *A Variety of Personality Pictures.* 1945.

33. BECKER, J.: *Einführung in die Charakterkunde.* Nürnberg, die Egge, 1947, pp. 118.

34. BECKHAM, A. S.: "Albinism in Negro Children." *Jour. of Genet. Psychol.,* 1946, vol. 69.

35. BELL, J. E.: *Projective Techniques; A Dynamic Approach to the Study of the Personality.* N. Y.: Longmans, 1948.

36. BENEDEK, T.: *Insight and Personality Adjustment.* N. Y.: Ronald, 1946.

37. BENNET, M. E.: *Designs for Personality.* N. Y.: McGraw-Hill, 1938.

38. BENTON, A. L.: *The Interpretation of Questionnaire Items in a Personality Schedule.* N. Y.: Archives of Psy. No. 190, 1935.

39. BERG, D. E.: *Personality Culture by College Faculties.* N. Y.: Institute for Public Service, 1920.

40. BERG, L.: *The Human Personality.* N. Y.: Prentice-Hall, 1933.

41. BERGLER, E.: "Personality Traits of Alcohol Addicts." *Quart. Jour. Stud. Alcohol,* 1946, vol. 7.

42. BERNREUTER, R. G.: *Personality Inventory.* Stanford University Press, 1931.

43. BERNREUTER, R. G.: "The Measurement of Self-sufficiency." *Jour. of Abnorm. Soc. Psychol.,* 1933, vol. 28, pp. 291—

44. BERNREUTER, R. G.: "Validity of the Personality Inventory." *Person. Jour.* 1933, vol. 11, pp. 383—

45. BERNREUTER, R. G.: "The Theory and Construction of the Personality Inventory." *Jour. of Soc. Psychol.*, 1933, vol. 4, pp. 387—

46. BERTOCCI, P. A.: "Personality," in *Encyclopedia of Psychology*, (ed. by P. L. Harriman, N. Y.: Philosophical Library, 1946, pp. 455-477.

47. BERWIN, B.: *Moses Mendelssohn im Urteil seiner Zeitgenossen.* (Kantstudien, Ergänzungshefte, 1919).

48. BIDDLE, R. A.: "The Construction of a Personality Inventory." *Jour. of Educ. Res'ch.*, 1948, vol. 41.

49. BLAKE, W. D.: "Measurement of Personality," in *Encyclop. of Psychology* (ed. by P. L. Harriman), N. Y., Philosophical Library, 1946, pp. 488-490.

50. BLANCHARD, P.: "Adolescent Experience In Relation to Personality and Behavior," in *Personality and Behavior Disorders,* vol. II, (ed. by J. McV. Hunt, N. Y.: Ronald, 1944.

51. BLOCH, H. A.: "The Personality of Inmates of Concentration Camps." *Amer. Jour. of Sociol.*, 1947, vol. 52.

52. BLOS, P.: *The Adolescent Personality.* N. Y.: Appleton, 1941.

53. BOGERT, L. J.: *Diet and Personality.* Garden City, N. Y.: Garden City Pub. Co., 1947.

54. BOLGAR, H. and FISHER, L. K.: "Personality Projection in the World Test." *Amer. Jour. of Orthopsychiat.*, 1947, vol. 17, pp. 117-128.

55. BOORMAN, W. R.: *Personality in its Teens.* N. Y.: Macmillan, 1931.

56. BOOTH, G. C.: "Objective Techniques in Personality Testing." *Arch. of Neurol. and Psychiat.*, Chicago, 1939, vol. 42, pp. 514-530.

57. BOOTH, G. C.: "Personality and Chronic Arthritis." *Jour. of Nerv. and Ment. Dis.*, 1937, vol. 85, pp. 637-662.

58. BOTT, H.: *Personality Development in Young Children.* Toronto: Univ. of Toronto Press, 1934.

59. BREYSIG, K.: *Das Recht auf Persönlichkeit und Seine Grenzen.* Berlin: Gruyter, 1944.

60. BRIDGES, J. W.: *Personality, Many in One.* Boston: Stratford, 1932.

61. BRIGHTMAN, E. S.: *Personality and Religion.* N. Y.: Abingdon, 1934.

62. BROWN, W.: *Science and Personality.* New Haven: Yale Univ. Press, 1929.

63. BROWN, W.: *Personality and Religion.* London: Univ. of London Press, 1946.

64. BRUNER, J. S., POSTMAN, L., and MCGINNIES, E.: "Personal Values as Determinants of Perceptual Selection." *Amer. Psychologist,* 1947, vol. 2.

65. BURGESS, E. W.: "The Delinquent as a Person." *Amer. Jour. of Sociology,* 1922-1923, vol. 28, p. 66—

66. BURGESS, E. W.: *"Personality and the Social Group.* Chicago: Univ. Press, 1929.

67. BURKHART, A. D.: *The Person in Religion,* etc. Philadelphia: (Thesis) Univ. of Penn., 1930.

68. BURKS, B. S.: "Personality Theories in Relation to Measurement." *Jour. of Soc. Psychol.,* 1936, vol. 7, p. 140—

69. BURKS, B. S.: "A Study of Identical Twins Reared Apart," in *Studies in Personality* in Honor of Lewis M. Terman).

70. BURLOUD, A.: *Le Caractère.* Paris: Presses Universitaires de France, 1942.

71. CABOT, P. S.: *The Relationship Between Characteristics of Personality and Physique in Adolescents.* Provincetown, Mass., The Journal Press, 1938.

72. CAMPBELL, C. M.: *Human Personality and the Environment*. N. Y.: Macmillan, 1934.

73. CANTRIL, H.: "The Place of Personality in Social Psychology." *Jour. of Psychol.*, 1947, vol. 24, pp. 19-56.

74. CANTRIL, H., and ALLPORT, G. W.: *The Psychology of Radio*. Harper, 1935, pp. 276.

75. CARTER, G. C.: *Student Personalities as Instructors See Them*. Lafayette, Ind.: Purdue Univ., 1945.

76. CASTELNUOVO-TEDESCO, P.: "Ratings of Intelligence and Personality from Handwriting." *Amer. Psychologist*, 1946, vol. 1.

77. CATTELL, R. B.: "Temperament Tests." *Brit. Jour. Psychol.*, 1933, vol. 23, p. 308.

78. CATTELL, R. B.: *Description and Measurement of Personality*. Yonkers: World Book Company, 1946, pp. xx + 602.

79. CATTELL, R. B.: "Oblique, Second Order, and Cooperative Factors in Personality Analysis." *Jour. of Gener. Psychol.*, 1947, vol. 36.

80. CATTELL, R. B.: "Primary Personality Factors in the Realm of Objective Tests." *Jour. of Person.*, 1948, vol. 16, pp. 459-487.

81. CAVAN, R. S., and CAVAN, J. T.: *Building a Girl's Personality*. N.Y.: Abingdon, 1932.

82. CHAMBERS, O. R.: "Character Trait Tests and the Prognosis of College Achievement." *Jour. Abnorm. Soc. Psychol.*, 1925, vol. 20, p. 303—

83. CHEIN, I.: "Behavior Theory and the Behavior of Attitudes." *Psychol. Rev.*, 1948, vol. 55.

84. CHI., P. L.: "Statistical Analysis of Personality Ratings." *Jour. Exp. Educ.*, 1937, vol. p. 229—

85. CHURCHMAN, C. W., and ACKOFF, R. L.: "Towards an

Experimental Measure of Personality." *Psychol. Rev.,* 1947, vol. 54.

86. Cobb, S.: "Personality as Affected by Lesions of the Brain," in *Personality and the Behavior Disorders,* vol. I, (ed. by J. McV. Hunt N. Y.: Ronald, 1944.

87. Cobb, S.: *Borderlands of Psychiatry.* Cambridge, Harvard Univ. Press, 1943.

88. Conrad, H. S.: "The Personal Equation in Ratings. I: An experimental Determination." *Jour. Genet.* Psychol., 1932, vol. 41, p. 267—

89. Conrad, H. S.: "The Personal Equation in Ratings. II: A Systematic Evaluation." *Jour. Educ. Psychol.,* 1933, vol. 24, p. 39—

90. Creegan, R. F.: "Personal Document Analysis," in *Encyclopedia of Psychology,* (ed. by P. L. Harriman) N. Y.: Philosophical Library, 1946. .

91. Crinis, M. de: "Der menschliche Gesichtsausdruck und seine klinische Bedeutung." *Forschung u. Fortschritt,* 1940, vol. 16, pp. 361-363.

92. Cronbach, L. J.: "A Validation Design for Qualitative Studies of Personality." *Jour. Consult. Psychol.,* 1948, vol. 12, pp. 365-374.

93. Cross, O. H.: "Braille Edition of the Minnesota Multiphasic Personality Inventory for Use with the Blind." *Jour. of Appl. Psychol.,* 1947, vol. 31.

94. Crutcher, R.: *Personality and Reason.* London: Favil, 1931.

95. Curran, C. A.: *Personality Factors in Counseling.* N. Y.: Grune and Stratton, 1945.

96. Dai, B.: "Some Problems of Personality Development among Negro Children." *Proc. Inst. Child Res'ch. Clin. Woods Schs.,* 1945, vol. 12.

97. DAVIDSON, H.: *Personality and Economic Background.* N. Y.: King's Crown, 1943.

98. DAVIS, C. E.: "Minnesota Multiphasic Personality Inventory." *Jour. of Clin. Psychol.,* 1947, vol. 3, pp. 298-301.

99. DELGADO, H.: *La Personalidad y el Carácter.* (2nd ed.) Lima: Editorial Lumen, 1946.

100. DIAMOND, S.: *A Study of the Influence of Political Radicalism on Personality Development.* N. Y.: (Archives of Psy., No. 203), 1936.

101. DITTRICH, O.: *Individualismus, Universalismus, Personalismus.* Berlin: Reuther and Reichard, 1917.
This was missed in my previous bibliographies.

102. DELAY, J.: *Les Dérèglements de L'humeur.* Paris: Presses Universitaires de France, 1946.

103. DESPERT, J. L.: "A Method for the Study of Personality Reactions in Preschool Age Children by means of Analysis of their Play." *Jour. of Psychol,* 1940, vol. 9, pp. 17-29.

104. DONAHUE, W. T.: "Interest and Personality Tests" in *An Introduction to Clinical Psychology.* (ed. by L. A. Pennington, and I. A. Ber, N. Y.: Ronald Press 1948.

105. DOWNEY, J. E.: "Familial Trends in Personality." *Character and Personality,* 1932, vol. 1, pp. 35—

106. DUFFY, E.: "Level of Muscular Tension as an Aspect of Personality." *Jour. of General Psychol.,* 1946, vol. 35.

107. DUFFY, E.: "A Systematic Framework for the Description of Personality." *Jour. of Abnorm. & Social Psychol.,* 1949, vol. 44, pp. 175-190.

108. DU MAS, F. M.: "On the Interpretation of Personality Profiles." *Jour. of Clin. Psychol.,* 1947, vol. 3, pp. 57-65.

109. EDWARDS, C. F.: "A Study of the Relationship of Spontaneity to Personality." *Speech Monogr.,* 1946, vol. 13.

110. ELLIS, A.: "Discussion of Heinlein's Comment on 'The Validity of Personality Questionnaires'." *Psychol. Bull.*, 1947, vol. 44.

111. DYSINGER, D. W.: "Signs of Personality Disintegration in *An Introduction to Clinical Psychology.* (ed. by L. A. Pennington, and I. A. Ber, N. Y.: Ronald Press, 1948.

112. ELLIS, A.: "Personality Questionnaires." *Rev. of Educ. Res'ch.*, 1947, vol. 17.

113. ELLIS, A.: "The Validity of Personality Questionnaires." *Psychol. Bull.*, 1946, vol. 43.

114. ESCALONA, S. K.: "An Application of the Level of Aspiration Experiment to the Study of Personality" *Teach. Coll. Contr. Educ.*, 1948, No. 937, pp. 132.

115. ESTES, S. G.: *The Judgment of Personality on the Basis of Brief Records of Behavior.* Ph.D. Thesis *(unpublished)* Harvard University Library, 1937.

116. EYSENCK, H. J.: *Dimensions of Personality.* London: Kegan Paul, 1947.

117. FISCHER, G. H.: *Ausdruck und Persönlichkeit.* Leipzig: Barth, 1934.

118. FISHER, V. E., and MARROW, A. J.: "Experimental Study of Moods." *Character and Personality,* 1934, vol. 2, p. 201—

119. FLANAGAN, J. C.: *Factor Analysis in the Study of Personality.* Stanford University Press, 1935.

120. FRANK, L. K.: "The Emergence of Personality." *Tr. N. Y. Acad. Sci.*, 1944, Ser. II, vol. 6, No. 5, pp. 149-156.

121. FRANK, L. K.: "Freedom for the Personality." *Psychiatry,* 1940, vol. 3, pp. 341-349.

122. FRANK, L. K.: "Personality and Rank Order." *Amer. Jour. of Sociol.*, 1929, vol. 35, pp. 177-186.

123. FRANK, L. K.: "Projective Methods for the Study of Per-

sonality." *Jour. Psychol.*, 1939, vol. 8, pp. 389-413. (Also in *Tr. N. Y. Acad. Sci.*, 1939, vol. 1, pp. 129-132),

124. FRANKL, V. E.: "Persönlichkeit und Verantwortung." *Schweiz. Zeitsch f. psychol. Anwend.*, 1947, vol. 6, p. 83—

125. FRANKLIN, G. H. & others: "Relationship of Total Bodily Movements to Some Emotional Components of Personality." *Jour. of Psychol.*, 1948, vol. 26, pp. 499-506.

126. FREEDMAN, H. L. and ROCKMORE, M. J.: "Marihuana; a Factor in Personality Evaluation and Army Maladjustment." *Jour. Clin. Psychopath and Psychother.*, 1946, vol. 7.

127. FREEMAN, W., and WATTS, J. W.: *Psychosurgery.* Springfield (Ill.), Thomas, 1942, pp. xii + 337.

128. FRENKEL-BRUNSWIK, ELSE, and SANFORD, R. N.: "The Anti-Semitic Personality; a Research Report" in *Anti-Semitism*, (ed. by E. Simmel). N. Y.: Internat. Universities Press, 1946.

129. GANNON, J. T.: *A Statistical Study of certain Diagnostic Personality Traits of College Men.* Washington, D. C.: Catholic Univ., 1939.

130. GARNETT, A. C.: *Instinct and Personality.* N. Y.: Dodd, Mead, 1928.
    Omitted in previous bibliographies by the present author.

131. GIBBS, C. A.: "Personality Traits by Factorial Analysis." *Austral. Jour. of Psychol. & Philos.*, 1942, vol. 20, pp. 1-15.

132. GILLIN, J.: "Personality Formation from the Comparative Cultural Point of View." *Proc. Inst. Child Res. Clin. Woods Schs.*, 1945, vol. 12.

133. GILLIS, H. W.: "A Study of some Characteristics of Successful Speech Majors." *Stanford Univ. Bul.*, 1945, Ser. 7, No. 119.

134. GOODENOUGH, F. L.: "The Use of Free Association in the Objective Measurement of Personality," in *Studies in Personality*, (in Honor of L. M. Terman) 1942.

135. GOODENOUGH, F. L.: "Semantic Choice and Personality Structure." *Science*, 1946, vol. 104, pp. 451-456.

136. GRAY, H.: "Jung's Psychological Types in Relation to Occupation, Race, Body-build." *Stanford Med. Bull.*, 1946, vol. 4.

137. GREGG, F. M.: *The Psychology of a Growing Personality*. Lincoln, Neb.: Personality Press, 1938.

138. GUILFORD, J. P., and GUILFORD, R. B.: "Personality Factors *S, E* and *M*, and their Measurement." *Jour. of Psychol.*, 1936, vol. 2, p. 109.

139. GULDE, C. and ROY, H. L.: "A Note on the Scoring of the Minnesota Multiphasic Personality Inventory." *Jour. of Consult.-Psychol.*, 1947, vol. 11, pp. 221-222.

140. GUTHRIE, E. R.: "Personality in Terms of Associate Learning," in *Personality and the Behavior Disorders*, vol. I, (ed. by J. McV. Hunt), N. Y.: Ronald, 1944, pp. 49-68.

141. HALL, C. S.: "Diagnosing Personality by the Analysis of Dreams." *Jour. Abnorm. & Soc. Psychol.*, 1947, vol. 42, pp. 68-79.

142. HAMLEY, H. R.: "Character Formation in Relation to Education," in *Modern Trends in Psychological Medicine*, (ed. by N. G. Harris). N. Y., Harper, 1949, pp. 450, pp. 335-346.

143. HART, H. N.: *Personality and the Family*. N. Y.: Heath, 1941.

144. HAVIGHURST, R. J. & others: "Personality Development." *Rev. of Educ. Res'ch.*, 1947, vol. 17, pp. 333-344.

145. HAVIGHURST, R. J. and H. TABA: *Adolescent Character and Personality*. N. Y.: Wiley, 1949, pp. 315.

146. HEALY, W.: *Personality in Formation and Action.* N. Y.: Norton, 1938.

147. HEATH, C. W.: *What People Are.* Cambridge, Harvard Univ. Press, 1945, pp. 141.

148. HEINLEIN, C. P.: "Comment on 'The Validity of Personality Questionnaires.'" *Psychol. Bull.,* 1947, vol. 44—

149. HENRY, W. E.: "An Exploration of the Validity and Usefulness of the Thematic Apperception Technique in the Study of Culture-personality Relations," *Univ. of Chicago Library,* 1947.

150. HILGARD, E. R.: "Human Motives and the Concept of Self." *Amer. Psychologist,* 1949, vol. 4, pp. 368-383.

151. HILL, J. M.: "Nailbiting; Incidence, Allied Personality Traits and Military Significance." *Amer. Jour. Psychiat.,* 1946, vol. 103.

152. HIRSCH, N. D.: *Twins; Heredity and Environment.* Cambridge, Harvard Univ. Press, 1930, pp. 159.

153. HOFFEDITZ, E. L.: "Family Resemblances in Personality Traits." *Jour. of Soc. Psychol.,* 1934, vol. 5, p. 214.

154. HOLLINGWORTH, H. L.: *Vocational Psychology and Character Analysis.* N. Y.: Appleton, 1929.

155. HOLT, E. B.: *Animal Drive and the Learning Process,* 1931.

156. HOLT, R. R.: "The Measurement of Self-insight and Some of its Personological Correlates." *Amer. Psychologist,* 1947, vol. 2.

157. HOOPINGARNER, N. L.: *Business Personality and Its Develment.* Vol. I. *Personality and Business Ability Analysis.* Vol. II. *Personality and Business Development.* Chicago & N. Y., Shaw, 1927.

158. HUNGERFORD, E.: *The Personality of American Cities.* N. Y.: McBride, Nast, 1913.

159. HUNT, J. McV.: *Personality and the Behavior Disorders.* vols. 1 & 2, N. Y.: Ronald, 1944.

160. HUNTINGTON, E.: *Season of Birth.* N. Y.: Wiley, 1938.

161. IBRAHIM, Z: "Non-integration of Personality." *Egypt. Jour. of Psychol.,* 1947, vol. 3, pp. 107-112. (*in Arabic*).

162. IRWIN, J. R.: "Galen on the Temperaments." *Jour. General Psychol.,* 1947, vol. 36.

163. JANET, P.: *L'évolution Psychologique de la Personnalité* etc. Paris: Chahine, 1929.
    A transcript of his lectures at the Collège de France.

164. JENNINGS, H. H.: *Leadership and Isolation, A Study of Personality in Interpersonal Relations.* N. Y.: Longmans, 1943.

165. JOHNSON, W. B.: "The Effect of Mood on Personality Traits as Measured by Bernreuter." *Jour. of Soc. Psychol.,* 1934, vol. 5, p. 515—

166. JOHNSON, W. B., and TERMAN, L. M.: "Personality Characteristics of Happily Married, Unhappily Married, and Divorced Persons." *Character and Personality,* 1935, vol. 3, p. 290—

167. JONES, E. S.: "Subjective Evaluations of Personality," in *Personality and the Behavior Disorders,* vol. I, (ed. by J. McV. Hunt, N. Y.: Ronald, 1944, pp. 139-169.

168. JONES, M. C., and BURKS, B. S.: *Personality Development in Childhood.* Washington, D. C.: National Research Council, 1936.

169. JONES, R. E.: "Personality Changes in Psychotics Following Prefrontal Lobotomy." *Jour. of Abnorm. and Social Psychol.,* 1949, vol. 44, pp. 315-328.

170. JONES, V.: "Character Development in Children—an Objective Approach" in *Manual of Child Psychology.* (ed. by L. Carmichael, N. Y.: Wiley, 1946, pp. 582-632.

171. JRGENSEN, J.: "Some Preliminary Remarks Concerning the Concept of Personality Types." *Acta Psychiat., Copenhagen,* 1946, vol. 21.

172. KAMIAT, A. H.: *Social Forces in Personality Stunting.* Cambridge, Mass.: Sci. Art., 1939, pp. 256.

173. KATZ, D., and ALLPORT, F. H.: *Students' Attitudes.* Syracuse, N. Y.: Craftsman Press, 1931.

174. KECKEISSEN, M. G.: "Moral Problems and Character Traits of High School Pupils." *Cath. Educ. Rev.*, 1947, vol. 45.

175. KEHL, R.: *Psicologia da Personalidade.* Rio de Janeiro, Alves [1941] pp. 354. (*in Portuguese*).

176. KELLY, E. L.: "Personality as related to Source and Adequacy of Sex Instruction," in *Studies in Personality* (*in Honor of L. M. Terman*), 1942.

177. KELLY, G. A., and BISHOP, F.: "A Projective Method of Personality Investigation." *Psychol. Bull.*, 1942, vol. 39.

178. KIMBER, J. A. M.: "Interests and Personality Traits of Bible Institute Students." *Amer. Psychologist,* 1946, vol. 1.

179. KINDER, E. F.: "Development of Personality Characteristics." *Amer. Psychologist,* 1947, vol. 2.

180. KLEIN, G. S.: "A Clinical Perspective for Personality Research." *Jour. of Abnorm. & Soc. Psychol.*, 1949, vol. 44, pp. 42-49.

181. KLOPFER, W. G.: "Personality Patterns of Old Age." *Rorschach Res'ch., Exch.,* 1946, vol. 10.

182. KLUCKHOHN, C. and MOWRER, O. H.: "Personality and Culture — a Conceptual Scheme." *Amer. Anthropol.*, 1944, vol. 46.

183. KLUCKHOHN, C.: *Mirror for Man.* Whittlesey House, 1949.

184. KROUT, M. H.: "A Preliminary Note on Some Obscure Symbolic Muscular Responses of Diagnostic Value in the Study of Normal Subjects." *Amer. Jour. of Psychiat.*, 1931, vol. 11, pp. 29-71.

PERSONALITY

185. Krout, M. H.: *Major Aspects of Personality.* Chicago: College Press, 1933, pp. xviii + 364.

186. Kubie, L. S. & R. H.: "Destructive Personalities." *Applied Anthrop.,* 1948, vol. 7, pp. 36-40.

187. Laird, J.: *Problems of the Self.* London: Macmillan, 1917. This title is missing in the previous bibliographies by the present author.

188. Landis, C.: *Personality and Sexuality of the Physically Handicapped Woman.* N. Y.: Hoeber, 1942.

189. La Rue, D. W.: *Educational Psychology; Personality and What Shapes It.* N. Y.: Nelson, 1939.

190. Lashley, K. S.: *Studies in the Dynamics of Behavior.* Chicago: University, 1932.

191. Lashley, K. S.: "Structural Variation in the Nervous System in Relation to Behavior." *Psychol. Review,* 1947, vol. 54.

192. Laslett, H. R., and Bennett, E.: "A Comparison of Scores on Two Measures of Personality." *Jour. of Abnorm. & Soc. Psychol.,* 1934, vol. 28, p. 459—

193. LeBreton, M.: "Problème du Moi et Technique du Roman Chez Virginia Woolf." *Jour. d. Psychologie,* etc., 1947, vol. 40, pp. 20-34.

194. Lecky, P.: *Self-consistency, a Theory of Personality.* N. Y.: Island, 1945.

195. Ledgerwood, R.: "Vector Theory of Dynamic Personality Structure." *Jour. of Gen. Psychol.,* 1949, vol. 40, pp. 119-120.

196. Lemarié, O.: *Essai sur la Personne.* Paris: Alcan, 1936.

197. Lentz, T. F.: "Utilizing Opinion for Character Measurement." *Jour. of Social Psychol.,* 1930, vol. 1, p. 536—

198. Lerner, E., Murphy, L., Stone, L. J., Beyer, E., and

BROWN, E.: "Studying Child Personality." *Monogr. Social Res'ch. Child Develpm.*, 1941, vol. 6, No. 4.

199. LESENNE, R.: *Traité de caractérologie*. Paris: Presses Universitaires de France, 1946.

200. LEVINSON, D. J.: " 'Projective Questions' in the Study of Personality and Ideology." *Amer. Psychologist*, 1947, vol. 2, p. 288.

201. LEWIN, K.: *A Dynamic Theory of Personality*. N. Y.: McGraw-Hill, 1935.

202. LEWISOHN, A.: *Painters and Personality*, (rev. ed.) 1948

203. LICHT, M.: "The Measurement of One Aspect of Personality." *Jour. of Psychol.*, 1947, vol. 24.

204. LINK, H. C.: *The Rediscovery of Man*, 1947. N. Y.: Dutton, pp. 223.

205. LINTON, R.: *The Cultural Background of Personality*. N. Y.: Appleton-Century, 1945.

206. LLINAS, P. A.; "La Personalidad Psíquica del Libertador Simón Bolívar." *Rev. Med. Legal Colombia*, 1946, vol. 8.

207. LLOYD, W.: "Some Aspects of Language as Significant of Personality." *Psychol. Bull.*, 1941, vol. 38, p. 747.

208. LUBORSKY, L. B. & CATTELL, R. B.: "The Validation of Personality Factors in Humor." *Jour. of Person.*, 1947, vol. 15, pp. 283-291.

209. MCCARTHY, T. J.: *Personality Traits of Seminarians*. Washington, D. C.: Catholic Univ. Press, 1942.

210. MACKINNON, D.: "The Structure of Personality," in *Personality and the Behavior Disorders*, vol. I, (ed. by J. McV. Hunt, N. Y.: Ronald, 1944, pp. 3-48.

211. MAGOUN, F. A.: *Balanced Personality*. N. Y.: Harper, 1943.

212. MALLER, J. B.: "Personality Tests," in *Personality and the Behavior Disorders*, vol. I, (ed. by J. McV. Hunt), N. Y.: Ronald, 1944, 170-213.

213. MANSON, M. P., and GRAYSON, H. M.: "Keysort Method of Scoring the Minnesota Multiphasic Personality Inventory." *Jour. Appl. Psychol.,* 1946, vol. 30.

214. MARKEY, S. C.: "Consistency of Descriptive Personality Phrases in the Forced Choice Technique." *Amer. Psychologist,* 1947, vol. 2.

215. MARQUIT, S.: "A Technique of Inquiry into Individual Personality." *Psychol. Bull.,* 1941, vol. 38.

216. MARTIN, A. R.: "A Study of Parental Attitudes and their Influence upon Personality Development." *Educ.,* 1943, pp. 1-13.

217. MARTIN, G. C.: "A Factor Analysis of the Bernreuter Personality Inventory." *Educ. Psychol. Measm't,* 1948, vol. 8.

218. MARTIN-CHAUFFIER, L.: "Proust and The Double 'I'." *Partisan Review,* 1949, vol. 16, pp. 1011-1026.

219. MASLOW, A. H.: "Dynamics of Personality Organization." *Psychol. Rev.,* 1943, vol. 50, pp. 514-539, 541-558.

220. MAY, M. A.: "The Foundations of Personality" in *Psychology at Work* (edited by P. S. Achilles) 1932.

221. McCLATCHY, V. R.: "A Theoretical and Statistical Study of the Personality Trait, Originality, as herein Defined." *Jour. of Abnorm. & Soc. Psychol.,* 1928, vol. 23.

222. MEAD, M.: "The Cultural Approach to Personality," in *Encyclop. of Psychol.,* (ed. by P. L. Harriman), pp. 477-488.

223. MEAD, M.: "Age Patterning in Personality Development." *Amer. Jour. Orthopsychiat.,* 1947, vol. 17.

224. MEEHL, P. E.: "An Investigation of a General Normality or Control Factor in Personality Testing." *Psychol. Monogr.,* 1945, vol. 59.

225. MELVIN, A. G.: *Building Personality.* N. Y.: Day, 1934.

226. MONS, W.: *Principles and Practice of the Rorschach Personality Test.* London: Faber, 1947, pp. 164.

227. MOORE, THOMAS V., STAFFORD, JOHN W., and HSU, EN HSI: "Obverse Analysis of Personality." *Jour. of Personality,* 1947, vol. 16.

228. MORENO, J. L., and JENNINGS, H.: "Spontaneity Training, a Method of Personality Development." *Sociometric Rev.,* 1936.

229. MORRIS, C. W.: *Signs, Language and Behavior,* 1946.

230. MORRIS, C. W.: *The Open Self, 1948.*

231. MOTTRAM, V. H.: *The Physical Basis of Personality.* N. Y.: Penguin, 1944.

232. MOUNIER, E.: *Traité du caractère.* Paris: Editions du Seuil, 1946.

233. MOWRER, O. H.: and KLUCKHOHN, C. "Dynamic Theory of Personality," in *Personality and the Behavior Disorders,* (ed. by J. McV. Hunt), N. Y.: Ronald, 1944, vol. I, pp. 69-131.

234. MUNRO, W. B.: *Personality in Politics,* N. Y.: Macmillan, 1924.
Omitted in previous bibliographies by the present author.

235. MURPHY, G. and JENSEN, F.: *Approaches to Personality.* N. Y.: Coward-McCann, 1932.

236. MURPHY, G.: *Personality.* N. Y.: Harper, 1947.

237. MURPHY, L. B.: "Childhood Experience in Relation to Personality Development," in *Personality and Behavior Disorders,* (ed. by J. McV. Hunt), N. Y.: Ronald, 1944, vol. 2, pp. 652-690.

238. MURPHY, L. B.: "The Appraisal of Child Personality." *Jour. of Consult. Psychol.,* 1948, vol. 12.

239. MURRAY, H. A.: "Effect of Fear on Estimates of Maliciousness of other Personalities," in *Contemporary Psycho-*

pathology, (ed. by S. S. Tomkins). Cambridge: Harvard Univ. Press, 1943, pp. 545-561.

240. MURRAY, H. A. and others: *Explorations in Personality*, N. Y.: Oxford Univ. Press, 1938.

241. MURRAY, H. A. and KLUCKHOHN, C.: (Editors) *Personality in Nature, Society and Culture.* N. Y.: Knopf, 1948, pp. xxi + 561.

242. NAPOLI, P. J.: "Finger-Painting and Personality Diagnosis." *Genet. Psychol. Monogr.*, 1946, vol. 34.

243. NEVER, M. L.: "Persönlighetstyper." *Norsk Pedag. Tidskr.*, 1947, vol. 6 (in Danish).

244. NEWCOMB, T. M.: *Personality and Social Change.* N. Y.: Dryden, 1943.

245. NEWMAN, I.: "Character Types" *Amer. Jour. of Psychother*, 1948, vol. 2, pp. 372-382.

246. NIMKOFF, M. F.: "Personality Development," in *Encyclopedia of Psychology*, (ed. by P. L. Harriman). N. Y.: Philosophical Library, 1946.

247. NORTHWAY, M. L.: "Personality and Sociometric Status; a Review of the Toronto Studies." *Sociometry*, 1946, vol. 9.

248. OAKS, R. E.: "The Child: his Painting and his Personality." *Childh. Educ.*, 1946, vol. 24.

249. O'GORMAN, W. D. & KUNKLE, E. C.: "Study of the Relation Between Minnesota Multiphasic Personality Inventory Scores and 'pilot error' in aircraft Accidents." *Jour. Aviat. Med.*, 1947, vol. 18, pp. 31-38.

250. PEAR, T. H.: "Personality in its Cultural Context." *Bull. John Rylands Libr., Manchester*, 1946, vol. 30.

251. PEILLAUBE, E.: *Caractère et Personnalité.* Paris: Tequi, 1935.

252. PENROSE, L. S.: "Heredity"; in *Personality and the Be-*

havior Disorders, (ed. by J. McV. Hunt), N. Y.: Ronald, 1944, vol. I.

253. PÉRIOT, M.: *Hippocrate avait Raison; Synthèse de la Personnalité Humaine par le Tempérament.* Marseilles: Leconte, 1941.

254. PETO, ENDRE: "The Psycho-Analysis of Identical Twins— with Reference to Inheritance." *Intern. Jour. of Psycho-Anal.,* 1946, vol. 27.

255. PLANT, J. S.: *Personality and the Cultural Pattern.* N. Y.: Commonwealth Fund, 1937.

256. PRADOS, M.: "Personality Studies of Homosexuals." *Rev. Psychol., Montreal,* 1946, vol. 1.

257. PREU, P. W.: "The Concept of Psychopathic Personality," in *Personality and the Behavior Disorders,* (ed. by J. McV. Hunt). N. Y.: Ronald, 1944, vol. I, pp. 922-937.

258. PRINCE, M.: *Clinical and Experimental Studies in Personality* (edited by A. A. Roback) 2nd edition, Cambridge, Sci-Art, 1939, pp. 672.

259. PRINZHORN, H.: *Persönlichkeits-psychologie.* Leipzig: Quelle & Meyer, 1932.

260. PULLIAS, E. V.: "Notes on Personality Development," *Ment. Hyg.,* 1948, vol. 32, pp. 261-270.

261. RABIN, A. I.: "Effects of Electric Shock Treatment upon some Aspects of Personality and Intellect." *Amer. Psychologist,* 1947, vol. 2.

262. RAMM, K. M.: "Personality Maladjustment among Monotones." *Smith Coll. Stud. Soc. Wk.* 1947, vol. 17.

263. RAMZY, I.: "Personality tests: II. Rorschach Test." *Egypt. Jour. Psychol.,* 1946, vol. 2.

264. RAND, H. A.: *Graphology; a Handbook.* (Introduction by A. A. Roback), Cambridge, Mass.: Sci-Art Publishers 1947, pp. 200.

[409]

265. READ, H.: "The Personality of the Poet," in *Collected Essays in Literary Criticism*. London: Faber, [1938], pp. 366.

266. REQUARD, F.: "Physik und Erbcharakter." *Zeitschr. f. d. ges. naturwiss'ft*, 1940, vol. 6, pp. 172-184.

267. REVERS, W. J.: *Persönlichkeit und Vermassung*. Würzburg: Schönengh, 1947.

268. RHEINFELDER, H.: *Das Wort 'Persona.'* Beihefte zur Zeitsch. f. roman. Philologie, 1928, No. 77, pp. 200.

269. RIBBLE, M. A.: "Infantile Experience in Relation to Personality Development," in *Personality and Behavior Disorders*, (ed. by J. McV. Hunt), N. Y.: Ronald, 1944, vol. II, pp. 621-651.

270. RICHMOND, W. V.: *Personality: its Development and Hygiene*. N. Y.: Farrar & Rinehart, 1937.

271. ROBACK, A. A.: "Meaning in Personality Manifestations." *Ninth International Congress of Psychology* (Proceedings and Papers), 1930, pp. 362-363.

272. ROBACK, A. A.: *Personality; The Crux of Social Intercourse*. Cambridge, Sci.-Art, 1931, pp. 144.

Contains a bibliography of 128 titles, not included in the present bibliography.

273. ROBACK, A. A.: "Personality Tests—Whither?" *Character and Personality*, 1933, vol. 1, pp. 214-224.

274. ROBACK, A. A.: "Peretz's Treatment of Personality," in *I. L. Peretz, Psychologist of Literature*, 1935, Cambridge, Sci-Art, pp. 356-383.

275. ROBACK, A. A.: *The Psychology of Common Sense*. Cambridge, Sci-Art, 1939, pp. 350.

276. ROBACK, A. A.: *The Psychology of Character* (3rd revised and enlarged edition). London: Routledge & Kegan Paul, 1950, pp. 724.

277. ROE, A.: "Painting and Personality." *Rorschach Res. Exch.*, 1946, vol. 10.

278. ROE, A.: "Personality and Vocation." *Trans. N. Y. Acad. Sci.*, 1947, vol. 9.

279. ROE, A.: "The Personality of Artists." *Educ. Psychol. Measm't*, 1946, vol. 6.

280. ROGERS, C. R.: "Some Observations on the Organization of Personality." *Amer. Psychol.* 1947, vol. 2, pp. 358-368.

281. ROHDE, A. R.: "Explorations in Personality by the Sentence Completion Method." *Jour. of Applied Psychology*, 1946, vol. 30, pp. 169-181.

282. ROHRACHER, H.: *Persönlichkeit und Schicksal,* Wien: Braumüller, 1926.
    Omitted in the author's previous bibliographies.

283. RORSCHACH, H.: *Psychodiagnostik.* Bern, Huber, 1921 (2d. ed. 1932) also translated into English, 1942.

284. ROSENZWEIG, S.: "Fantasy in Personality and its Study by Test Procedures." *Jour. of Abnorm. Soc. Psychol.*, 1942, vol. 37, pp. 40-51.

285. ROSSILLI, V. D.: "A Study and Evaluation of the use of Drama as an Aid to Personality Development and Speech Correction." *Speech Monogr.*, 1946, vol. 13.

286. ROTHACKER, E.: *Die Schichten der Persönlichkeit.* Leipzig: Barth, 1938.

287. ROTTER, J. B. and WILLERMAN, B.: "The Incomplete Sentences Test as a Method of Studying Personality." *Jour. of Consult. Psychol.*, 1947, vol. 11.

288. RUESCH, JURGEN, & BOWMAN, KARL M.: "Personality and Chronic Illness." *Jour. Amer. Med. Ass.*, 1948, vol. 136.

289. RUNDQUIST, E. A., and SLETTO, R. F.: *Personality in the Depression.* University of Minnesota Press, 1936.

290. RUTTEN, T.: "Persoonlijkheid in de Spiegel der Samen-leving," in *Miscellanea Psychologica Albert Michotte,* pp. 391-411, (*in Dutch*) "Personality in the Mirror of Social Life."

291. RYLANDER, G.: *Personality Changes after Operations on the Frontal Lobe.* London: Oxford, 1939, pp. 327.

292. SALTER, J. A.: *Personality in Politics.* London: Faber, 1947.

293. SAPIR, E.: "The Emergence of the Concept of Personality in a Study of Culture." *Jour, of Soc. Psychol.,* 1934, vol. 5, pp. 408-415.

294. SANFORD, F. H.: "Speech and Personality: a Comparative Case Study." *Character & Personality,* 1942, vol. 10, pp. 169-198.

295. SANFORD, F. H.: "Speech and Personality." *An Introduction to Clinical Psychology.* (ed. by L. A. Pennington, and I. A. Berg) N. Y.: Ronald Press, 1948.

296. SARGENT, H.: "Projective Methods: their Origins, Theory and Application in Personality Research." *Psychol. Bull.,* 1945, vol. 42, pp. 257-293.

297. SAUL, L. J.: *Emotional Maturity; the Development and Dynamics of Personality.* Philadelphia: Lippincott, 1947.

298. SCHAER, K. F.: "Blutgruppe, Charakter, Konstitution." *Schweiz. Zeitschr. f. Psychol. Anwend.,* 1942, vol. 1, pp. 75-80.

299. SCHETTLER, C.: "Objective Measurements of Personality Traits." *Jour. Personality,* 1947, vol. 15, pp. 292-299.

300. SCHILLER, L.: "Ganzheitliche Auffassung und Persönlich-keitstypus." *Ztschr. f. Psychol.,* 1942, vol. 153, pp. 43-80.

301. SCHNEIDER, E.: *Psychologie der Person.* Stuttgart: Enke, 1947.

302. SCHOEN, M.: *Human Nature,* 1930.

303. SCHOTTKY, J. (ed.): *Die Persönlichkeit im Lichte der Erblehre.* Leipzig: Teubner, 1936.

304. SCOTT-JAMES, R. A.: *Personality in Literature.* London: Secker, 1913.
A misnomer.

305. SEARS, R. R.: "Personality Development in Contemporary Culture." *Proc. Amer. Phil. Soc.,* 1948, vol. 92, pp. 363-370.

306. SHANNON, J. R.: "Traits of Research Workers." *Jour. Educ. Res.,* 1947, vol. 40.

307. SHEERER, E. T.: "The Relationship Between Acceptance of Self and Acceptance of Others." *Jour. of Consult. Psychol.,* 1949, vol. 13, pp. 169-175.

308. SHEFFIELD, A. E.: *Case Study Possibilities.* Boston, 1922.

309. SHELDON, W. H.: *The Varieties of Human Physique; an Introduction to Constitutional Psychology.* N. Y.: Harper, 1940.

310. SHELDON, W. H.: *Varieties of Human Temperament.* N. Y.: Harper, 1942, pp. x + 520.

311. SHELDON, W. H.: "Constitutional Factors in Personality," in *Personality and the Behavior Disorders,* (ed. by J. McV. Hunt), N. Y.: Ronald, 1944, vol. I.

312. SHIPLEY, W. C., GRAY, F. E., and NEWBERT, N.: "The Personal Inventory — its Derivation and Validation." *Jour. Clin. Psychol.,* 1946, vol. 2.

313. SHUEY, A. M.: *Personality Traits of Jewish and Non-Jewish Students.* N. Y.: (Arch. of Psychol., 1944 No. 290).

314. SKAGGS, E. B.: "Ten Basic Postulates of Personalistic Psychology." *Psychol. Rev.* 1947, vol. 54.

315. SLETTO, R. F.: "A Critical Study of the Criterion of Internal Consistency in Personality Scale Construction." *Amer. Sociol. Rev.,* 1936, vol. 1.

316. SLETTO, R. F.: *Construction of Personality Scales by the Criterion of Internal Consistency.* Hanover, N. H.: Sociological Press, 1937.

317. SMITH, B. M. and HUMPHREY, B. M.: "Some Personality Characteristics Related to ESP Performance." *Jour. Parapsychol.,* 1946, vol. 10, pp. 269-289.

318. SPOERL, D. T.: "Personality and Drawing in Retarded Children." *Character & Personality,* 1940. vol. 8, pp. 227-239.

319. STAGNER, R.: *Psychology of Personality.* N. Y.: McGraw-Hill, 1937. 2d. ed. 1948.

320. STEARNS, A. W.: "Unfit Personalities in the Military Services," in *Personality and the Behavior Disorders,* (ed. by J. McV. Hunt), N. Y.: Ronald, 1944, vol. II, pp. 822-832.

321. STEIN, M. I.: "The Use of A Sentence Completion Test for the Diagnosis of Personality." *Jour. of Clin. Psychol.,* 1947, vol. 3, pp. 47-56.

322. STERN, K., and PRADOS, M.: "Personality Studies in Menopausal Women." *Amer. Jour. of Psychiat.,* 1946, vol. 103.

323. STERN, L. W.: *Studien zur Personwissenschaft.* Leipzig: Barth, 1930.

324. STEVENSON, G. S.: "The Prevention of Personality Disorders," in *Personality and the Behavior Disorders,* (ed. by J. McV. Hunt, N. Y.: Ronald, 1944; vol. II, pp. 1164-1192.

325. STOCK, D.: "The Self Concept and Feelings Toward Others." *Jour. of Consult. Psychol.,* 1949, vol. 13, pp. 176-180.

326. SVENSON, GUNNAR: "The Creation of Ideals: a Question of the Energy-Distribution in the Personality Field." *Jour. of General Psychol.,* 1947, vol. 37.

327. SYMONDS, P. M.: *Diagnosing Personality and Conduct.* N. Y.: Century, 1931.

328. SYMONDS, P. M.: *Psychological Diagnosis in Social Adjustment.* N. Y.: Amer. Book Co., 1934.

329. SYMONDS, P. M.: "Evaluation of Teacher Personality." *Teach. Coll. Rec.,* 1946, vol. 48.

330. SYMONDS, P. M., and SAMUEL, E. A.: "Projective Methods in the Study of Personality." *Rev. of Educ. & Res'ch.,* 1941, vol. 11, pp. 80-93.

331. TAYLOR, H. C.: "Social Agreement on Personality Traits as Judged from Speech." *Jour. of Soc. Psychol.,* 1934, vol. 5, p. 244—

332. TERMAN, L. M., and MILES, C. C.: *Sex and Personality.* N. Y.: McGraw-Hill, 1936.

333. TERMAN, L. M.: (Contributed in Honor of) *Studies in Personality,* 1942.
    The most relevant studies are listed separately.

334. THOMSON, D.: *Personality in Politics.* N. Y.: Nelson, 1939.

335. THORPE, L. P.: *Personality and Life.* N. Y.: Longmans, 1941.

336. THORPE, L. P.: *Psychological Foundations of Personality.* N. Y.: McGraw-Hill, 1938.

337. TOLMAN, E. C.: *Purposive Behavior in Animals and Men.* N. Y.: Century, 1932.

338. TOLMAN, C. C.: *Drives Toward War.* N. Y.: Appleton-Century, 1942.

339. TRESSELT, M. E.: "A Study of the Factors in the Identification of Handwriting." *Jour. of Soc. Psychol.* 1946, vol. 24.

340. TYLER, H. T.: *The Bearing of Certain Personality Factors Other Than Intelligence on Academic Success.* N. Y.: Columbia Univ., 1931.

341. TYRRELL, G. N. M.: *The Personality of Man*. West Drayton, Middlesex: Penquin, 1948.

342. URIBE, C. G.: "Simón Bolívar y su Personalidad genial." *Rev. Med. Legal Colombia,* 1946. vol. 8.

343. VAUGHAN, R. M.: *The Significance of Personality.* N. Y.: Macmillan, 1930.

344. VERNON, P. E.: "Tests of Temperament and Personality." *Brit. Jour. Psychol.,* 1929, vol. 20.

345. VERNON, P. E.: "Some Characteristics of the Good Judge of Personality." *Jour. of Social Psychol.,* 1933, vol. 4.

346. VERNON, P. E.: "The measurement of Personality and Temperament." *Human Factor,* 1934, vol. 8.

347. VERNON, P. E.: "The Attitude of the Subject in Personality Testing." *Jour. of Appl. Psychol.,* 1934, vol. 18.

348. VERNON, P. E.: "The Matching Method Applied to investigations of Personality." *Psychol. Bull.,* 1936, vol. 33.

349. VERNON, P. E.: *The Assessment of Psychological Qualities by Verbal Methods* — A survey of Attitude Tests, Rating Scales and Personality Questionnaires, London: 1938, pp. 124.

350. VERNON, P. E., and ALLPORT, G. W.: "A Test for Personal Values." *Jour. of Abnormal & Soc. Psychol.,* 1931, vol. 26.

351. WALLACE, W. J.: "Personality Variation in a Primitive Society." *Jour. of Personality,* 1947, vol. 15, pp. 321-328.

352. WEKSTEIN, L.: "X-raying the Personality." *Scient. Monthly,* 1947, vol. 65, pp. 133-142.

353. WELLS, F. L.: "Evaluation of Personality and Character Tests." *Amer. Jour. of Orthopsychiatry,* 1932, vol. 2, pp. 327-334.

354. WELLS, F. L.: "Personal History, Handwriting, and Specific Behavior." *Jour. of Personality,* 1946, vol. 14, pp. 295-314.

355. WERNER, H.: "William Stern's Personalistics and Psychology of Personality." *Character and Personality*, 1938, vol. 7, pp. 109-125.

356. WHEATLEY, L. A. and SUMNER, F. C.: "Measurement of Neurotic Tendency in Negro Students of Music." *Jour. of Psychol.*, 1946, vol. 22.

357. WILKIE, J. S.: "An Experiment on Reading Character from Portraits." *Jour. of General Psychol.*, 1949, vol. 40, pp. 11-35.

358. WILLOUGHBY, R. R., and MORSE, M. E.: "Spontaneous Reactions to a Personality Inventory." *Amer. Jour. of Orthopsychiat.*, 1936, vol. 6.

359. WILLOUGHBY, R. R.: "A Note on Personality Factors Affecting the Rehabilitation of Problem Families," in *Studies in Personality* (in Honor of Lewis M. Terman), 1942.

360. WINFREY, M. E.: *A Personality Study of College Girls.* Nashville, Tenn.: Peabody College, 1936.

361. WINTHROP, H.: "Semantic Factors in the Measurement of Personality Integration." *Jour. of Soc. Psychol.*, 1946, vol. 24.

362. WINTHROP, H.: "Two Concepts of Personality Disintegration." *Jour. of General Psychol.*, 1949, vol. 40, pp. 177-218.

363. WOLF, R., and MURRAY, H. A.: "An Experiment in Judging Personalities." *Jour. of Psychol.*, 1936, vol. 3.

364. WOLFF, W.: "Projective Methods for Personality Analysis of Expressive Behavior in Preschool Children." *Character & Personality*, 1942, vol. 10, pp. 309-330.

365. WOLFF, W.: *The Expression of Personality.* N. Y.: Harper, 1943.

366. WOLFF, W.: *The Personality of the Pre-school Child; the Child's Search for his Self.* N. Y.: Grune and Stratton, 1946

367. WOLFF, W.: *Diagrams of the Unconscious; Handwriting and Personality in Measurement, Experiment, and Analysis,* N. Y.: Grune & Stratton, 1948.

368. WOODRUFF, A. D.: "The Concept-value Theory of Human Behavior." *Jour. of General Psychol.,* 1949, vol. 40, pp. 141-154.

369. WOODWORTH, R. S.: *Heredity and Environment.* Social Science Research Council, 1941, Bulletin 47, pp. 90.

370. YOUNG, K.: "Variations in Personality Manifestations in Mormon Polygynous Families" in *"Studies in Personality* (in Honor of Lewis M. Terman), 1942.

ADDENDA

371. ALLPORT, G. W.: *The Use of Personal Documents in Psychological Science,* N. Y.: Social Science Res'ch Council, 1942.

372. BOWLBY, J.: *Personality and Mental Illness.* N. Y.: Emerson Books, 1942.

373. BRINKMANN, D.: "Uber das Grundprinzip der Psychologischen Typerlehre," *Schweiz. Zeitschr. f. Psychol. Anwendung,* 1948, vol. 7, pp. 191-207.

374. BURT, C.: "The Factorial Study of Temperamental Traits." *Brit. Jour. of Psychol.,* (Statist. Sect.), 1948, vol. 1, pp. 178-203.

375. CATTELL, R. B.: "The Primary Personality Factors in Women Compared with those in Men." *Brit. Jour. Psychol.,* (Statist, Sect.), 1948, vol. 1, pp. 114-130.

376. CREEGAN, R. F.: "The Phenomenological Analysis of Personal Documents." *Jour. of Abnorm. & Soc. Psychol.,* 1944, vol. 39.

377. HUNT, E. E., Jr.: "A Note on Growth, Somatotype, and Temperament." *Amer. Jour. & Phys. Anthrop.,* 1949, vol. 7, pp. 79-89.

378. GOLDBERG, L. H.: "The Biology of Temperament." *Jour. Aviat. Med.,* 1949, vol. 20, pp. 120-123; 129.

379. Janse de Jonge, A. L.: *Karakterkunde.* Baarn: Bosch and Keuning, 1949, pp. 287.

380. Jastak, J.: "A Plan for the Objective Measurement of Character." *Jour. of Clin. Psychol.,* 1948, vol. 4, pp. 170-178.

381. Johnson, W.: "Speech and Personality." *Rev. of General Semant.,* 1949, vol. 6, pp. 84-102.

382. Kriekemans: *Inleiding tot de Karakterkunde* (Introduction to the Science of Character). Antwerp, [1936] Standard Boekhandel, pp. 148 (in *Dutch*).

383. McGill, V. J.: "A Psychological Approach to Personality," in *Philosophy for the Future the Quest of Modern Materialism.* (ed. by B. W. Sellars, V. J. McGill, and M. Farber) N. Y.: Macmillan, 1949.

384. McQuitty, L. L.: "Diversity of Self Endorsements as a Measure of Individual Differences in Personality." *Educ. Psychol. Measm't.,* 1949, vol. 9, pp. 3-14.

385. Ruesch, J.: "The Infantile Personality; The Care Problem of Psychosomatic Medicine." *Psychosom. Medicine,* 1948, vol. 10, pp. 134-144.

386. Ryan, E. J.: "The Relation between Body Types and Temperament." *Jour. Amer. Dental Ass'n.,* 1948, vol. 37, pp. 13-19.

387. Sapir, S.: "Personality" in the *Encyclopedia of the Social Sciences,* vol. 12, pp. 85-88.

388. Seltzer, C. C.: "The Relationship between the Masculine Component and Personality" in *Personality in Nature, Society and Culture,* N. Y.: Knopf, pp. 84-96.

389. Sherif, M. and Cantril, H.: *The Psychology of Ego-Involvements,* N. Y.: Wiley, 1947, pp. v + 525.

390. Stephenson, W.: "The Q-technique Study of Personality." *Trans. N. Y. Acad. Sci.,* 1949, vol. 11, pp. 215-219.

391. Waldrop, R. S.: "A Statistical Examination of Sheldon's Concept of Primary Components of Morphology." *Microfilm Abstr.,* 1949, vol. 9 (1), pp. 161-162.

REGISTER OF PERSONAL NAMES
AND
INDEX OF SUBJECTS

REGISTER OF PERSONAL NAMES

(Characters in fiction are italicized)

Abelson, E. A., 389
Abramson, H. A., 389
Abel, T. M., 389
Abélard, 286
Abelson, H. H., 389
Ackoff, R. L., 395
Adams, H. F., 390
Adler, A., 36, 265
Albert of Bollstadt, 353
Albert the Great, 354
Albino, R. C., 390
Allan, D. M., 390
Allen, A., 390
Allport, F. H., 81, 160, 403
Allport, G. W., 70, 79, 80, 82,
   85, 129, 132, 146, 147-152, 160,
   212, 237, 390, 395, 418.
Alschuler, R. H., 259, 390
Amatora, M., 390
Amoroso, M. D., 391
Anastasi, A., 39
Anderson, A. L., 390
Anderson, W. E., 390
Angyal, A., 391
Aquinas, T., 46, 353
Archimedes, 351
Argelander, A., 391
Aristotle, 264, 273
Arius, 45
Arluck, E. W., 391
Aschaffenburg, G., 253
Atreya, B. L., 391
Aveling, F., 391
Babbitt, 205, 239, 280
Ax, A. E., 391

Bach, J. S., 222-225
Bacon, F., 285, 354
Bacon, R., 354
Baldwin, M., 21
Balken, E. R., 391
Ball, R., 9
Balzac, H., 65
Barnes, T. C., 391
Barr, A. A., 391
Barrett, D. M., 391
Bateson, G., 391

Batouala, 314, 315
Baud, F., 391
Baumgarten, F., 132, 392
Bayet, A., 75, 392
Beau Brummel, B., 282
Beck, S. J., 257, 392
Becker, J., 392
Beckham, A. S., 392
Beethoven, 56, 222-225
Bekhterev, VI., 141, 160
Bell, Ch., 201
Bell, J. E., 392
Benedek, E., 392
Bennet, M. E., 392, 404
Benton, A. L., 392
Berg, D. E., 392
Berg, L., 392
Bergler, E., 392
Berman, L., 63
Bernard, L. L., 155, 286
Bernreuter, R. G., 392, 393
Bertocci, P. A., 393
Berwin, B., 287, 393
Bethe, R., 141, 160
Beyer, E., 404
Biddle, R. A., 393
Binet, A., 210, 211, 234, 260, 280
Bishop, F., 403
Bismarck, 200, 281
Blake, W. D., 393
Blanchard, P.,
Bloch, H. A., 393
Blos, P., 393
Boccacio, 48
Bock, A. V., 174
Bogert, L. J., 393
Bolgar, H., 393
Boorman, W. R., 393
Booth, G. C., 393, 394
Boswell, J., 57
Bott, H., 394
Bovary, 49
Bowlby, J., 418
Bowman, K. M., 411
Bowne, B. P., 46
Brändström, E., 292, 294-296
Breuning, G., *von*, 56

REGISTER OF PERSONAL NAMES

INDEX OF SUBJECTS

INDEX OF SUBJECTS